Praise for *The Way of Me*

Poland was at the epicenter of world history throughout the twentieth century. The vibrancy of Polish Catholicism gave birth to great saints over the centuries, but never more so than in our turbulent times. A pilgrimage along that itinerary of sanctity – as Stephen Binz proposes – invites us to live the Great Commission to be missionary disciples that each of us received at our baptism – and to do so with complete confidence that Jesus Christ is, in truth, the Lord of History.

George Weigel
Distinguished Senior Fellow and William E. Simon Chair in Catholic Studies, Ethics and Public Policy Center

This book will help pilgrims understand why Poland – *semper fidelis* (always faithful) – produced saints the caliber of St. John Paul II and St. Faustina Kowalska. Over 1,000 years of history, the Catholic faith has permeated the culture of Poland, and that faith has preserved the people's identity as a nation. Neither partitions, occupations, oppression, nor poverty could conquer the Polish spirit informed by a lively faith and trust in God and in the Queen of Poland, Our Lady of Częstochowa. Many of these marvels of Poland will become clearer to the readers of *The Way of Mercy: Pilgrimage in Catholic Poland*.

Most Reverend Thomas Wenski
Archbishop of Miami

Stephen J. Binz's inspiration to use the lens of mercy as the medium by which to see and learn about Poland's Catholic heritage is a source of great joy to me. It is through this lens of mercy that we enter into a deep understanding of the lives of the great Polish saints, only to discover a deeper meaning in our own life stories also. This is the unique contribution of Stephen's book: a combination of impressive historical knowledge with a deep spiritual approach and prayerful inspiration. Every pilgrim needs this in order to have a transformative experience when visiting a holy place. I pray for such experiences for the readers and congratulate Stephen on his beautiful work!

Sr. Gaudia Skass, OLM
Congregation of the Sisters of Our Lady of Mercy

As the son of Polish immigrants with deep Catholic roots, I have a great affection for Poland's long and faithful religious tradition. Therefore, I encourage you to take a close look at Stephen Binz's terrific new book that provides a beautiful tribute to the places, churches, and saints of Poland. The generous faith and values of my Polish ancestors helped shape me into the husband, father, grandfather, and leader that I am. They can teach us all about promoting a culture that values belief and principles. I invite you to enter this rich history through *The Way of Mercy: Pilgrimage in Catholic Poland*.

Mike Krzyzewski
Former Head Basketball Coach
Duke University (1980-2022) and U.S. Senior National Team (2005-16)

The chapter on St. John Paul II is very rich with many historic elements and descriptive details which transform the reader into a pilgrim. Particularly compelling is the author's explanation of the influence of Jan Tyranowski on Karol Wojtyła's spiritual life, and the references to the Carmelite and Marians paths which guided young Karol until the final hour of his pontificate.

Maxime Nogier
Executive Director, Saint John Paul II National Shrine

Stephen J. Binz has given us a work which reflects the insights of saints, persons, and places that have formed the rich spirituality of a Polish culture. I look forward to using these insights, as I conduct my next pilgrimage to Poland.

Most Reverend Jerome Listecki
Archbishop of Milwaukee

Pilgrimages to sacred places have been a part of Polish culture and faith for centuries. Poland's landscape is filled with holy sites, great and small, that provide constant, tangible reminders of God's presence in the lives of her people. Stephen J. Binz's *The Way of Mercy: Pilgrimage in Catholic Poland* provides a guide to some of the most important of these places, including those connected to St. Faustina Kowalska, St. Maximilian Kolbe, and Pope St. John Paul II. His tour provides English-speaking readers a glimpse into Poland's painful history in the 20th century and the abiding Catholic faith that sustained her people during times of war and repression.

John Radzilowski, Ph.D.
Director, Polish Institute of Culture and Research at Orchard Lake
Professor of History, University of Alaska

I wish I had had Binz's book on the last pilgrimage I led to Poland. I'm grateful that I'll have it on the next!

Christopher West, ThD
President, Theology of the Body Institute

Whether you are about to travel to Poland, or can only explore it from afar, Stephen J. Binz has crafted a book that will not only dutifully and delightfully lead you around the holy and historical places of that fine country, but will introduce you to the saints forged there down through Poland's history. As you get to know the individuals that, by God's grace, made Poland the Catholic country that it is, you might find yourself transformed from pedestrian to pilgrim, and sightseer to saint.

Most Reverend Thomas John Paprocki
Bishop of Springfield in Illinois

Whether you are making a spiritual pilgrimage to Poland or wishing to deepen your appreciation of the country's Catholic heritage from afar, *The Way of Mercy* serves as an invaluable resource. Stephen J. Binz provides readers with essential background information, helpful descriptions and photographs of key sites associated with the country's most prominent saints, and reflection questions and prayers to enhance the pilgrimage experience.

Robert E. Alvis
Author, *White Eagle, Black Madonna:
One Thousand Years of the Polish Catholic Tradition*

The twentieth century was a time of great trials, and in our own century the human race also faces grave threats. In the very midst of the horrors of the twentieth century, God raised up three of the greatest saints the Church has ever known – St. Maria Faustina, St. Maximilian Kolbe, and St. John Paul the Great. In our time, pilgrimage to Poland to venerate these saints and to rejoice in their extraordinary witness to Jesus Christ has become a necessity. The pilgrim to Poland discovers also the great Marian shrines and much more. Stephen Binz has given us a beautiful and rich guidebook to "crossing the threshold of hope" with the great Polish saints of wisdom, mercy, and sacrificial love.

Matthew Levering
James N. Jr. and Mary D. Perry Chair of Theology, Mundelein Seminary

THE WAY OF
MERCY

Pilgrimage in
Catholic Poland

STEPHEN J. BINZ

Available from:
Marian Helpers Center
Stockbridge, MA 01263
Prayerline: 1-800-804-3823
Orderline: 1-800-462-7426

Websites:
ShopMercy.org
Marian.org
TheDivineMercy.org

ISBN: 978-1-59614-571-9
Library of Congress Control Number: 2022914293

Imprimi Potest:
Very Rev. Chris Alar, MIC
Provincial Superior
The Blessed Virgin Mary, Mother of Mercy Province
August 14, 2022
Feast of St. Maximilian Mary Kolbe, priest and martyr

Nihil Obstat:
Robert A. Stackpole, STD
Censor Deputatus
August 14, 2022

Scripture quotations are from the *New Revised Standard Version Bible: Catholic Edition*, copyright © 1989, 1993 the Division of Christian Education of the National Council of the Churches of Christ in the United States of America. Used by permission. All rights reserved.

Saint Faustina image on page 41, © Congregation of Marian Fathers of the Immaculate Conception of the B.V.M.

All other photography herein is by the author. © Stephen J. Binz.

CONTENTS

PREFACE

Although I've been leading Christian pilgrimages for over 30 years, only in recent years have I discovered the wonders of Poland. My first trip to Poland was led by a Jewish survivor of the Holocaust, the late Eva Mozes Kor. She taught me about the rich Jewish tradition of Warsaw and Kraków, the tragedy of the ghettos, and the Nazi's "Final Solution." I explored this terrible history through the eyes of a woman tortured at Auschwitz by the Nazi doctor Josef Mengele, a woman who later in her life chose to free herself from bitterness by forgiving all her persecutors.

My next trip to Poland was during the Jubilee Year of Mercy, called by Pope Francis for 2016. In preparation for the extraordinary jubilee, I wrote a Bible study entitled *Divine Mercy*, and during the first five months of the year, I presented 30 parish missions and retreats across North America on the theme of Divine Mercy. Then in September, I led a pilgrimage of eager Catholics to explore the sites in Poland associated with the 20th-century saints of Divine Mercy: Faustina Kowalska, Maximilian Kolbe, and John Paul II.

Following these trips, I have traveled to Poland several more times, being enriched by more places, history, and sanctity in this fascinating land, and I hope to lead many more groups in the way of Divine Mercy in the future. It's the fruit of these experiences, along with my 30 years of experience in offering pilgrimages to sacred places throughout the world, that I hope to bring to this book. I will explore with you the land, rivers, cities, and towns of Poland, as well its sanctuaries, people, and cultures. And I will do so not just as an historian and tour guide, but especially as a pilgrim, inviting you to experience these places as sacred, and allowing them to deepen your faith and to form you more fully into disciples of Jesus.

My interest in pilgrimage is complemented by my enjoyment of photography. I enjoy making images because it helps me to see more clearly, to take notice of light, color, texture, and detail. The pictures throughout this book are my own, the fruit of several years of creating travel photography throughout the world. I hope they help you to imagine and remember your encounter with the sacred places of Poland.

I have written this guide for both the adventurous traveler, preparing for a physical journey to Poland, and the imaginative traveler, visualizing the places of this land from an armchair. Either way, I hope you will be able to envision these sites and experience them in the context of Christian faith and through an experience of prayer.

Author as a Polish Highlander.

I am grateful to Eva and to the CANDLES Holocaust Museum and Education Center in Terre Haute, Indiana, for introducing me to Poland and the horrors and courage manifested there during the Second World War. I also thank Agnieszka Nowak, an English-speaking guide in Poland, for her good advice in writing this work, Edita Krunic for encouraging me to explore Poland more thoroughly, Małgorzata Pyrtak for her generous help in Wrocław, Maria Kromp-Kropiowska for welcoming me to the Edith Stein House, Inesa Čaikauskienė at the Vilnius Pilgrim Center, and countless more who helped me along the way. I also thank Fr. Chris Alar, MIC, director of the Association of Marian Helpers at the National Shrine of The Divine Mercy; Dr. Joe McAleer of Marian Press; Curtis Bohner, designer; and Bob French, the copyeditor, among others, who helped see this book to its completion.

I am grateful too for all the pilgrims who have traveled with me to Poland and other pilgrimage sites throughout the world. And in particular, I dedicate this book to all Polish-Americans, whose ancestors have settled in this land and whose Polish pride I deeply admire.

MAP OF POLAND

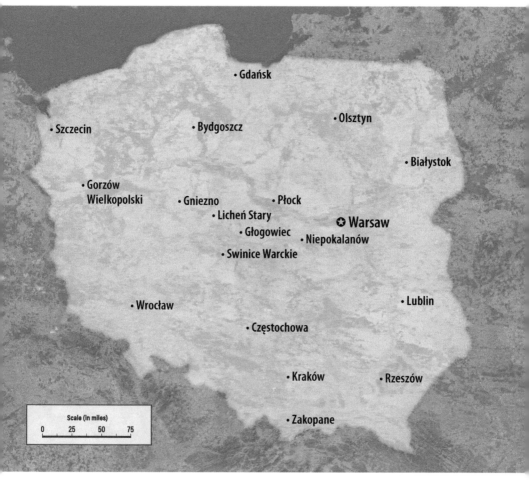

I. POLAND AND THE WAY OF DIVINE MERCY

In our own times, God's Spirit has voiced throughout the Universal Church a strong proclamation of Divine Mercy, which is often called the primary attribute of our God. This loving mercy of God, revealed throughout the history of ancient Israel and definitively through the Life, Death, and Resurrection of Jesus, was manifested in a distinctive way through the 20th-century struggles of the Polish people. Through the lives and witness of saints like Faustina Kowalska, Maximilian Kolbe, and Pope John Paul II, Divine Mercy has been revealed anew in our world by way of the Church in Poland.

Out of terrible suffering comes renewed grace. The trials of the Polish people throughout the 20th century, especially the assault of Nazi Germany from the west and the oppression of communist Russia from the east, made Poland the martyr of the nations, or in St. John Paul's words, the "Golgotha of the modern world." Yet, these sufferings have been transformed by God into a gift of mercy for the world. It seems to be the special mission of the Polish Church to be a witness of that gift and the bearer of the grace of Divine Mercy for our times.

Yet, as we explore this land, we begin to realize that the climactic events of the last century were only possible because of the rich Christian tradition of over a thousand years in Poland. The patron saints of Poland, like St.

Wojciech, St. Stanisław, and St. Jadwiga, are the sturdy pillars supporting the Church of Poland through the ages. On the shoulders of these faithful giants, the Polish saints of our era stand. They are some of the earliest of that remarkable cloud of witnesses — the martyrs, bishops, confessors, and holy ones — that has sustained the faith of Poland throughout its history.

Likewise, we recognize other saints, perhaps less well known than the most ancient and the most recent. We realize that there could never have been a Wojtyła without a Wyszyński, fortifying the Church as it passed through the fire of totalitarian rule. The inspiring insights of St. Faustina in the 20th century flowed from the beautiful compassion and care for the poor exhibited by St. Albert Chmielowski in the 19th century. The years of World War II were punctuated by brave rescuers, some just now coming to be known, saving Jewish victims from agonizing treatment under the Nazi rule. And Poland became a free country again at the end of the 20th century not only because of the bravery of Lech Wałęsa of Gdańsk and Pope John Paul II, but also because of the work of countless patriots and the martyrdom of Fr. Jerzy Popiełuszko. All of these great saints and witnesses are strands of the golden thread of Divine Mercy woven through the fabric of Poland's history.

As we see and touch the memorials of this gallery of saints and national heroes, perhaps too we can hear some of the beautiful music of Poland, from the sacred sounds arising from her cathedrals and shrines to the folk tunes that express the popular culture of her towns and cities. And like a rising crescendo, the music of Poland's greatest composer, Frédéric Chopin, forms a beautiful soundtrack for our journey.

Finally, we couldn't travel far in Poland without soon recognizing that the Holy Virgin Mary is the Queen of Poland. Her images, titles, and shrines abound throughout the country. But nowhere is Mary more honored as the nation's queen than at the Jasna Góra Monastery, where Our Lady of Częstochowa has received a coronation with papal crowns since 1717. In addition to her regal titles, Mary is honored as the Mother of Mercy. Her image often depicts the royal mother gathering her many children with tender compassion under her protective mantle. May she keep us in her care as we make our pilgrimage through her Polish realm.

1. Pilgrimage in Catholic Poland

Pilgrimage is a unique kind of travel. It is more than an experience of pleasant sightseeing. Pilgrimage involves both an external and an internal journey. For a successful pilgrimage, travelers must tour with eyes wide open, prepared to encounter people, places, and experiences along their external journey. But, at the same time, travelers must keep their minds and hearts open to the personal transformation that will occur along their internal journey.

Because people have traveled in this way from the dawn of history, there seems to be something deep within our human nature that longs to go on pilgrimage. This journey to sacred places in search of transcendence could be described as one of the archetypal experiences of humanity. Leaving behind our mundane cares and ordinary responsibilities, we enter into the universal experience of pilgrimage, joining the way of our ancestors with our minds, our hearts, and our feet.[1]

Our Christian faith is ideally suited for the ancient practice of pilgrimage. Because God is incarnate in the world through Jesus Christ, we are capable of encountering God in the people, places, and things of this world. This sacramental imagination allows us to search for God in all things, and to quest for the divine presence particularly in those places where God has been manifested in history. Through the lives of the saints and events of sacred history, certain places have come to be viewed as holy sites where the veil between Heaven and earth is particularly translucent.

Poland is the ideal land for learning the art of pilgrimage. Its history and culture is deeply religious; it is filled with memories of some of the Church's best-known saints; and famous churches and beautiful shrines cover the landscape. Increasingly, more and more pilgrims from throughout the world are discovering Poland as the ideal place for a transforming encounter with God. People of disparate languages, races, and nationalities are traveling to Poland, transcending their differences with the essential purpose of religious pilgrimage.

The Catholic culture of Poland allows pilgrims to experience a deeply mediated faith, where God is experienced through the saints and Sacraments of the Church. Because Jesus has manifested Himself to the world through the mediation of His Mother, Mary, Polish Catholicism understands that Marian spirituality is a beautiful way to deepen Christian faith. The lives of the Polish saints serve as models and mentors for one's own path to God, inspiring pilgrims with the places and events that mark their lives of sanctity. At their shrines throughout the land, their presence can be felt, and through their prayers we can draw closer to God through communion with them.

In the churches of Poland, the sacrifice of the Mass makes present the divine gift of Christ's one offering to the Father on the Cross. In sacred worship with the angels and saints, we share here and now in the graces

Pilgrims at the Divine Mercy Shrine in Płock.

of Christ's saving Life, Death, and Resurrection. For this reason alone, the churches of Poland are beautiful, while also filled with the skilled artistry of their builders. Because God is worshiped here and Christ is sacramentally present in these places, they embody in a unique way the work of Poland's finest architects and artisans over the centuries.

God uses the visible, material, and particular to mediate the invisible, immaterial, and universal divine presence. For this reason, pilgrimage functions in a way analogous to the Sacraments. Through the sacred words, symbolic elements, and ritual gestures of Sacraments, God offers us grace, which forms us more deeply into the image of Christ. Likewise, pilgrimage is concrete, relational, and embodied, enabling a divine encounter in the here and now.

The Gospel account of the journey along the road to Emmaus (see Lk 24:13-35) describes some of the most important aspects of Christian pilgrimage. The travelers along the way encounter Jesus, who accompanies them on their journey as they discuss their life experiences, read from Scripture, offer hospitality, and break bread together. Their travel is more than a journey; it is a pilgrimage because they experience the Risen Lord. He is present with them on the road, in the words they exchange, in the Scriptures, in the signs of hospitality, in the Eucharist, and in the community formed through their experience. The encounter with the Risen Lord on their journey offers new possibilities and new hope for their Christian lives. Christian pilgrims, then, are formed more fully into disciples of the Lord through the elements of genuine pilgrimage: journey, community, Scripture, sacrifice, hospitality, ritual, communal prayer, sacred places, Eucharist, and spiritual encounter.

Whether you travel virtually through this book or journey to Poland to explore the land, you can encounter the graces of pilgrimage by integrating these elements into your experience. Within this book you will find information to enrich your understanding of Poland's sacred places and images and to enhance your imagination. You will find questions for your reflection that will lead you into an experience of meditative prayer. Scriptural texts will expand your perception of God's mercy, and litanies of praise and petition will magnify your experience of travel into a sacred encounter with Christ and His Church.

2. A Millennium and More of Christianity

The Polish Catholic hierarchy, led by Cardinal Primate Stefan Wyszyński, guided the Church in the celebration of 1,000 years of Christianity in Poland in 1966. The millennial celebration was preceded by a nine-year Great Novena beginning in 1957, a time of preparation marked by fasting, prayer, and processions. The ruling Communist Party, seeking to match the festivities with its own secular observance, sought to restrict the Church's activities, refusing to allow Wyszyński to attend overseas celebrations and denying Pope Paul VI permission to visit Poland during the commemoration. Despite the restrictions, the remembrances of 1966 formed an ideal opportunity to review the always dramatic, often tragic, and forever-inspiring history of the faith in Poland.

The Christianization of Poland received its impetus with the baptism of Mieszko I, the first ruler of the future Polish nation, and much of his court. Mieszko's wife, Dąbrówka of Bohemia, is usually credited as a major influence on Mieszko's decision to accept Christianity. The ceremony took place on Holy Saturday of April 14, 966, an event that most historians mark as the beginning of Polish statehood. Within a few decades, Poland joined the rank of established European states recognized by the papacy and the Holy Roman Empire.

The spread of the faith across Poland led to the building of churches and the appointment of bishops. Mieszko's son Bolesław I the Brave established the Archdiocese of Gniezno in the year 1000. He cordially supported the missionary undertaking of St. Wojciech (Adalbert, bishop of Prague), who traveled to the pagan tribes of Poland when rejected by his own people. When Wojciech was martyred, Bolesław had his relics transferred to the

Gniezno Cathedral, which soon became a major pilgrimage site, increasing Poland's political power in Europe. Saint Wojciech is honored today as Poland's first patron saint.

Relations between the Church and the rulers of Poland were not always so unified, however, as exemplified by the dispute between St. Stanisław (1030-1079), the bishop of Kraków, and the king. Bishop Stanisław excommunicated King Bolesław II the Bold, probably because of the king's injustices and cruelty. While Stanisław was celebrating Mass at the church in Skałka, he was killed by the king and cut into many pieces. Today, St. Stanisław is honored as a martyr and Poland's second patron saint. Each year, thousands of pilgrims participate in a procession with the saint's relics from the Wawel Cathedral to the nearby Skałka church.

Jewish settlement in Poland began early in its history, and Poland contained the highest concentration of Jews in the world from the time of the Middle Ages until World War II. Compared to the situation of Jews in most other European countries, the Jewish people of Poland were secure and prosperous. The General Charter of Jewish Liberties, known as the Statute of Kalisz, was issued by the Duke of Greater Poland, Bolesław the Pious, in 1264. It granted Jews unprecedented legal rights, including exclusive jurisdiction over Jewish matters in Jewish courts, and specified a broad range of freedoms of religious practices, movement, and trade. The act exempted the Jews from enslavement or serfdom and was the foundation of future Jewish prosperity in the Polish kingdom. Following a series of expulsions of Jews from Western Europe, Jewish communities were established throughout Poland in the 13th and 14th centuries.

The Piast dynasty that began with Mieszko I continued until the death of Kazimierz III the Great, who reigned as king of Poland from 1333 to 1370. Kazimierz inherited a kingdom weakened by war and made it prosperous and wealthy. He doubled the size of the kingdom, reformed the army, and renewed the judicial system. He introduced the codes of law of Greater and Lesser Poland as an attempt to end the overwhelming superiority of the nobility. He was known for siding with the weak when the law did not protect them from nobles. During his reign, all three major classes — the nobility, priesthood, and bourgeoisie — were more or less counterbalanced, allowing Kazimierz to strengthen his monarchy. Many large-scale brick building projects were undertaken during his reign, including the construction of churches in the Polish Gothic style and over 40 castles. He also founded the University of Kraków, the oldest Polish university, and he confirmed privileges and protections previously granted to Jews and encouraged them to settle in Poland in great numbers.

The Jagiellonian Dynasty

After the Piast dynasty failed to produce a male heir, the Polish nobility decided that the young Jadwiga should be crowned as the first female monarch of the Kingdom of Poland at the age of 11. She reigned from 1384 until her death. With her mother's consent, Jadwiga's advisors opened negotiations with Jogaila, Grand Duke of Lithuania, who was still a pagan, concerning his potential marriage to Jadwiga. Jogaila signed the Union of Krewo, pledging to convert to Catholicism and to promote the conversion of his pagan subjects. After lengthy prayer, seeking divine guidance, Jadwiga agreed to marry him.

Jogaila was baptized in Kraków's Wawel Cathedral and took the Christian name Władysław. He married Jadwiga in 1386, becoming King Władysław II Jagiełło of Poland and coruler with Queen Jadwiga. The partnership formed a Polish-Lithuanian union, bringing vast territories controlled by the Grand Duchy of Lithuania into Poland's sphere of influence, and proved beneficial for both the Polish and Lithuanian people. Queen Jadwiga died in 1399, after giving birth to a premature daughter, who also died. Jadwiga, known as the mother of the poor, weak, and ill of Poland, was buried together with her daughter in Wawel Cathedral.

After the death of Jadwiga, Władysław II Jagiełło reigned in Poland a further 35 years, laying the foundation for the centuries-long Polish-Lithuanian union and the Jagiellonian dynasty, which ruled until 1572. During his reign, the Polish-Lithuanian state was the largest in the Christian world. Its victory over the Teutonic Knights at the Battle of Grunwald in 1410 secured the Polish-Lithuanian borders and marked the beginnings of the Polish Golden Age.

In the Jagiellonian period, Poland developed as a feudal state with an increasingly dominant landed nobility. The *Nihil novi* act adopted by the Polish Sejm (parliament) in 1505 transferred most of the legislative power in the state from the monarch to the Sejm, forbidding the king to issue laws without the consent of the nobility (*szlachta*). This event marked the beginning of the period known as "Golden Liberty," when the state was ruled by the members of the Polish nobility, which constituted up to 10 percent of the population, a greater proportion than in other countries. In principle the nobility were all free and equal, but some possessed a small patch of land that they tended themselves, while the magnates owned networks of estates with several hundred towns and villages and many thousands of subjects.

Baptism of King Władysław II Jagiełło, co-ruler with Queen Jadwiga.

The golden age of Polish culture continued through the 16ᵗʰ-century reigns of Zygmunt I and Zygmunt II, the last two Jagiellonian kings. This cultural flowering had its material base in the prosperity of the elites, comprising both the landed nobility and patrician families of urban centers like Kraków and Gdańsk. During this Polish Renaissance, science, painting, sculpture, architecture, music, and literature flourished, and some of Poland's most notable cultural works were created.

The Polish-Lithuanian Commonwealth

Zygmunt II's childlessness added urgency to the idea of turning the personal union between Poland and the Grand Duchy of Lithuania into a more permanent and tighter relationship. The signing of the Union of Lublin in 1569 created the Polish-Lithuanian Commonwealth, the "Republic of the Two Nations," stretching from the Baltic Sea and the Carpathian mountains to present-day Belarus and western and central Ukraine. The new federation became a multinational entity with a common monarch, parliament, monetary system, and foreign-military policy, in which only the nobility enjoyed full citizenship rights.

The death of Zygmunt II in 1572 without an heir ended the Jagiellonian rule and initiated the so-called Republic of Nobles, in which the nobility elected the new king. The process was increasingly marked by corruption, with votes being openly bought and sold, resulting in a series

Creation of the Polish-Lithuanian Commonwealth in 1569.

of foreign rulers. There was little allegiance to these elected monarchs, and the country became increasingly regionally divided, sowing the seeds of the destruction of Poland as a strong European power. The third of the elected rulers, the Swedish Zygmunt III Wasa, moved the capital from Kraków to Warsaw in 1596, an act the Krakovians have not forgiven.

The Polish-Lithuanian Commonwealth was multiethnic and multireligious. Among the population were Poles, Lithuanians, Latvians, Ukrainians, Estonians, Jews, Armenians, and Muslim Tatars. The main social segments of the population included 70 percent peasants, 20 percent residents of towns, and 10 percent nobles and clergy. The Slavic populations of the eastern lands were primarily Eastern Orthodox. At a time when religious wars and persecutions raged across Europe, the Commonwealth was an oasis of tolerance, and persecuted religious groups flocked there. While in the rest of Europe, Jews were walled in ghettoes or expelled, they were given privileges by the Polish kings. Numerous Armenian merchants settled in Poland, as did evangelical Protestant sects. Following the Reformation, most Polish nobles adopted Calvinism, and only about 40 percent of the Polish-Lithuanian Commonwealth's population remained Catholic.

Yet, Poland emerged as one of the great successes of the Catholic Counter-Reformation, reversing the gains of Protestantism, such that the mid-16th century to the mid-18th century witnessed the increasing ascendancy of the Catholic faith. A key figure in this work was Bishop Stanisław

Hozjusz, who drafted a profession of faith at the Synod of Piotrków, later expanded into his celebrated *Confessio catholicae fidei Christiana* ("Christian Confession of Catholic Faith"). Protestantism never established a significant following among the masses of Polish peasantry. The arrival of the Jesuit order in 1564 and their vigorous activities over the coming decades contributed greatly to the accomplishments of Catholicism. Jesuits like Piotr Skarga, an outstanding orator and popular writer, provided an internal unity to the Catholic response in opposition to the more dispersed and less organized Protestant efforts.

Poland's internal decline culminated in the so-called *Potop*, or Deluge, of the 17th century. In 1648, the Cossacks led a rebellion aimed at gaining Ukrainian independence. Hundreds of thousands of Poles and Jews were killed in the process. Seven years later, Poland's neighbor to the north, Sweden, invaded and ransacked much of the country. At the shrine at Jasna Góra in Częstochowa, the Poles were able to fend off the Swedish invaders, crediting the miraculous icon of the Black Madonna with the victory. The Poles then regrouped and mounted an impressive offensive, regaining much of the lost territory. Peace with Sweden was secured with the Treaty of Oliwa in 1660, but much of the Commonwealth lay in ruins, with its landmass greatly reduced and nearly half of its population dead through war and disease.

After a period of recovery from these tragic events, Poland's finest hour militarily came in 1683 when King Jan III Sobieski convincingly defeated the Ottoman Turks at the Siege of Vienna. While the Austrian emperor was indecisive, the Polish king and his Polish army of winged hussars stormed to the city and saved Christian Europe from an Islamic onslaught. Impressed by Sobieski's skill, Pope Innocent XI proposed that Sobieski head his new Holy League to defend Europe against Islam.

Partition, Death, and Rebirth

Following the spectacular victory at Vienna, Poland-Lithuania grew internally weak and fractured. Poland's stronger neighbors — Peter the Great's Russia, Frederick II's Prussia, and Maria Theresa's Austria — took advantage of this, and in a series of three partitions in 1772, 1773, and 1795, divided the country among themselves. After the first partition, in which Poland lost a third of its territory and half of its inhabitants, the Sejm took steps toward political reform which culminated in Europe's first written constitution, the second in the world following that of the United States of America. The May 3 Constitution, as it became known, is still a source of Polish pride and commemorated by a national holiday. Nevertheless, in the final partition, Poland, one of Europe's oldest nations, ceased to exist for over a century.

Yet incredibly, during these years, Polish culture not only survived; it thrived. Since the nation and the Catholic faith were intimately united, the Church was arguably the institution most responsible for preserving Polish culture. Although Poland's masters had banned the teaching of the Polish language in schools, the Poles continued to teach it. Polish composers like Frédéric Chopin and poets like Adam Mickiewicz and Juliusz Słowacki gained international celebrity. The Poles continued to fight against their oppressors, although their insurrections most often led to brutal repression.

Following the First World War, the Bolshevik Revolution and the Treaty of Versailles had destroyed the empires that oppressed Poland, and national independence was restored to Poland in 1918, with Józef Piłsudski serving as Chief of State. Shortly thereafter, Bolshevik Russia tried to invade its neighbor to the West, hoping to use Poland as a springboard for exporting communist revolution to all of Europe. A Soviet commander wrote these orders in 1920: "To the West! Over the corpse of White Poland lies the road to worldwide conflagration. March upon Vilnius, Minsk, Warsaw!" and "onward to Berlin over the corpse of Poland!"[2]

Few believed that the Poles could win the Polish-Bolshevik War, but the Poles prayed hard for victory with special Masses and religious processions across the country. They scored a stunning victory at the Battle of Warsaw, and more Polish military successes followed, forcing the Soviets to pull back. In what became known as the "Miracle on the Vistula," the Poles defeated the Bolsheviks, forcing Vladimir Lenin and the Soviet leadership to postpone their objective of linking up with European revolutionary leftist collaborators to spread the communist revolution across Europe.

The Second World War

As the political climate in Europe became increasingly menacing in 1939, the foreign ministers of Germany and the Soviet Union signed a nonaggression pact that included a secret protocol for dividing Poland between them. So, on September 1, Nazi Germany invaded Poland from the West, the opening event of World War II. Sixteen days later, communist Russia followed suit, invading Poland from the East. Despite lacking the troops and equipment of its aggressors, the Poles fought bravely for five weeks and never surrendered. The Nazi-Soviet occupation was more brutal in Poland than anywhere else. Before the end of the war, 6 million Polish citizens had been killed — half of them were ethnic Poles and the others were Jews, nearly 90 percent of the country's Jewish population, murdered by the Nazis.

Poles were regarded by the Nazis as *untermenschen* — a racially inferior species, like the Jews. Their final aim was the destruction of the Polish people, along with the extermination of the Jews and gypsies, and the settlement of Germans in these "liberated" areas. In tandem with the German terror, the Soviet Union set about the annexation of occupied East Poland and began the "Russification" of these territories. This involved the expulsion of whole sections of the Polish population from their homeland. Stalin sought to force the Poles to lose their self-esteem and identity. It is estimated that 1.65 million Polish citizens were deported in cattle wagons to hard-labor camps for "re-education" in remote Soviet territories of the Arctic and Siberia, where their chances of survival were minimal.

Perhaps the greatest single war crime in modern history was committed by the Soviet Union in the spring of 1940 near the village of Katyn in Russia. The Katyn massacre entailed a series of mass executions of Polish military officers and intelligentsia carried out by Soviet troops and approved by the Soviet Politburo led by Joseph Stalin. Of the total killed, about 8,000 were officers imprisoned during the 1939 Soviet invasion of Poland, another 6,000 were police officers, and the remaining 8,000 were Polish intelligentsia, those deemed to be intelligence agents, landowners, factory owners, lawyers, and priests. Katyn Forest has become a symbol of the suffering of the Polish people at the hands of the Soviets.

During the war, the Poles formed an extensive underground resistance movement and a Polish government-in-exile that operated first in Paris, then in London. Hundreds of thousands of Poles joined the underground Polish Home Army, a part of the Polish Armed Forces of the government-in-exile, eventually boasting the fourth-largest Allied army. About 200,000 fought on the Western Front in the Polish Armed Forces, loyal to the government-in-exile, and about 300,000 in the Polish Armed Forces in the East under the Soviet command on the Eastern Front. By blowing up bridges and rail tracks, the Poles disrupted the German supply lines to such an extent that they played a substantial part in their defeat.

As the implementation of the Nazi Final Solution began, the Holocaust in Poland proceeded with force. The Warsaw Ghetto Uprising was triggered by the liquidation of the Warsaw Ghetto by German SS units. The elimination of Jewish ghettos in German-occupied Poland took place in many cities. As the Jewish people were being removed to be exterminated, uprisings were waged against impossible odds by the Jewish Combat Organization and other desperate Jewish insurgents.

The greatest single undertaking of the Polish resistance movement was the Warsaw Uprising that began on August 1, 1944. The uprising, in which most of the city's population participated, was instigated by the underground Home Army and approved by the Polish government-in-exile in an attempt to establish a noncommunist Polish administration ahead of the arrival of the Red Army. The bitterly fought uprising lasted for two months and resulted in the death or expulsion from the city of hundreds of thousands of civilians. The Russian army impassively observed the battles from across the Vistula River, ignoring Polish attempts to make radio contact with them and refusing to advance their forces or to assist from the nearby Soviet air base,

108 Blessed Polish Martyrs of World War II, killed by Nazi Germany and beatified by Pope John Paul II in 1999.

thus allowing the Polish resistance to be crushed. After the Poles surrendered, the Germans razed the Polish capital to the ground with heavy bombardment.

Approximately 90 percent of Poland's war casualties were the victims of prisons, death camps, raids, executions, annihilation of ghettos, epidemics, starvation, excessive work, and ill treatment. Many of the victims were among Poland's brightest and most creative citizens. In addition, the war left 1 million children orphaned and over half a million persons disabled. Poland lost 38 percent of its national assets (whereas comparatively, Britain lost only 0.8 percent and France only 1.5 percent), and two-thirds of its industrial potential had been destroyed. The cities and landscape were ravaged, and barren areas haunted the scenery with remnants of the death camps.

The war was an especially agonizing time for Poland's Catholic Church, which was seen by the occupation as the carrier of social resistance. Half of Poland's Catholic clergy were sent to concentration camps. Most of the inmates in Dachau's infamous priest block were Polish. In some dioceses, almost all priests were murdered. Fascinated with St. John of the Cross and St. Teresa of Avila, the future Pope St. John Paul II initially wanted to become a Carmelite, but his bishop discouraged him from doing so, saying that Poland desperately needed diocesan priests as so many were being killed by the Nazis. A large number of Polish Catholics acted heroically during these wretched times, and quite a few have been beatified or canonized, including, most famously, St. Maximilian Kolbe, the Franciscan friar who gave his life for a fellow inmate at Auschwitz.

Enslaved by Communism and Freed by Solidarity

By 1945, Poland was overrun by the Red Army, and although the people of Poland had contributed mightily to the Allied war effort, they were sold out to Stalin by his allies Roosevelt and Churchill. While postwar Western Europeans and North Americans enjoyed prosperous decades marked by blue jeans, Coca-Cola, and convertibles, postwar Poland experienced censorship, ration cards, and political prisoners. For nearly half a century, the Poles would be ruled by a communist regime. Stalin famously remarked that imposing communism on Poland was akin to "fitting a saddle onto a cow."[3] The hallmarks of Stalinism in Poland were the imposition of Marxist-Leninist ideology, the amassment of huge armed forces, centralized economic planning, and a concentration on heavy industry. With the Communist Party wielding all power, the government was, in effect, a dictatorship of the party over the people.

The Polish people's refusal to embrace communism had largely to do with the strength of the Catholic Church. As a result of the Holocaust and border changes, the Polish population was for the first time in the nation's history more than 90 percent Catholic, and Polish Catholicism during this painful period of communist rule became stronger than ever. This spiritual potency was due in large part to Cardinal Stefan Wyszyński, Primate of Poland from 1948 until his death in 1981, who became an uncompromising thorn in the side of the communist government. As he continually reminded the Poles of their heritage, their faith became stronger and stronger.

Although the financial assets of the Church had been confiscated by 1950, the Church was one of the few institutions that retained a level of independence against the regime. Priests and laity were often attacked and threatened with arrest, accused of anti-state attitudes. The communist purpose sought to create a new, socialist person, freed from any religious aspirations. But the attempted eradication of transcendent ideals from Polish society proved to be a disastrous failure for these rulers. In 1956, 1968, 1970, and 1976, the Polish people challenged the regime in a series of uprisings. However, each period of unrest was met with bloody repressions that fragmented and terrified the people.

All this changed on October 16, 1978, when Cardinal Karol Wojtyła of Kraków was elected pope. He was 58 years young and the first non-Italian bishop of Rome since 1523. A year later, Pope John Paul II traveled on a nine-day pilgrimage in his homeland. Millions of Poles attended Masses with him; millions more watched him on television or listened on the radio. In addresses that avoided direct politics, he spoke of the God-given dignity of human beings in Christ — words with revolutionary potential.

Solidarność becomes a nonviolent movement struggling for the liberation of Poland.

In August 1980, the Solidarity union, led by the charismatic electrician Lech Wałęsa, was formed at the Lenin Shipyards in Gdańsk. Solidarność quickly became much more than a labor union — above all it was a nonviolent movement fighting for the liberation of the Polish nation. Pope John Paul II was a strong supporter of Solidarity, and Poland's communist rulers were in a panic. Solidarity's Catholic nature was unmistakable as striking workers said the Rosary and celebrated Mass while supported by priests and parishes throughout the country. The Church became the primary place where Poles could live as if they were free.

On orders from Moscow to crush Solidarity, Poland's communist dictator General Wojciech Jaruzelski declared martial law from 1981 to 1983 and jailed 20,000 Solidarity activists. Yet Solidarity's strength could not be squashed. The Church was a forum for political discussions, lectures, and the dissemination of publicity and illegal literature. The Church paid a heavy price for all this, and the fearless priest Fr. Jerzy Popiełuszko was tortured and murdered by members of the security police in 1984. Following John Paul's pilgrimage to Poland in 1987, the communists agreed to negotiate with the union over basic political, social, and economic reforms and to hold semifree elections. On June 4, 1989, the voters overwhelmingly chose Solidarity, which formed a new government. Before Pope John Paul II was elected, no sane person would have expected to see the Soviet Bloc crumble in his or her lifetime. But later that same year, dissident movements inspired by Solidarity toppled communist regimes throughout the Soviet

Bloc, and by 1991, the Soviet Union was on the ash heap of history. In 1999, Poland became a member of the North Atlantic Treaty Organization (NATO), a return to its historical role over a millennium as defender of Europe. The nation swiftly adapted to a free-market economy and attracted investments worldwide.

The flag that flies over Poland today displays two horizontal stripes of white and red, the national colors associated with Poland since its beginnings in the 10ᵗʰ century. White represents the majestic white eagle that Poland's mythical founder, Lech, discovered as he walked across the land. As he approached, the great bird expanded its massive wings across the red light of the setting sun. In another story, Lech was impressed with the mother eagle so valiantly defending her young that she began to bleed. Inspired by the sight, Lech adopted the white eagle over the red background as the symbol of Poland. The white of today's flag represents the eagle's heroic spirit, and the red represents its blood and sacrifice. The red and white is often seen flying with the yellow and white of the Holy See and the white and blue Marian flag. Since becoming a member of the European Union in 2004, the Polish flag flies with the banner of Europe. Although the European Union does not acknowledge the symbolism, the flag's blue background and crown of 12 stars (Rev 12:1) is an ancient emblem of Mary, Our Lady and Queen.

The hymn "God Save Poland" ("*Boże, coś Polskę*") is a solemn prayer for the nation, sung in Polish churches and included in every songbook:

> O God, who, through so many centuries,
> surrounded Poland with the brilliance of power and glory,
> who has protected it with the shield of your defense,
> against the disasters that were meant to defeat it. ...

Heard during the insurrections, wars, and foreign occupations that plagued Poland through the centuries, the refrain of this anthem has reflected the changing history of the nation up to the present day. Its refrain, "To your altars we carry a prayer," ended with "Save our King, Lord" in 1816; was modified to "Return our homeland to us, Lord!" in 1830; replaced with "Return our free homeland to us, Lord!" in 1980; evolved to "Bless our homeland and freedom, Lord!" in 1989; and finally became "Bless our free homeland, Lord!" in 1996.

While Poland continues to face many challenges, including the grow-ing threat of Western secularism and consumerism, it is incredible that Poland has preserved its unique culture and is free to practice its Catholic faith today. The fact that Poland saved European civilization from Islamic

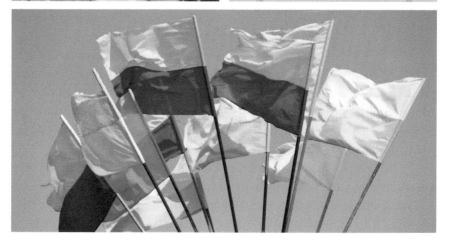

Virgin Mary statue; the white eagle over the red background, the symbol of Poland; the Polish flag flies with the yellow and white of the Holy See and the white and blue Marian flag.

invaders in 1683, drove back the Bolsheviks in 1920, and in the 1980s formed a mass movement that ultimately toppled the Soviet behemoth is truly astounding. Perhaps this same great nation may show the way for Western Europe and North America to overcome its waning faith and provide an example of spiritual renewal leading to a culture of life and a civilization of love.

*Merciful Jesus offers Himself in the
Sacrifice of the Mass.*

3. The Gospel of Divine Mercy

Although we rationally understand that God is infinite, eternal, and almighty, this philosophical understanding of God can seem abstract and distant from the real life of God's people. The Scriptures present a God who is also close to His people, showing personal care for their plight and deep compassion in their suffering. When God saw the misery of His people in bondage, He came to liberate and redeem them. This is not an indifferent God in the heavens, nor is this a rash and vengeful God who responds from afar. Over and over, Israel's Scriptures describe God as "merciful and gracious, slow to anger and abounding in steadfast love" (Ps 103:8). When God's people merited death because of continual transgression, rebellion, and sin, God granted them space for new life through Divine Mercy. Biblical history testifies that God takes no satisfaction in the death of the sinner but finds delight when the sinner repents and returns to Him to live with joy and abundance.[4]

Sin creates a distorted image of God in the human heart. Because of sin, we tend to view God as a divine avenger, who counts our transgressions and dispenses an equivalent punishment. But, as Fr. Michael Gaitley, MIC, has said, "The whole of the Bible can be summarized as one long 'school of trust,' where our good and merciful God is simply trying to get us skittish, fearful creatures to give up our fear of him and trust in his love and goodness."[5] God is continually trying to heal our false image of Him so that we can trust in Him as the God of mercy. He is the one to Whom we can turn with contrite hearts and from Whom we can ask for mercy, expecting to receive it.

The gift of Jesus Christ — His Incarnation, Ministry, Death, and Resurrection — is the supreme expression of God's mercy. Each account of healing, exorcism, and forgiveness by Jesus in the Gospels is a cameo of Divine Mercy. In Jesus, God's mercy is extended to the afflicted, the poor, the lost, and the sinners of Israel. Through His public ministry, the primary facets of God's mercy are given a tangible and personal shape. The mercy of Jesus expresses itself in the inclusion of social outcasts in His company, the forgiveness of repentant sinners, the healing of those sick in mind and body, acknowledgement of the needs of the poor, compassion for tired and hungry crowds, and even pardon for those who violently put Him to death.

Jesus's demonstration of Divine Mercy in individual acts throughout the Gospels illustrates the redemption that God extends to the whole world through the sacrificial Death and Resurrection of His Son. In the Cross of Jesus Christ, standing as a sign over the world, over history, and over every human life, the mercy of God is most clearly displayed. The One Who is Lord over life and death has suffered and died, conquering death and restoring life. When we look to the crucified Christ, we see love to the full, compassion in its most tangible form, and Divine Mercy in its most extravagant presentation.

Although God offers everyone the saving grace of His merciful love, we must open our hearts to receive it in order to experience its transforming power. Our salvation depends on our free response to the offer of God's love. In His mercy, God holds the possibility of salvation open to all human beings who are willing to allow their heart to be changed, even if their guilt is ever so great and their former life ever so messed up. Every person is able to trust in the immeasurable mercy of God. The "no" of someone's refusal is always weak alongside the unconditional "yes" that God has spoken to humanity in the Death and Resurrection of Christ. In ways unfathomable to us, God never ceases to court human beings to the very end of their lives. God even enlists the intercession of all the angels and saints of Heaven on behalf of every individual so that they might choose eternal life over the rejection of God's mercy that results in unending death.

Jesus Christ, as judge of the living and the dead, holds the mantle of God's mercy over us. In God's plan of salvation, the biblical message of mercy has the first as well as the last word. The mercy embodied in Jesus is the uplifting, hope-inducing message on which we can rely in every situation, both in life and in death. It is our refuge, our comfort, and the source of our confidence.

In His Resurrection appearance to His disciples in the Upper Room, Jesus gave them what would later be described as an image of Divine Mercy. Although the disciples had abandoned Jesus during His Passion and locked the doors of their hearts out of fear, the Risen Lord showed them the sacred wounds of His hands and side, and He gave them His joy, forgiveness, and peace, urging them to trust in Him.

Yet, because the image of God is still distorted by sin, we continue to have a hard time trusting in Divine Mercy. For this reason, God has continued to manifest His mercy throughout the history of the Church and throughout the world. Wherever and whenever the Church suffers, it suffers as the Body of Christ. The Church unites its suffering with that of Christ, and this suffering has a healing and saving effect. This is especially true of the witness of the martyrs, about whom it is said, "The blood of the martyrs is the seed of the Church."[6]

The Saints of God's Mercy Prepare Poland for Great Suffering

Throughout its history as a Christian country, Poland has suffered greatly, often for the sake of other nations and peoples. Poland was chosen many times to save Western Christianity from being devoured. At the end of the 18th century, Poland was consumed by its neighbors and obliterated from the map of Europe. Then she rose again from the ashes of World War I, only to be ravished in the next world war, suffering an 18 percent casualty rate during the bloodiest conflict in human history. After being oppressed in their own land under their communist overlords, enduring decades of brutal humiliation, the Polish people rose again in solidarity and freed not only themselves but the peoples of Central and Eastern Europe in a nonviolent revolution. Out of some of the greatest darkness and deepest suffering in human history there arose in Poland an era blessed for recognizing God's grace and mercy.

Arising from the simple life and mystical experiences of a young Polish consecrated woman named Faustina Kowalska, the devotion to Divine Mercy is spreading throughout the world. Born in 1905, Faustina joined the Congregation of the Sisters of Our Lady of Mercy in Warsaw at the age of 20. Throughout her short life, Sr. Faustina reported having visions of Jesus and conversations with Him, which she noted in her diary, later published as *The Diary of Saint Maria Faustina Kowalska: Divine Mercy in My Soul* (Marian Press: Stockbridge, MA, 2003). While living at a convent in Płock, she experienced a vision of Jesus wearing a white garment with red and pale rays emanating from His heart. Jesus told her to have this image painted with the signature: "Jesus, I trust in You" (in Polish: "*Jezu, ufam Tobie*"). Jesus told her that He desired this image be venerated "first in your chapel, and [then] throughout the world" (*Diary*, 47).

In 1933, Sr. Faustina was transferred to the convent in Vilnius, where she worked as the gardener. Shortly after arriving, she met Fr. Michael Sopoćko, the newly appointed confessor to the sisters, who grew to trust and support Faustina's mystical experiences. He directed her to write a diary to record the conversations and messages from Jesus that she was reporting and was instrumental in having the first Divine Mercy image painted by an artist. Thanks to the work of Bl. Fr. Sopoćko, the Divine Mercy devotion began to spread throughout Poland by way of pamphlets that included the Divine Mercy Chaplet, the Divine Mercy Novena, and the Litany of Divine Mercy. Faustina did not live to see the fruit of her mystical revelations, dying at the age of 33 of tuberculosis on October 5, 1938, in Kraków.

Before her death Sr. Faustina predicted the terrible war that began with the invasion of Poland by Nazi Germany and the Soviet Union. The Divine Mercy devotion became a source of strength and inspiration for many people in Poland during those dreadful years. The message revealed to Sr. Faustina is nothing new, just a reminder of what the Church has always taught and believed: that God is merciful, faithful, and forgiving. This devotion to Divine Mercy involves a decision to accept God's mercy with gratitude, to trust completely in the mercy of Jesus, and to be merciful as He is merciful.

Another Polish saint from the first half of the 20th century, Maximilian Kolbe, was a Franciscan friar who used his intense zeal for God for the good of the Church. It is said that when Maximilian was a youth, he asked Our Lady what was to become of him. She then came to him in a

St. Faustina Kowalska, the first canonized saint of the Great Jubilee in 2000.

St. Maximilian Kolbe, Franciscan priest and martyr at Auschwitz.

vision holding two crowns, one white, the other red, asking if he was willing to accept either. If he accepted the white, it meant he would live a life of heroic virtue; accepting the red meant dying as a martyr. He responded, "I will accept them both."

Reading the work of St. Louis de Montfort, *True Devotion to Mary*, Kolbe was particularly struck by de Montfort's claim that total consecration to Jesus through Mary is the "surest, the easiest, the shortest and the most perfect means" to becoming a saint.[7] When sinners open their hearts to Mary, she leads them through the grace of conversion to her divine Son. Father Kolbe knew that becoming a saint is the way to give the greatest possible glory to God, so he dedicated his apostolic life to facilitating Marian consecration for as many people as possible.

In 1917, embracing the motto "Through the Immaculate to the Heart of Jesus," Kolbe gathered six other friars and formed the *Militia Immaculatae*, a spiritual army to convert sinners and win the world for God. Its essence is living the consecration — being an instrument of God's mercy in Mary's hands as she is an instrument of Divine Mercy in God's hands — belonging totally to her and being used by her for the work of mercy. They began publishing the magazine *Knight of the Immaculata*, and in 1927, founded a new Franciscan community near Warsaw called Niepokalanów, meaning "City of the Immaculata."

By the end of 1938, a few months before the Nazis invaded Poland, Niepokalanów was the largest Franciscan community in the world and the *Knight of the Immaculata* reached a pressrun of a million copies a month. The community also printed a daily newspaper as well as other magazines and books, including several anti-Nazi works. On the eve of the war, millions of Poles had been drawn to Marian consecration and a deeper experience of God's mercy through the Mother of Mercy.

Through the hidden spirituality of Sr. Faustina Kowalska and the energetic intensity of Fr. Maximilian Kolbe, Poland was prepared to pass through the fire of suffering brought by the Second World War. While Sr. Faustina died on the eve of the war, Fr. Maximilian continued to work until 1941, when the community was shut down by the Gestapo and he and four other friars were arrested and imprisoned. Kolbe was transferred to Auschwitz, where he witnessed to other prisoners through his faith and compassion. Finally, Kolbe volunteered to take the place of the father of a family in the starvation bunker, where he died after two weeks of agony.

Although Poland was the place in which the worst of the 20th century happened, it is also the place from which God's response to those evils arose.

Even as oppressive suffering closed in on Poland from the West and from the East, mercy radiated from the heart of the Risen Christ as a sign to Poland and to the world of God's personal and boundless love. The two horrific systems, brutal Nazism and atheistic communism, which killed tens of millions of people, choked off humanity's sense of hope and left the world reeling in despair. Divine Mercy was the gift through which the people of the earth could again offer repentance and experience forgiveness and healing.

"This Is the Time for Mercy"

Although there is no evidence that Karol Wojtyła knew either Sr. Faustina or Fr. Maximilian personally, despite the fact that at one time they all lived in close proximity to each other near Kraków, the direct connections between them came about after their deaths, while Wojtyła was Archbishop of Kraków and later the Pope.

During the Nazi occupation of Poland, while Wojtyła worked long hours in forced labor at a quarry and chemical plant, he read the writings of St. Louis de Montfort and consecrated himself to Jesus through Mary. The consecration so marked his life that he would adopt St. Louis' phrase *"Totus Tuus"* (Totally Yours) as his motto as bishop and later as Pope. After the war, Wojtyła heard about the heroic self-offering of Maximilian Kolbe at Auschwitz and was influenced by his Marian writings. As Pope, John Paul II was a promoter of Fr. Maximilian the mariologist and martyr, canonizing him in 1982 and calling him an "apostle of a new Marian era."

As it happens, the quarry and chemical plant where the youthful laborer worked, while also clandestinely enrolled at the underground seminary of Kraków, was located just a few hundred yards past the convent where Sr. Faustina had lived during her final years. Young Karol would often stop and pray at the convent chapel after a hard day of labor. In his years as a young priest, and later as a bishop and archbishop of Kraków, Karol Wojtyła would often visit the convent and lead the sisters in reflective retreats.

As the first Polish pope, John Paul II promoted the Divine Mercy devotion of St. Faustina and her cause for canonization. In 1981 he wrote an encyclical entitled *Dives in Misericordia* (*Rich in Mercy*), illustrating that the heart of the mission of Jesus was to reveal the merciful love of the Father. As the Great Mercy Pope, John Paul II preached about God's mercy, wrote about it, and most of all lived it — offering forgiveness to the man who shot him in St. Peter's Square and doing everything in his power to heal the wounds caused by the historic conflicts between Catholics and other Christian churches and between the Church and the Jewish people.

Merciful Jesus extends redeeming grace to the peoples of the world (by Vaidotas Kvašys).

Pope John Paul II extends Divine Mercy by offering forgiveness to the man who shot him in Rome.

In 2000 he canonized Sr. Faustina, making her the first canonized saint of the new millennium, and established the Octave Sunday of Easter as "Divine Mercy Sunday" for the Universal Church. And, finally, he died on the eve of Divine Mercy Sunday, receiving Communion during the anticipated Mass for the feast. Then the relationship between Pope John Paul II and the saints of mercy came full circle when he was canonized on Divine Mercy Sunday, 2014, becoming himself one of the saints of Poland who brought the world a new awareness of the merciful love of God.

The Divine Mercy devotion and the Polish saints of mercy arose in the 20th century, the bloodiest era in human history, in order to usher in the 21st century, the third millennium, as a time of conversion and renewal. As Pope John Paul proclaimed and Popes Benedict and Francis have repeated, "This is the time for mercy,"[8] a time of unprecedented grace for the whole Church and the entire world. The devotional prayers, the lives of these saints, and the sacred places described in this pilgrimage offer us tangible ways to bring the message of Divine Mercy from the head to the heart. Even if we know that God is merciful, our wounded hearts often feel otherwise. As Jesus told St. Faustina, "The graces of my mercy are drawn by means of one vessel only, and that is — trust.

The more a soul trusts, the more it will receive" (*Diary*, 1578). Let us not be afraid to allow Jesus to transform us — through our Mother of Mercy, the grace of the Scriptures and Sacraments, and the saints and prayers of His Church — to be His Body in the world, radiating the image of God.

4. Preparation and Prayer for Pilgrimage

While we prepare our minds for pilgrimage by reading, we must also prepare our hearts for the spiritual encounters that await us. The better we prepare, the more able we will be to experience God's grace through the sacred places of our journey.

Because going on pilgrimage is a calling, various people and circumstances in our lives align to prepare us to hear the prompting of God in our heart to travel on a sacred journey. As we get ready to take a pilgrimage to Poland, we might best prepare by reviewing and being grateful for the ways that God and other people have cleared the way for us. Then we may seek to lessen any fears we may have by trusting in God for protection and guidance, realizing we are escorted by heavenly companions.

Along with trust in God comes a sense of expectation. If God has brought us to this moment, then we ought to have an open mind and heart, expecting Him to work within us in new and surprising ways. So to prepare, let us consider what we hope to receive from God as a result of this pilgrimage.

Like the pilgrims traveling to Emmaus, Christ walks with us along our way. Let us make quiet spaces in our lives so we may hear the Lord speak in the silence of our hearts and wait for Him to show us His presence. While we look for Christ, we realize that He is really the one looking for us. Let us ask for a contemplative spirit so that we may encounter the Lord's living presence in the holy people and places we find on our journey.

To ensure that our journey embodies these elements of pilgrimage, we should try to walk in the way that many have traveled before us, and follow some basic guidelines:

• Travel lightly by keeping our clothing and our baggage simple so we don't get weighed down.

• Travel expectantly by looking forward to the learning and change we will experience through our encounters.

• Travel humbly by visiting the people of this land with respect and reverence for their traditions and way of life.

- Travel gratefully by realizing we are guests in this land and displaying appreciation for the people who are providing for us.

- Travel softly by seeking an attitude of inner quietness and attentive listening, making time for silence when we stand on holy ground.

- Travel courteously by showing consideration for our hosts and fellow travelers and by helping to smooth the way through difficulties.

- Travel patiently by staying flexible and adaptable, realizing that unexpected changes, delays, and glitches are part of the whole experience.

- Travel relaxed by letting go of tensions and deciding to have a good time.

Learning to Pray the Chaplet of Divine Mercy

As we prepare to travel in the way of Divine Mercy, the Chaplet of Divine Mercy, which Jesus gave St. Faustina (*Diary*, 475), will help us focus and trust, preparing our hearts for the experiences ahead. Saint Faustina heard Jesus telling her, **"The souls that say this chaplet will be embraced by my mercy during their lifetime and especially at the hour of their death"** (*Diary*, 754). The prayers focus on three themes: asking for the mercy of God, trusting in Christ's abundant mercy, and showing mercy to others and acting as a conduit of God's mercy toward them.

You may begin with the optional opening prayers:

> You expired, Jesus, but the source of life gushed forth for souls, and the ocean of mercy opened up for the whole world. O Fount of Life, unfathomable Divine Mercy, envelop the whole world and empty Yourself out upon us.

> (Repeat three times) O Blood and Water, which gushed forth from the Heart of Jesus as a fount of Mercy for us, I trust in You!

Using Rosary beads, begin with the Sign of the Cross. Pray one Our Father, one Hail Mary, and the Apostles Creed.

On each of the five decades (Our Father bead of the Rosary), pray:

> Eternal Father, I offer you the Body and Blood, Soul and Divinity of Your Dearly Beloved Son, Our Lord, Jesus Christ, in atonement for our sins and those of the whole world.

Feast day procession.

On each of the ten Hail Mary beads, pray:

> For the sake of His sorrowful Passion, have mercy on us and on the whole world.

For the concluding prayer, repeat three times:

> Holy God, Holy Mighty One, Holy Immortal One, have mercy on us and on the whole world.

You may also add this optional closing prayer:

> Eternal God, in whom mercy is endless and the treasury of compassion inexhaustible, look kindly upon us and increase Your mercy in us, that in difficult moments we might not despair nor become despondent, but with great confidence submit ourselves to Your holy will, which is Love and Mercy itself.

Prayer for Pilgrimage

God our Father, Who created us and sustains us,
God the Son, Who redeemed us and gives us new life,
God the Holy Spirit, Who sanctifies us and guides our church,
May your blessings be upon us as we travel on pilgrimage.

Give us the heart of a pilgrim,
trusting in your guidance and dependent on the hospitality of others.
Fill our hearts with joy,
freed from needless anxiety and lightened from our daily burdens.
Unbind us to live in Your freedom,
seeking holiness and focusing on the things that matter most.

Bread of Heaven, Who feeds Your people on their journey,
Living water, Who quenches your people's thirsts,
nourish us along our pilgrim way, with insights for our minds,
with fervor for our hearts, and with music for our souls.

Move in our lives, O God, during this pilgrimage,
as we leave our homes, the familiar and comfortable.
Open our eyes to goodness and beauty,
our ears to hear Your voice speaking,
our noses to the aromas of sanctity,
our mouths to life's flavors and spices,
our memories to savor all that You give us along the way.

Mary, Mother of Mercy and Queen of Poland,
accompany us on the journey with your maternal presence.
Loving daughter of the Father, teach us to listen to the Word of God.
Mother of the Son, show us how to love Jesus and stay close to Him.
Spouse of the Holy Spirit, direct our hearts to seek spiritual gifts.
You who are the highest honor of our race,
hear the plea of your children as we cry to you, now and at the hour of death.
Amen.

II. *Saint Faustina Kowalska*

The mystical experiences of St. Faustina inspired the worldwide devotion to Divine Mercy and earned her the title of "Apostle of Divine Mercy." Through the Divine Mercy devotion, she teaches us to trust completely in God and to live each day in His mercy.

After entering the Congregation of the Sisters of Our Lady of Mercy, Faustina Kowalska lived her consecrated life in several convents throughout Poland. Working as a cook, gardener, and porter, she faithfully followed the rule of religious life and hid within herself an extraordinary union with God. During her lifetime, few knew anything of her rich interior life, which she recorded in her *Diary*.

After her death from tuberculosis at age 33, her *Diary* and elements of the Divine Mercy devotion began to spread throughout Poland and became a source of strength and inspiration for many during the Second World War. By 1941, the devotion had reached the United States through the efforts of Fr. Józef Jarzębowski, a Polish-born member of the Marian Fathers of the Immaculate Conception of the Most Blessed Virgin Mary. Throughout the 1950s, the movement continued to spread with the worldwide distribution of millions of printed images and prayer cards.

Beginning in 1959, however, the Holy Office in Rome banned the spread of the Divine Mercy devotion because of alleged theological errors caused by inaccurate translations of Faustina's *Diary*. Meanwhile in 1965, with Rome's approval, Archbishop Karol Wojtyła opened the informative process into Faustina's life and virtues, interviewed witnesses, and requested the start of the official process leading to her beatification. In 1978 the ban was lifted, leading to Faustina's beatification in 1993 and canonization in 2000, when she became the first canonized saint of the Great Jubilee Year. At her canonization, Pope John Paul II said, "By this act, I intend today to pass this message on to the new millennium."[9]

By visiting the places associated with the life of St. Faustina, we accompany her on her spiritual pilgrimage and she accompanies us on ours. Through the various aspects of the Divine Mercy devotion — the veneration of the Divine Mercy Image; the celebration of Divine Mercy Sunday; the prayer of the Chaplet to the Divine Mercy; the prayer at the 3 o'clock Hour of Mercy; and the spreading of the devotion of the Divine Mercy — we become increasingly trustful of God's mercy and desire to be channels of that mercy by doing spiritual and corporal works of mercy for others. May this pilgrimage be a means for us to invite Jesus into our innermost hearts, as St. Faustina did, and to experience our lives as permeated by God's mercy.

1. Głogowiec, Świnice Warckie, and Łódź: *The Early Life of St. Faustina*

Helena Kowalska (the baptismal name of St. Faustina) was born in 1905, at a time when Poland had not appeared on any map of the world for over a hundred years. The village of Głogowiec, where she lived her first 16 years, could not be reached by a paved road and was inhabited by farming families who were mostly illiterate. Helena was born into a poor and religious family of peasants, the third of 10 children. Pope John Paul II said that it was to precisely this poor girl, "a girl from nowhere," that God entrusted the mission of announcing to the whole world the most important message of the 20th century.[10]

The modest home of Helena's parents, Marianna and Stanisław Kowalski, is today a small museum featuring mementos of their family life. The limestone house was completed in 1900 and sat on a few acres of farmland. The house consisted of two rooms, divided by a hallway, with a family room on the left and a kitchen on the right, which served also as the father's carpentry workshop in the winter. The family life was centered in faith, as evidenced by the pictures hung on the walls and other articles of devotion. Marianna is remembered as hard-working, organized, warm, and sincere. The scent of freshly baked bread often wafted from her kitchen. While

Shrine of St. Faustina's Birth and Baptism.

supporting his family through farming and carpentry, Stanisław owned an impressive collection of books. As one of the few people able to read and write in the area, he read aloud to his family in the evenings and taught his children to do the same. He would begin each day at dawn by singing the Little Office of the Immaculate Conception, known as "*Godzinki*," expressing a deep and heartfelt faith.

Two days after her birth, Helena was brought for baptism to the family's parish church, St. Kazimierz Church in nearby Świnice Warckie. This was the family's parish church, where Helena and her family attended Sunday Mass and other devotions and where she went to her first Confession and first Holy Communion. In the diary, Faustina wrote about her experiences from her childhood:

> From the age of seven, I experienced the definite call of God, the grace of a vocation to the religious life. It was in the seventh year of my life that, for the first time, I heard God's voice in my soul; that is, an invitation to a more perfect life. But I was not always obedient to the call to grace. I came across no one who would have explained these things to me (*Diary*, 7).

Saint Kazimierz Church was already a place of worship in 1300; the present church was built in 1859, and today it is the Shrine of the Birth and Baptism of St. Faustina. Three baroque altars are found in the sanctuary: The center features an image of the Merciful Jesus, the left altar displays an image of Our

Family home of Marianna and Stanisław Kowalski in Głogowiec.

Lady of Częstochowa, and the right altar highlights an image of St. Faustina and the baptismal font at which she was received into Christ's life. The parish confessional is also displayed in a side room, a witness to her first encounters with God in this Sacrament of mercy.

Several years later, as a religious sister, Faustina returned to her home and childhood church in order to visit her severely sick mother. At that time, she wrote in her diary about her experiences in this church:

> How easy it was to pray in that little church! I remembered all the graces that I had received there, and which I had not understood at the time and had so often abused. I wondered how I could have been so blind. And as I was thus regretting my blindness, I suddenly saw the Lord Jesus, radiant with unspeakable beauty, and He said to me with kindness, **My chosen one, I will give you even greater graces that you may be the witness of My infinite mercy throughout all eternity** (*Diary*, 400).

No primary school was available in the region during the years of Russian rule, but in 1917, a school was built. Helena was 12 at the time, so she attended school for less than three years. At age 16, she begged her parents' permission to take up gainful employment to lighten their burdens. She left her family home for the nearby city of Aleksandrów, where she worked as a domestic servant to support herself and help her parents. During this period the desire to join a convent was gradually growing inside her. Since her parents were against it, young Helena tried to muffle God's call.

She moved to the large city of Łódź, where two of her sisters were also living, and worked at 29 Abramowski Street doing housework and caring for three small children. There she bought fashionable clothing and tended to her physical appearance, but the pleasant, freckle-faced redhead could not find genuine happiness. In July 1924, Helena went with her sisters to a dance in Venice Park (now Juliusz Słowacki Park). There in the park after dancing, she experienced a vision of Jesus during his Passion. Covered with wounds, He looked at her and said: "How long shall I put up with you and how long will you keep putting me off?" (*Diary*, 9). She then made her way to the nearby Cathedral of St. Stanisław Kostka, where she had

The sanctuary honoring the birth and baptism of St. Faustina in Swinice Warckie.

frequently attended Mass. She fell prostrate before the Blessed Sacrament and begged God to tell her what to do next. She then heard a voice in her soul: "Go at once to Warsaw; you will enter a convent there" (*Diary*, 10). The next day she packed her few possessions and took the train to Warsaw.

MEDITATION

• Why does God choose those who are simple, poor, and lowly to do the work of Christ?

• How does the young Helena inspire me to seek God's will?

Reading: 1 Corinthians 1:27-31
God chose what is foolish in the world to shame the wise...

Response: "Lead me, O LORD, in the way everlasting."

O Lord, you have searched me and known me.
You know when I sit down and when I rise up;
   you discern my thoughts from far away.
You search out my path and my lying down,
   and are acquainted with all my ways. R.

Even before a word is on my tongue,
   O Lord, you know it completely.
You hem me in, behind and before,
   and lay your hand upon me.
Such knowledge is too wonderful for me;
   it is so high that I cannot attain it. R.

Where can I go from your spirit?
  Or where can I flee from your presence?
If I ascend to heaven, you are there;
  if I make my bed in Sheol, you are there.
If I take the wings of the morning
  and settle at the farthest limits of the sea,
even there your hand shall lead me,
  and your right hand shall hold me fast. **R.**

For it was you who formed my inward parts;
  you knit me together in my mother's womb.
I praise you, for I am fearfully and wonderfully made
  Wonderful are your works; that I know very well
  (Ps 139:1-10, 13-14). **R.**

Prayer: Lord God, You know us far better than we know ourselves. From the womb, from our families, from our communities, You have chosen us and offered us the calling that is ours. Help us continually discern Your movements in our hearts, guide our way according to Your will, and lead us where you would have us go. As You chose St. Faustina from the simple and lowly of the world to be Your Apostle of Divine Mercy, guide us along Your way to everlasting life.

2. Warsaw, Sisters of Our Lady of Mercy

After being directed to Warsaw to enter a convent, Helena Kowalska went to the first church she saw, St. James Church, to seek God's guidance. She told her story to the parish priest, Fr. Jakub Dąbrowski, who decided to send her to the home of his friends, Aldona and Samuel Lipszyc, to stay while she sought a convent to join. Helena took care of the house and their four children, while they awaited the birth of their fifth. From the Lipszyc house in Ostrówek, she periodically went into the city of Warsaw to seek a convent to join, but her extreme poverty caused her to be refused by each one she visited.

One day in 1924, however, Helena came to the convent of the Sisters of Our Lady of Mercy on Żytnia Street. The portress announced her arrival and the superior of the house, Mother Michaela Moraczewska, received her in the parlor. Seeing that the girl had a pleasant smile and exhibited a great deal of simplicity, sincerity, and common sense, she chose to accept her. Sister Faustina recalls another detail of this meeting in her diary:

When Mother Superior … came out to meet me, she told me, after a short conversation, to go to the Lord of the house and ask whether He would accept me. I understood at once that I was to ask this of the Lord Jesus. With great joy, I went to the chapel and asked Jesus: "Lord of this house, do you accept me?". … Immediately I heard this voice: **I do accept you; you are in my Heart.** When I returned from the chapel, Mother Superior asked first of all: "Well, has the Lord accepted you?" I answered, "Yes." "If the Lord has accepted, [she said] then I also will accept" (*Diary*, 14).

Cathedral of St. Stanislaus Kostka in Łódź, where St. Faustina pleaded to God to tell her what to do next with her life.

But realizing that the girl had no dowry or personal effects, Mother Michaela suggested that she go into service for a time and save money for her wardrobe. Helena willingly accepted the idea and returned to the Lipszyc household. She worked for another year, saving her income and bringing it periodically to the convent for safekeeping. Then, Helena said her goodbyes to the family and promised never to forget them. She kept her promise, and many years later after Faustina's death, none of the Lipszyc family lost their lives in the Holocaust. In fact, Aldona Lipszyc, now a widow, saved many people of Jewish descent during the Nazi occupation, keeping many of them at her home in Ostrówek. She died in 1980, and in 1996 was honored with the title "Righteous Among the Nations" for her brave rescues.

On August 1, 1925, Helena began her postulancy at the convent, a trial period to determine if she had a vocation to religious life. Describing her feelings when joining the convent, she wrote: "It seemed to me that I had stepped into the life of Paradise. A single prayer was bursting forth from my heart, one of thanksgiving" (*Diary*, 17). The congregation's apostolic work consisted of helping girls and women who were then described as gone astray and in need of moral conversion. Provided with spiritual and

The Church of Divine Mercy at the Shrine of St. Faustina in Warsaw.

social help from the sisters, they could then return to normal life in society. In those days, the sisters were divided into two groups: The first choir were generally better educated and worked directly with the girls' instructions, and the second choir, mainly from lower social levels, did the support work in the kitchen and garden. All the sisters, however, were obligated to pray and to be concerned about the salvation of those entrusted to them.

The Warsaw convent is the birthplace and motherhouse of the Congregation of the Sisters of Our Lady of Mercy, founded by Mother Teresa Potocka. After her husband's death, she joined a community in France that looked after prostitutes who desired to change their lives. She soon returned to Warsaw and founded there the first "mercy house," with a chapel and house for girls, based on the French model. The dedication on November 1, 1862, by Archbishop Feliński, is adopted as the date of the creation of the Sisters of Our Lady of Mercy in Poland. Today the congregation continues to imitate and serve Christ in his mercy toward all types of humanity's spiritual miseries, imploring God's mercy for the world through prayer and sacrifice.

Following her novitiate in Kraków, where she took the name Sr. Maria Faustina, she returned to the convent in Warsaw and was assigned to work in the kitchen. It was here that her health began to fail, and she was confined to the infirmary for about a month. Some of the sisters complained that she was only pretending to be ill, and Faustina found refuge only in contemplating the Passion of Jesus. When she complained to Jesus that she was being a burden to the sisters, she heard Jesus say to her, "You are not living for yourself but for souls, and other souls will profit from your sufferings. Your prolonged suffering will give them the light and strength to accept My will" (*Diary*, 67).

Faustina began to experience an increasingly close relationship with Jesus and deepening mystical encounters. Many of her confessors and superiors doubted the genuineness of her experiences, and Faustina began to doubt herself. God's grace became for her a source of great suffering. Yet, the more Faustina doubted, the more God immersed her in His favor. Mother Michaela herself told Faustina, "Sister, along your path, sufferings just spring up out of the ground. I look upon you, Sister, as one crucified. But I can see that Jesus has a hand in this. Be faithful to the Lord" (*Diary*, 149).

Here also, in 1932, Sr. Faustina began her third probation, a five-month period of spiritual preparation for perpetual vows. During this time, she began to understand that she was being invited by God to be a "victim soul," one who would generously accept great sufferings, united with Christ's own Passion, for the sake of others. "Suffering," she realized, "is a great grace; through suffering the soul becomes like the Savior; in suffering love becomes crystallized; the greater the suffering, the purer the love" (*Diary*, 57).

Jesus urged Faustina to meditate on His Passion so that she could know more profoundly the love that burns in His heart for souls. He said to her:

Call upon My mercy on behalf of sinners; I desire their salvation. When you say this prayer, with a contrite heart and with faith on behalf of some sinner, I will give him the grace of conversion.

This is the prayer: O Blood and Water, which gushed forth from the Heart of Jesus as a fount of Mercy for us, I trust in You (*Diary*, 186-187).

The site of the convent is today the Shrine of St. Faustina in Warsaw, which includes the Church of Divine Mercy and St. Faustina as well as a museum. During World War II, the convent was near the ghetto wall, and there is documentation of fleeing Jewish girls being assisted and going into hiding in the convent. During the Warsaw Uprising in 1944, the Nazis evicted all the sisters and their 200 protégés, herding them to a concentration camp. The convent buildings were burned and remained in ruins throughout the 20 century. In the 1980s, the ruined grounds became the hub of independent artists and creative opposition to the oppressive government. Reconstruction of the site began in the early 21ˢᵗ century, transforming the convent chapel into an active parish church. In 2017 the church was named a shrine of St. Faustina.

MEDITATION

- With what kind of people did Jesus associate in the Gospels? What does this tell me about Him?
- What did St. Faustina learn through her experiences of rejection followed by acceptance?

Reading: Matthew 9:10-13
As [Jesus] sat at dinner in the house, many tax collectors and sinners came…

Response: "You are merciful and gracious, O Lord."

Incline your ear, O Lord, and answer me,
   for I am poor and needy.
Preserve my life, for I am devoted to you;
   save your servant who trusts in you. R.

Gladden the soul of your servant,
   for to you, O Lord, I lift up my soul.
For you, O Lord, are good and forgiving,
   abounding in steadfast love to all who call on you. R.

Give ear, O Lord, to my prayer;
   listen to my cry of supplication.
In the day of my trouble I call on you,
   for you will answer me. R.

For you are great and do wondrous things;
   you alone are God.
Teach me your way, O Lord,
   that I may walk in your truth;
   give me an undivided heart to revere your name. R.

O God, the insolent rise up against me;
   a band of ruffians seeks my life,

and they do not set you before them.
But you, O Lord, are a God merciful and gracious,
  slow to anger and abounding in steadfast love and faithfulness. R.

Turn to me and be gracious to me;
  give your strength to your servant;
  save the child of your serving girl.
Show me a sign of your favor,
  so that those who hate me may see it and be put to shame,
  because you, Lord, have helped me and comforted me (Ps 86:1-2, 4-7, 10-11, 14-17). R.

Prayer: Divine Physician, You extend the medicine of mercy to the outcasts and sinners. Because You have been merciful and gracious, abounding in steadfast love and faithfulness, we can trust in You and pray with confidence. Teach us Your ways that we may walk in Your truth; give us undivided hearts to revere Your Holy Name.

3. Płock, Divine Mercy Sanctuary

The convent of the Congregation of the Sisters of Our Lady of Mercy in Płock is the place where Jesus first revealed Himself to Sr. Faustina as the Merciful Lord and gave her instructions to paint the image according to the vision she received. Here, too, Jesus expressed to Sr. Faustina his desire for a Feast of Mercy on the Sunday after Easter.

The sisters came to Płock at the end of the 19th century, where they worked as tutors and teachers at the Guardian Angel Institute for girls and women in need of moral renewal. Near the city's Old Market, the sisters lived a life of prayer and work, teaching

Convent of the Congregation of the Sisters of Our Lady of Mercy in Płock.

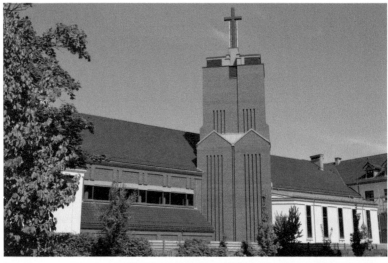

The newly constructed Shrine of Divine Mercy in Płock;
the place where St. Faustina was instructed to paint the image of the Merciful Jesus.

skills in doing laundry, sewing, and embroidering. The sisters also had a convent and farm in the village of Biała, about six miles from Płock. Here the wards learned the skills of farming, providing the economic base for the Guardian Angel Institute. In 1950 the communist authorities deported the sisters from Płock to Biała and nationalized the work of the institute. After 40 years of forced absence, the sisters were able to return and resume their work. Although the historical building was in ruins, it was rebuilt and a temporary chapel was dedicated in 1990.

Sr. Faustina arrived at the convent in Płock in May of 1930. After a period of exhausting work in the kitchen, she was sent to convalesce from fatigue at the convent in Biała during the final months of the year. After her recovery, Faustina returned to Płock and was assigned to the bakery shop. Every day, many inhabitants of Płock bought baked goods and were served by Sr. Faustina.

On February 22, 1931, Sr. Faustina experienced her mystical vision of the Merciful Jesus, which she describes in her diary:

> In the evening, when I was in my cell, I saw the Lord Jesus clothed in a white garment. One hand [was] raised in the gesture of blessing, the other was touching the garment at the breast. From beneath the garment, slightly drawn aside at the breast, there were emanating two large rays, one red, the other pale. In silence I kept my gaze fixed on the Lord; my soul was struck with awe, but also with great joy. After a while, Jesus said to me, **Paint an image according to the pattern you see, with the signature: Jesus, I trust in You. I desire that this image be venerated, first in your chapel, and [then] throughout the world** (*Diary*, 47).

In 1991, Pope John Paul II visited Płock and blessed the image of the Merciful Lord Jesus recently painted by Elżbieta Plewa-Hoffmann. The image began a procession throughout the diocese until the Feast of Divine Mercy in 2000, when it was placed permanently in the chapel, and the grounds were declared a Shrine of Divine Mercy. Construction began on an extension of the Divine Mercy Shrine in 2016. Today the shrine contains a chapel where the Merciful Jesus first revealed Himself to St. Faustina. It also includes a church, facilities for pilgrims, and a museum.

The museum features numerous photographs, documents, and memorabilia related to the life and holiness of St. Faustina. Some of the most precious relics of the shrine include the authentic bakery with the preserved kiln and tools used for baking bread and the floor on which St. Faustina walked. There is also a reconstruction of her convent cell.

MEDITATION

• What aspects of the image of the Merciful Lord Jesus most touch my heart?

• In what ways do I desire God to transform my heart through the "vessel" of the image?

Reading: John 20:19-21
He showed them his hands and his side…

Response: "Jesus, I trust in you."

God's presence filled my soul, and I heard these words, My daughter, I desire that your heart be formed after the model of My merciful Heart. You must be completely imbued with my mercy" (*Diary*, 167). R.

I promise that the soul that will venerate this image will not perish. I also promise victory over [its] enemies already here on earth, especially at the hour of death. I Myself will defend it as My own glory (*Diary*, 48). R.

I am offering people a vessel with which they are to keep coming for graces to the fountain of mercy. That vessel is this image with the signature: Jesus, I trust in You (*Diary*, 327). R.

I desire that the Feast of Mercy be a refuge and shelter for all souls, and especially for poor sinners. On that day the very depths of My tender mercy are open. I pour out a whole ocean of graces upon those souls who approach the Fount of My Mercy (*Diary*, 699). R.

Souls who spread the honor of My mercy I shield through their entire lives as a tender mother her infant, and at the hour of death I will not be a Judge for them, but the Merciful Savior. At that last hour, a soul has nothing with which to defend itself except My mercy. Happy is the soul that during its lifetime immersed itself in the Fountain of Mercy, because justice will have no hold on it (*Diary*, 1075). R.

"I am Love and Mercy Itself. There is no misery that could be a match for My mercy, neither will misery exhaust it, because as it is being granted — it increases. The soul that trusts in My mercy is most fortunate, because I Myself take care of it" (*Diary*, 1273). R.

Prayer: Merciful Lord Jesus, who revealed Your image to Saint Faustina, we desire to glorify Your compassionate heart and trust completely in You. Let Your mercy be impressed like a seal upon our hearts so that we may give You honor and express Your love to others. Through the Blood and Water which gushed forth from your Sacred Heart, deliver us from fear, forgive us from sin, and make us ministers of Your mercy.

4. Vilnius, Divine Mercy Pilgrimage

Although Vilnius is today the capital of Lithuania, when St. Faustina lived in the city between the world wars, it was part of Poland. Since the 17th century, pilgrims have been drawn to Vilnius to visit the miraculous image of the Holy Mother of Mercy. The dark Madonna is positioned in a chapel above the gate of the city known as the Gate of Dawn (in Polish, *Ostra Brama*, or Sharp Gate), her neck humbly bent, graciously looking over the city. Throughout its history, the residents of Vilnius, Catholic and Orthodox alike, have lovingly cared for victims of famine, floods, wars, and fire, earning it the title "City of Mercy" under the patronage of their holy Mother.

The Sisters of Our Lady of Mercy came to Vilnius in 1908 and established a convent on Antakalnis Hill. They cared for women who were former prisoners and juvenile offenders, tended to a military hospital, and earned income through baking bread and washing clothes. In 1933, after professing her perpetual vows in Kraków, Sr. Faustina was directed by her superiors to go to the convent house in Vilnius, where she lived until 1936. Outwardly she served as the gardener, while inwardly she experienced some of the most important moments of divine intimacy that would form the foundations of the Divine Mercy devotion.

The only remaining building of the convent, the one in which St. Faustina lived, has been restored and is open for visitors at 29 Grybo Street. The superior of the convent was Mother Irena Krzyżanowska, who was a great support for Faustina's mystical life and actively encouraged the Divine Mercy devotion. More significantly, here Sr. Faustina met Fr. Michael Sopoćko, her long-sought spiritual director, for whom she had been praying for a long time. She immediately recognized him when he came to the convent as confessor because she had seen him in a vision before her arrival in Vilnius. In Faustina's recreated cell and in other rooms of the restored convent, relics of St. Faustina and Bl. Fr. Michael Sopoćko are venerated along with other mementos of their lives.

Father Sopoćko was a professor of theology at the university and a confessor for many congregations. Before agreeing to become Sr. Faustina's spiritual director, he sent her to a psychiatrist and inquired among her superiors. Then receiving favorable judgments from all, he allowed her to begin to reveal to him the experiences of her soul. After seeking the advice of other learned priests, he began to realize that she had been enriched by God with unusual graces.[11]

As Sr. Faustina insisted that God desired the Merciful Jesus image to become a means of grace for an aching world, Fr. Sopoćko arranged for a well-known Vilnius artist, Eugeniusz Kazimirowski, to paint the image. He obtained permission from Mother Irena for Faustina to visit the artist regularly to give him precise instructions about the painting. At this time, as it happened, Kazimirowski had his studio on the ground floor of the same building in which Fr. Sopoćko was living on the floor above. The artist worked on this first image of the Merciful Jesus for six months, completing it in June of 1934. When Faustina saw the completed image, she had difficulty concealing her disappointment. The image was not in the least as beautiful as her vision. Returning to the convent chapel, she burst into tears. Then she heard Jesus say: "Not in the beauty of the color, nor of the brush lies the greatness of this image, but in My grace" (*Diary*, 313).

Father Sopoćko hung the finished painting in the corridor of the Bernardine Sisters' convent, near St. Michael's Church, where he was the rector. But Sr. Faustina insisted that Jesus desired the image to be venerated in a place of honor. Fittingly, the first place that the image of Merciful Jesus was publicly venerated was at the Gate of Dawn, with the icon of the Holy Mother of Mercy. In April 1935, for three days leading up to the first Sunday after Easter, the worldwide Church marked the solemn closing of the Jubilee of Redemption, the 19th centenary of Christ's Death and Resurrection. When Fr. Sopoćko was asked to preach at this event at the *Ostra Brama*, he agreed, but on the condition that the Merciful Jesus painting be placed in a high window of the Gate of Dawn where it could be seen by crowds of faithful people. As he preached an impassioned homily about the mercy of God, he pointed frequently to Kazimirowski's painting. Sister Faustina, who attended the liturgy during these holy days, wrote in her *Diary* that she saw the arm of Jesus blessing all the people gathered there and that the rays shining from Him were penetrating into people's hearts (*Diary*, 416-417).

In this convent, Sr. Faustina began writing her beloved *Diary*, which she kept over a period of four years until three months before her death in 1938. As previously mentioned, it began at the request of Fr. Sopoćko, who asked her to write down all her spiritual experiences in a notebook, which he would then study at his leisure. Although she feared that no words could express her experiences, she began to write out of obedience to God's will. The final result was six notebooks, revealing the wise and holy personality of the author and documenting the instructions of Jesus as to how He desired the devotion to Divine Mercy to be formed.

Here, too, in this convent, the Chaplet of Divine Mercy was dictated to St. Faustina on September 13-14, 1935. "Say unceasingly the chaplet that

*Miraculous image of the Holy Mother of Mercy in a chapel above the
Gate of Dawn in Vilnius.*

House of St. Faustina in Vilnius, the convent where she received the revelation of the Chaplet of Divine Mercy.

I have taught you. Whoever will recite it will receive great mercy at the hour of death," Jesus said to her. "Even if there were a sinner most hardened, if he were to recite this chaplet only once, he would receive grace from My infinite mercy" (*Diary*, 687). The chaplet is prayed every day at the convent at 3:00 p.m., the Hour of Great Mercy.

This original image of the Merciful Jesus, painted in Vilnius, has a fascinating history. Two years after its first public veneration at the *Ostra Brama*, the painting was hung in the Church of St. Michael next to the main altar. Although the church was closed in 1948 by the communist government, the image remained undisturbed until 1951, when two women ransomed the image from the caretaker of the abandoned church and gave it to the priest at the Church of the Holy Spirit. In 1956, the painting was taken from Lithuania to Belarus, to a small church near Grodno. There it remained for a number of years with people coming to see it and pray. In 1970, the church was shut down by the government and looted, but the Merciful Jesus image remained miraculously untouched.

Finally in the autumn of 1986, the holy image was spirited back to Vilnius without raising the suspicion of the government. It was again given into the care of the Church of the Holy Spirit and inconspicuously hung on a side altar. For over 50 years, the painting had suffered neglect and damage. So, in the spring of 2003, the professional restorer Edita Hankov-sa-Červinska removed previous signs of preservation and repainting from the image, revealing the image exactly as it was in 1934 when Kazimirowski painted it. In 2004, it was moved to the nearby Church of the Holy Trinity, which after its restoration became the beautiful Shrine of Divine Mercy.

While in Vilnius, Sr. Faustina received messages in her soul that God desired her to establish a new religious congregation, a community that would dedicate themselves to spreading the message of Divine Mercy in deed, word, and prayer to the ends of the earth. While she didn't follow this direction during her lifetime, God's desire is now being fulfilled through the great global movement of Divine Mercy, involving consecrated men and women and laypersons who wish to live in a spirit of trust in God and mercy toward their neighbors, proclaiming Divine Mercy and invoking it for the world.[12]

After Sr. Faustina's death and in response to her requests, Fr. Sopoćko facilitated the formation of what is now the Congregation of the Sisters of Merciful Jesus. The first six candidates for the rising congregation took temporary vows during the war, but during the Soviet occupation, they left Vilnius and established the motherhouse of the congregation in Myślibórz, Poland. Today the Sisters of Merciful Jesus form a few dozen congregation houses in Poland and abroad.

In the spring of 2000, the Sisters of Merciful Jesus returned to Vilnius and requested permission from Cardinal Audrys Bačkis to establish a house there. He decided to give the sisters the historical site at 4 Rasu Street, a small two-floor brick house, formerly belonging to the Visitation Sisters but which had served during the Soviet era as the administration office for the nearby jail. Nevertheless, the place is permeated with the gentle footsteps of Sr. Faustina, who many decades before had traveled back and forth to visit the artist Eugene Kazimirowski, whose studio was in this house. Today the Sisters of Merciful Jesus live here and run a hospice for the dying. The chapel of their convent is located in the former workshop where the original image of the Merciful Jesus was painted. In 2005, the Brothers of Merciful Jesus were formed in Vilnius with the approval of Cardinal Bačkis. Today they have a house and church near the train station and serve others through the spiritual and corporal works of mercy.

Today's Vilnius is a vibrant city filled with many churches, both Catholic and Orthodox. The Cathedral Basilica of Saints Stanisław and Władysław dates back to 1387. Rebuilt several times, it acquired its current Neoclassical style at the beginning of the 19th century. Father Sopoćko delivered homilies on Divine Mercy here during Lenten devotions, drawing crowds from all over the city. The cathedral was closed throughout the Soviet occupation and housed the Vilnius Art Gallery, but in 1988, it was returned to the faithful and solemnly reconsecrated. The relics of St. Kazimierz Jagiellon were also returned and are now venerated in the magnificent Chapel of St.

Kazimierz. Other distinguished noblemen, rulers, bishops and other clergy are buried in the crypts.

The Church of St. Michael the Archangel, where Fr. Sopoćko was rector from 1934 to 1938, and the former Bernardine Franciscan Sisters Convent, where he was chaplain, form an impressive Renaissance-era ensemble. Saint Michael's today is the Church Heritage Museum. Father Sopoćko lived in the building beside St. Michael's that is opposite the Church of St. Francis of Assisi and St. Bernardine of Siena (the Bernardine Church). When the war began and the Soviets occupied Vilnius, Fr. Sopoćko organized secret meetings of Catholic intellectual groups and of the Marian Sodality. On March 3, 1942, while Sopoćko was offering Mass at the Bernardine Church, Nazis had entered his lodgings with the intention of arresting him. Forewarned not to return to his rooms, he left for Juodšiliai with the help of the Ursuline Sisters, crediting Divine Mercy for his successful escape to safety.

The Dominican Church of the Holy Spirit, which held the image of the Merciful Jesus after its return from Belarus, was visited by St. John Paul II in 1993 on his visit to Vilnius. In 2004, when the image was transferred to the nearby Church of the Holy Trinity, the church was then given the title Shrine of Divine Mercy. The image of the Merciful Jesus is today permanently displayed in the center of the shrine above the altar. On each side are graffiti made by Nijolė Vilutytė: the Holy Mother of Mercy of the Gate of Dawn and the prayer "Jesus, I trust in You" in 11 languages.

MEDITATION

- What does the history of the original painting of the Merciful Jesus tell me about the significance of tangible, sensory images for intangible, interior faith?

- How are the red and pale rays coming from the Heart of Jesus penetrating my life?

Reading: John 19:31-37
One of the soldiers pierced his side with a spear, and at once blood and water came out...

Response: "Have mercy on us and on the whole world."

Everyone who believes that Jesus is the Christ has been born of God. ... By this we know that we love the children of God, when we love God and obey his commandments. R.

For the love of God is this, that we obey his commandments. And his commandments are not burdensome, for whatever is born of God conquers the world. And this is the victory that conquers the world, our faith. R.

This is the one who came by water and blood, Jesus Christ, not with the water only but with the water and the blood. R.

And the Spirit is the one that testifies, for the Spirit is the truth. There are three that testify: the Spirit and the water and the blood, and these three agree. R.

Those who believe in the Son of God have the testimony in their hearts. ... And this is the testimony: God gave us eternal life, and this life is in his Son. R.

Whoever has the Son has life. ... I write these things to you who believe in the name of the Son of God, so that you may know that you have eternal life (1 Jn 5:1-4, 6-13). R.

Prayer: Lord Jesus, You gave Yourself completely to us at Your death as You delivered over Your Spirit and poured out water and blood from Your side in testimony to Your merciful love. Show us Your truth and enkindle our faith so that we will know in what font we have been cleansed, by Whose blood we have been redeemed, and by Whose Spirit we have been reborn to eternal life.

5. Białystok, Bl. Fr. Michael Sopoćko

The life of Fr. Michael Sopoćko, the spiritual director of St. Faustina, was inextricably linked with the message of Divine Mercy. St. Faustina was the visionary, the recipient of the revelations; Bl. Sopoćko was the messenger, chosen by God to make them known throughout the Church. She wrote of him, "As a result of his efforts, a new light will shine in the Church of God for the consolation of souls. ... I have never before come upon such great faithfulness to God as distinguishes this soul" (*Diary*, 1390). His authentic life of faith, great apostolic fervor, theological studies, and developed pastoral sensitivity let him know that this was a message from God.[13] Through his research, writing, teaching, and his own suffering after the death of Sr. Faustina, he brought the mystery of Divine Mercy from her heart to the whole world.

The Shrine of Divine Mercy in Białystok.

Both during and after the Second World War, Fr. Sopoćko sought to keep his teachings hidden from the Soviet authorities in Vilnius, but he faced increasing dangers, including the threat of deportation to Siberia. So, in 1947, he accepted an invitation from Archbishop Jałbrzykowski to come to work in Białystok, Poland. Here he taught at the seminary and pursued other educational and pastoral activities. But his most important undertaking was always spreading the devotion of Divine Mercy, to which he was ardently devoted to the end of his life.

As in Vilnius, Fr. Sopoćko served as confessor to communities of religious sisters. Among them were the Missionaries of the Holy Family, who then resided on Poleska Street. Thanks to his efforts, a chapel under the invocation of the Holy Family was consecrated in the religious house of the sisters. When his physical ability deteriorated and ailments struck, he was forced to retire from full-time ministry. He then moved permanently to the convent grounds, where he conducted his writing and pastoral work.

His rich personality and spirituality, accompanied by humility, continued to attract many, but prayer and writing became the base of his vocation. A quotation from his diary constitutes a testimony of how he understood his final service:

Memorial room of Bl. Michael Sopoćko, run by the community he founded, the Congregation of the Sisters of Merciful Jesus.

Old age should be treated as a vocation to greater love of God and neighbor. God has new plans for the elderly, plans of deepening the human being by revealing to him, face to face, his inner life. The only effective action that we are capable of is prayer. In this active passivity everything prepares us, everything counts, everything works for our gain.[14]

When the Holy Office in Rome issued the 1959 decree prohibiting the propagation of images and documents presenting the Divine Mercy devotion because of the spread of faulty publications, Fr. Sopoćko humbly obeyed that decision. Yet he continued to research and write about the theological foundations of the devotion, including a four-volume work, *The Mercy of God in His Works*. His work for the benefit of Divine Mercy was furthered by the beatification process for Sr. Faustina, begun in 1965 by the Kraków archbishop, Karol Wojtyła.

Father Sopoćko remained in Białystok through the remainder of his life. Though disabled by age, spreading the message of Divine Mercy remained the driving force of his life until his death on February 15, 1975, in his room on Poleska Street. Sadly, he did not live to see the prohibition lifted in 1978 or the flowering of the Divine Mercy devotions in later years.

The house where Fr. Sopoćko spent the final years of his life, at 42 Poleska Street, presently belongs to the Congregation of the Sisters of Merciful Jesus, the community that he founded. A memorial room to Bl. Fr. Michael Sopoćko was established in the apartment where he lived.

Chapel of St. Faustina Kowalska and Bl. Michael Sopoćko in Białystok.

The Shrine of Divine Mercy in Białystok contains the sarcophagus holding the mortal remains of Bl. Fr. Sopoćko. Above his tomb, Bl. Michael is depicted as a young priest, wearing a worn-out cassock, signifying his simplicity and hard work. He is holding a Rosary and a breviary, while the image of Merciful Jesus hovers above his shoulder with the rays of mercy flowing through him.

Sopoćko's case for beatification was started at the Vatican in 1987, and in 2004, Pope John Paul II issued a decree on Sopoćko's virtues. His solemn beatification took place in 2008, at the shrine. Around the altar, there was a colorful banner quoting the words of Jesus to St. Faustina about Bl. Fr. Sopoćko: "He is a priest after My own Heart" (*Diary*, 1256). The homily was delivered by Cardinal Stanisław Dziwisz, former secretary for John Paul II and then Archbishop of Kraków, who said this:

> There was a need for Fr. Michael's wisdom, spiritual sensitiv-
> ity, and holiness of life in order to recognize, in the visions of
> the simple nun, God's message directed to the whole world.
> … Blessed Fr. Sopoćko proclaimed the mercy of God not only
> through direct and complete involvement in this task, which was

initiated by Sr. Faustina. He himself was a man of infinite trust in the mercy of God. This was his deepest spiritual attitude. This was his "personal song." This was a special characteristic of his Christian and priestly identity.[15]

MEDITATION

• Why is Bl. Fr. Michael Sopoćko often called a second "apostle of Divine Mercy"?

• How does Bl. Michael help me understand the vocation of old age?

Reading: 2 Corinthians 4:1-7
Since it is by God's mercy that we are engaged in this ministry, we do not lose heart...

Response: "Jesus, I trust in You."

Holy Spirit, give me the grace of unwavering trust when I think of Our Lord's merits, and of fearful trust when I think of my own weakness. R.

When poverty comes knocking at my door. R.

When sickness lays me low, or injury cripples me. R.

When the world pushes me aside, and pursues me with its hatred. R.

When I am besmirched by calumny, and pierced through by bitterness. R.

When my friends abandon me and wound me by word and deed. R.

Spirit of love and Mercy, be to me a refuge, a sweet consolation, a blessed hope, that in all the most trying circumstances of my life I may never cease to trust in You.[16] R.

Prayer: Most Merciful Jesus, You chose Bl. Michael Sopoćko as spiritual director to St. Faustina, strengthening her in fidelity to your voice and guiding her to the heights of holiness. Show us, through his study, teaching, service, and suffering, how to respond to Your calling, to be obedient to Your will, and to be absorbed in the mystery of Your unlimited mercy.

Convent and Chapel of the Sisters of Our Lady of Mercy in Kraków-Łagiewniki.

6. Kraków-Łagiewniki, Convent and Tomb of St. Faustina

Sister Faustina spent the final months of her short life at the sisters' convent in Łagiewniki, located in the southern part of Kraków. She knew this convent well, having spent her novitiate years here, and she received her habit, took the name Mary Faustina, and made her final vows with the Sisters of Our Lady of Mercy in the chapel. Here, too, Sr. Faustina wrote much of her *Diary* and experienced extraordinary mystical graces.

In Faustina's day, the "House of Mercy" for women and girls seeking moral renewal offered embroidery, weaving, and bookbinding workshops; a washhouse; and a garden and agricultural farm. The entire complex was placed under the patronage of St. Joseph, and the sisters referred to it simply as Józefów, Joseph's Place. Today, the Youth Educational Center is named after St. Faustina and operates as a facility for girls who are not socially adjusted. The sisters run a dormitory, a junior high school, a three-year high school, and a two-year vocational school of gastronomy and hairdressing.

Sister Faustina began working as a gardener here in her final months of life, but was reassigned as the porter at the convent gate when her illness prevented such strenuous toil. In the building for guest accommodations today, the cell of Sr. Faustina has been reconstructed, and a plaque commemorates the experience in which Jesus came to the gate as a poor young man, which St. Sr. Faustina describes in her *Diary*. After she fed Him some soup with breadcrumbs, He let her know that "He was the Lord of heaven and earth" and vanished from her sight. When she reflected on this encounter at the gate, she heard these words in her soul:

My daughter, the blessings of the poor who bless Me as they leave this gate have reached My ears. And your compassion, within the bounds of obedience, has pleased Me, and this is why I came down from My throne — to taste the fruits of your mercy (*Diary*, 1312).

During her final years, Sr. Faustina's lifelong experience of the interweaving of suffering and grace heightened, as she submitted herself completely to the will of God. She began undergoing an invisible stigmata, feeling the sufferings of Christ in His Passion without the visible wounds. She was also in the last states of advanced tuberculosis, which would soon take her life.

About a year before her death, Sr. Faustina received instructions from the Lord concerning another element of the Divine Mercy devotion; namely, the Hour of Great Mercy at 3 p.m., the time of the Lord's death on the Cross:

I remind you, my daughter, that as often as you hear the clock strike the third hour, immerse yourself completely in My mercy, adoring and glorifying it; invoke its omnipotence for the whole world, and particularly for poor sinners; for at that moment mercy was open wide for every soul. In this hour you can obtain everything for yourself and for others for the asking; it was the hour of grace for the whole world — mercy triumphed over justice (*Diary*, 1572).

When Mother Irena visited Sr. Faustina shortly before her death, Faustina beckoned her to come nearer and said to her without a hint of pride, "The Lord Jesus wants to elevate me and make me a saint." On October 5, 1938, Sr. Faustina knew it was the day of her death. At nine o'clock in the evening, the sisters gathered at her bedside to pray, while Faustina was conscious and grateful for their presence. At 10:45 p.m., St. Faustina peacefully went to her reward, while almost immediately her emaciated body seemed to take on an unearthly beauty. On the convent building at the entrance to the chapel, a plaque points to the cell in the former convent infirmary where St. Faustina was called home to the Lord.

The greatest part of Sr. Faustina's mission began after her death, as she had said it would. Although few of the community members had any hint of her extraordinary mystical experiences during her lifetime, they soon began to learn that a saint had lived among them. During World War II, the devotion to Divine Mercy spread throughout Poland, offering hope for many, especially for those in the many concentration camps throughout the country. After the war, Faustina's message widened through refugees and soldiers throughout the world. The convent in Łagiewniki became the chief center for the devotion, as the faithful came to pray in the chapel and visit the grave of Sr. Faustina in the community's cemetery.

Plaque outside the room where Sr. Faustina died on October 5, 1938.

The chapel, which was consecrated in 1891, joins the two wings of the convent. A statue of Our Lady of Mercy has the central place at the main altar, while on the left side stands St. Stanisław Kostka, the patron of youth, and on the right St. Mary Magdalene, the patron of penitents. On the side altar on the right rests a picture of St. Joseph, to whom the chapel was dedicated.

The miraculous image of Merciful Jesus painted by Adolf Hyła is placed above the side altar on the left. It was blessed by Fr. Józef Andrasz, SJ, the spiritual director of Sr. Faustina at this convent, on Divine Mercy Sunday, 1944. As part of the cause for Sr. Faustina's beatification, promoted by Archbishop Karol Wojtyła, her remains were exhumed and transferred to the convent chapel in 1966. Below the image of Merciful Jesus, the saint's remains rest in a white marble coffin. Visitors may pray at her tomb and join in praying the chaplet every day at 3 p.m.

Chapel of the Sisters of Our Lady of Mercy;
tomb of St. Faustina and miraculous image of Merciful Jesus by Adolf Hyła.

MEDITATION

- Do I experience suffering and grace as separate aspects of my life or are they interwoven?
- How could I learn to observe the Hour of Great Mercy?

Reading: 1 John 4:13-21
By this we know that we abide in him and he in us, because he has given us of his Spirit...

Response: "Oh Blood and Water which gushed forth from the Heart of Jesus as a fount of mercy for us, I trust in you!" (*Diary*, 309).

Great love can change small things into great ones, and it is only love which lends value to our actions. And the purer our love becomes, the less there will be within us for the flames of suffering to feed upon, and the suffering will cease to be a suffering for us; it will become a delight! By the grace of God, I have received such a disposition of heart that I am never so happy as when I suffer for Jesus, whom I love with every beat of my heart (*Diary*, 303). R.

When I see that the burden is beyond my strength, I do not consider or analyze it or probe into it, but I run like a child to the Heart of Jesus and say only one word to Him: 'You can do all things.' And then I keep silent, because I know that Jesus Himself will intervene in the matter, and as for me, instead of tormenting myself, I use that time to love Him (*Diary*, 1033). R.

Neither graces, nor revelations, nor raptures, nor gifts granted to a soul make it perfect, but rather the intimate union of the soul with God. These gifts are merely ornaments of the soul, but constitute neither its essence nor its perfection. My sanctity and perfection consist in the close union of my will with the will of God (*Diary*, 1107). R.

O my Jesus, each of Your saints reflects one of Your virtues; I desire to reflect Your compassionate heart, full of mercy; I want to glorify it. Let Your mercy, O Jesus, be impressed upon my heart and soul like a seal, and this will be my badge in this and the future life (*Diary*, 1242). R.

O bright and clear day on which all my dreams will be fulfilled; O day so eagerly desired, the last day of my life! I look forward with joy to the last stroke the Divine Artist will trace on my soul, which will give my soul a unique beauty that will distinguish me from the beauty of other souls. O great day, on which divine love will be confirmed in me. On that day, for the first time, I shall sing before heaven and earth the song of the Lord's fathomless mercy (*Diary*, 825). R.

Prayer: O Treasure of my heart, I want to adore You in my soul as You are adored on the throne of Your eternal glory. I pray that the sufferings of my life may become opportunities to experience Your grace more intensely. Give me a great and pure love for You so that in my troubles I may run to Your heart like a child, trusting that You can do all things. Unite my will with Your own will, so that I may reflect Your compassionate heart, full of mercy, now and at the great day of my death.

Basilica of Divine Mercy in Kraków-Łagiewniki.

7. Kraków-Łagiewniki, Basilica of Divine Mercy

As Pope John Paul II consecrated the new Basilica of Divine Mercy in 2002, he dedicated the whole world to Divine Mercy, saying:

> Today, therefore, in this Shrine, I wish *solemnly to entrust the world to* Divine Mercy. I do so with the burning desire that the message of God's merciful love, proclaimed here through Saint Faustina, *may be made known to all the peoples of the earth* and fill their hearts with hope. May this message radiate from this place to our beloved homeland and throughout the world. May the binding promise of the Lord Jesus be fulfilled: from here there must go forth "the spark which will prepare the world for his final coming."[17]

The worldwide apostolic movement of Divine Mercy began to develop when Fr. Michael Sopoćko began to publish images of the Merciful Jesus with the chaplet, novena, and litany toward the end of St. Faustina's earthly life. The movement grew during the war and the postwar years. New communities, churches, institutions, and apostolates multiplied, all undertaking the work of spreading the devotion and imploring Divine Mercy for the world.

As mentioned previously, the spontaneous development of the movement was slowed by the Holy See's notification of 1959, which placed a ban on propagating the devotion to Divine Mercy. Yet, the 19-year prohibition turned out to be a blessed time, allowing for the study of Sr. Faustina's life and writings, which formed a more solid theological foundation for the movement. A new wave of development occurred after the withdrawal of the notification in 1978 by Pope Paul VI and the pastoral visits and encouragement of Pope John Paul II. Finally, the beatification followed by the canonization of St. Faustina in 2000 caused the devotion to Divine Mercy to radiate throughout the world. Today the apostolic movement of Divine Mercy embraces millions of people on every continent, who in different ways continue the mission of St. Faustina.

The basilica is a large white oval church that seats 4,000 persons on the grounds of the convent. During his visit to Łagiewniki in 1997, Pope John Paul II blessed the cornerstone brought from Mount Calvary in Jerusalem. After construction was complete in 2002, he returned to dedicate the church on his last pastoral visit to Poland.

Behind the large stone altar of the upper church rests the tabernacle in the shape of the globe with the continents outlined on it. It is surrounded by the form of a bush being tossed by strong winds, symbolizing the moving currents of the modern world. As God spoke to Moses in the burning bush, God continues to speak in the midst of today's world. The image of Merciful Jesus, painted by Jan Chrząszcz, stands within the bush above the tabernacle, reminding us that peace is found only in the mercy of God. The central image is flanked by paintings of St. John Paul and St. Faustina. Further to the left and right there is an image of Our Lady of the Gate of Dawn and the text of the act of entrustment of the world to Divine Mercy, delivered here in 2002 by John Paul II.

Opposite the area of the altar, a huge stained-glass window above the choir depicts a luminous cross against the background of the sun, sky, and sea. The colors harmonize with the vertical stained-glass windows on each side of the basilica, creating the effect of a ship sailing on the sea.

Five unique chapels are located in the lower part of the basilica. The decor of each is a gift from the churches of other European countries. The central place is occupied by the Chapel of St. Faustina, donated by the Church in Italy, and the other chapels are arranged radiantly around it. The interior is simple and bright, the walls lined with light sandstone slabs. Front and center rests a painting of St. Faustina with her *Diary*. Below stands the tabernacle in the shape of an opening flower, which refers to the

Basilica of Divine Mercy altar with tabernacle and storm-tossed bush.

Carillon bells named for the saints of Poland.

words of the *Diary*, "The Love of God is the flower — Mercy the fruit" (see *Diary*, 948). The altar, pulpit, and the base of the reliquary are made of light travertine. In front of the altar, the relic of the saint is placed in a reliquary in the shape of a rose.

The Communion of Saints Chapel is a gift of the Church in Hungary. The mosaics on the side walls depict saints and blessed men and women of Hungary, Poland, and other European countries. They are led by Mary, the Mother of God, and their images are accompanied by the text of the Beatitudes, which reads like a commentary on their lives. Above the marble altar there is a mosaic of the Merciful Jesus with St. Faustina listening intently to his words, and around its edges are the words, "Jesus, I trust in You," in several languages. In front of the altar, in a hand-shaped reliquary, rests a relic of St. Stephen, King of Hungary.

The Chapel of St. Andrew the Apostle is a Greek Catholic chapel where the Divine Liturgy may be celebrated in the Eastern Rites. The icon screen follows the Eastern tradition, and the painted walls depict the Cathedral of the Mother of God, Baptism of Kievan Rus (a mass baptism of Christians initiated by Vladimir the Great in the first Eastern Slavic state around 988 A.D.), the Old Testament Trinity, Christ Acheiropoietos (a well-known icon of Christ, "made without hands"), and the Exaltation of the Holy Cross.

The Chapel of the Holy Cross is a gift from the faithful in Germany. Behind the altar is a wooden cross and a crown of thorns. To the side is a bronze sculpture of St. Teresa Benedicta of the Cross, also known as Edith Stein. The expressive Stations of the Cross include the faces of Sts. John Paul II, Teresa of Calcutta, Francis of Assisi, and Maximilian Kolbe.

The Chapel of Our Lady of Sorrows was donated by the Church in Slovakia. Behind the altar is a tender carved Pietà and the scene of Christ's entombment and Resurrection etched in glass. On the walls are images of Sts. Cyril and Methodius, the apostles to the Slavs, the words of the Magnificat in Old Church Slavonic, Latin, Greek, and Hebrew, and representations of the Seven Sorrows of Mary: the prophecy of Simeon, the flight into Egypt, the loss of Jesus in the temple, meeting Jesus on the way to Golgotha, Jesus' Crucifixion and Death, Jesus' body being taken down from the Cross, and Jesus' entombment.

Nine carillon bells have been hung at the front of the basilica. The following names are inscribed on the bells: Jesus, St. Faustina, St. John Paul, St. Stanisław, St. Jacek (Hyacinth), St. Jadwiga, St. John Cantius, St. Rafał

Kalinowski, and St. Brother Albert Chmielowski. Below are the words of Psalm 89, "We will sing of the mercies of the Lord forever" (Ps 89:1).

Next to the basilica stands the Chapel of Perpetual Adoration of the Blessed Sacrament, which is open day and night. The stained glass from top to bottom is decorated with floral design. The altar is the shape of a blazing fire with the monstrance within it. A perpetual lamp with the fire of Mercy burns over the monstrance as a sign of the message of God's Mercy spreading from this place to the whole world. Shortly before his death, Pope John Paul II wrote, "Nothing makes the work of mercy, which was accomplished through the cross and resurrection, more present than the Eucharistic presence of the Lord. May this presence, therefore, be a source of strength and hope for all pilgrims."[18]

A 250-foot tower topped with a cross overlooks the basilica. A viewing platform offers a panorama of the city and the surrounding area, extending even to the Tatra Mountains on a clear day. It can be reached by elevator or 315 steps. Above the entrance to the tower is a statue of St. John Paul as a pilgrim of peace. He is releasing a dove that will carry the message of God's mercy to the world.

MEDITATION

- How does the Basilica of Divine Mercy offer me a sense of Christ's Universal Church?

- In what ways does the message of Divine Mercy fill my heart with hope?

Reading: Ephesians 3:14-19
I bow my knees before the Father, from whom every family in heaven and on earth takes its name…

Response: "St. Faustina, pray for us."

Witness of the Father's mercy, humble servant of Jesus, and obedient instrument of the Holy Spirit. R.

Trustful daughter of Our Lady of Mercy and great apostle of the mercy of God. R.

Guide on the Way of the Cross and partaker in the Lord's Passion and Resurrection. R.

Persistent with steadfast faith, persevering in unwavering hope, and enkindled with ardent love. R.

Hope of the despairing, strength of the sick, safeguarding the hearts of the dying. R.

Offering your suffering for the salvation of sinners and imploring God's mercy for the whole world. R.

Prayer: O God, Who in a wondrous manner revealed the inexhaustible riches of Your mercy to St. Faustina, may Your Church sing of Your mercy from generation to generation. By gazing with trust upon the pierced side of Your Son, give us the grace to perform works of mercy for our neighbors and finally to praise Your mercy forever in Heaven.

III. Saint Maximilian Kolbe

When Raymond Kolbe was born and baptized in 1894, the nation of Poland was only a future hope based on a noble past, as its territory had been completely conquered by surrounding nations. He was the second of five sons, raised by parents who were both fervent Catholics and zealous Polish patriots. The heart of this Polish patriotism was and is the shrine of Our Lady of Częstochowa, the queen of her people, inspiring chivalrous exploits in the pursuit of freedom and the defense of the faith. In his youth, the future saint had a passionate interest in all things military and dreamed of a military career to liberate his beloved Poland from its enemies. He revered those heroes of Poland's past who didn't hesitate to make the supreme sacrifice of their lives for their cherished religion and their beloved country. The boy knew that somehow, in service of his Blessed Mother and Queen, he would attain the two promised crowns, the white crown of heroic virtue and the red crown of martyrdom.

At age 13, Kolbe entered a Franciscan junior seminary in Lwów. The youth was the most talented in his class, excelling in mathematics and physics, and his teachers predicted a brilliant future for him in science or as a military strategist. But, in 1910, he was received as a novice and took the habit of the Conventual Franciscans with the new name of Maximilian, after a young Roman who was beheaded for declaring that, as a Christian, he

Saint Maximilian Kolbe, priest, Pole, patriot, and prisoner.

could not serve in the Roman army or swear allegiance to the emperor. The young Maximilian Kolbe knew that he still wanted to struggle and fight, but he would not be waging battle with the sword. He took his final vows in 1914, the same year his father was captured by the Russians and hanged for his part in fighting for an independent Poland.

The young friar spent the years 1912 to 1919 studying philosophy and theology in Rome. During his studies, he realized that the most important fight against evil was a spiritual one. On October 16, 1917, with six Franciscan companions, he founded a new type of army, the Militia of the Immaculata (*Militia Immaculatae*), with the aim of converting hearts to Jesus and bringing all to love Mary Immaculate. While his health began to deteriorate with advanced tuberculosis, his zealous love for Mary Immaculate became the devouring characteristic of his life. For her, he strove to develop all the good that was in him, and he wanted to encourage others to do the same.

When Fr. Maximilian returned to Poland in 1919, he rejoiced that Poland was free once again, a liberation that he attributed to Poland's heavenly Queen. He set out to extend the influence of his Militia and formed cells all over Poland, inviting people from all ranks of society to consecrate their lives to the mission of Mary to extend as far as possible the kingdom of the most Sacred Heart of Jesus. Kolbe's style of consecration emphasizes a radically apostolic dimension — working under the command of Mary Immaculate as she labors to bring all souls to Christ. "We must be the best possible instruments in her immaculate hands and let her lead us in everything," Kolbe said. For every strayed and indifferent soul Mary enters, she obtains the grace of conversion and growth in holiness.

In 1922, Kolbe and his Franciscan militia began to publish a monthly magazine, the *Knight of the Immaculata*, with an initial print run of 5,000. The publication began to grow, and five years later 70,000 copies per issue were printed. At that time, Fr. Maximilian began to look for a larger site and was offered property by Prince Jan Drucko-Lubecki at Teresin, west of

Warsaw. Father Maximilian promptly erected a statue of Mary Immaculata there, and the monks began the arduous work of construction. On December 8, the friary was consecrated and given the name Niepokalanów, the City of the Immaculata.

Kolbe's vision for the Militia of the Immaculata would not be confined to Poland. In 1930 he left Poland with four Franciscan brothers on a journey to the Far East. Traveling by way of Port Said in Egypt, then Saigon and Shanghai, they landed at Nagasaki in Japan. They were received warmly by the local archbishop, rented a house near the cathedral, and within a month they were printing the *Knight* in Japanese. The next year, they purchased land and inaugurated a new friary, Mugenzai no Sono (Garden of the Immaculate), built on the slopes of Mount Hikosan. The location was dictated by poverty, built on steep ground sloping away from the city, but in 1945, when the atomic bomb all but levelled Nagasaki, the friary was protected by the mountain and was able to take in refugees from the city. The friary, novitiate, seminary, and publishing house continued to grow, and today the Garden of the Immaculate remains the center of a Franciscan province.

In 1936, Kolbe was recalled to Poland because of his poor health. The publications coming from Niepokalanów continued to multiply, and by the time the war broke out, the *Knight* had a circulation of over a million copies. Priests in parishes all over Poland reported a tremendous upsurge of faith due to the literature coming from Niepokalanów. After the war, the Polish bishops claimed that Fr. Kolbe's magazine had prepared the Polish nation to endure and survive the horrors of the war.

As the Germans invaded Poland, they occupied the friary and destroyed much of it. Many of the Franciscans, including Kolbe, were deported to Germany. But that exile lasted only three months, and the prisoners were set free. Returning to Niepokalanów, Fr Maximilian was galvanized to transform the grounds into a shelter for 3,000 Polish refugees, among whom were 2,000 Jews. The friars housed, fed, and clothed them all. Inevitably the community came under suspicion and was closely watched, and, in the last edition of the *Knight* before his death, Fr. Kolbe wrote the following:

> No one in the world can change Truth. What we can do and should do is to seek truth and to serve it when we have found it. The real conflict is the inner conflict. Beyond armies of occupation and the hecatombs of extermination camps, there are two irreconcilable enemies in the depth of every soul: good and evil, sin and love. And what use are the victories on the battlefield if we ourselves are defeated in our innermost personal selves?[19]

1. Niepokalanów, the City of the Immaculata

At the heart of Niepokalanów, the foundation of St. Maximilian Kolbe's Militia of the Immaculata, stands the old wooden chapel. This is where it all started, the cradle of the community. In this chapel, the saint prayed, offered Mass, and preached conferences. Here, too, the brothers made their Franciscan vows of poverty, chastity, and obedience. Images of the four Franciscans arrested with Kolbe by the Gestapo are honored on the chapel walls. Just off the sacristy, visitors can see the first cell of St. Maximilian, where he lived from the founding in 1927 until 1930.

Outside the chapel, a small statue of Mary Immaculata is displayed. Kolbe placed the statue in the empty field as he was expecting to receive the land from Prince Jan Drucko-Lubecki in 1927. The figure expresses Fr. Maximilian's belief that Niepokalanów is a place chosen by the Immaculata and is exclusively dedicated to spreading devotion to her. All that is and will be at Niepokalanów, he declared, will belong to her.

When the "city" was consecrated on December 8, it consisted of no more than a few simple buildings with tar-paper roofs, but it soon flourished as more and more men from throughout Poland sought to join the community. Soon a junior seminary was built at Niepokalanów to prepare priests for the missions. Before long, Niepokalanów had become the largest friary in the world, shining forth with Franciscan zeal, simplicity, charity, and joy. In 1939 it housed 762 inhabitants: 13 priests, 18 novices, 527 brothers, 122 boys in the junior seminary, and 82 candidates for the priesthood. Among the inhabitants were doctors, dentists, farmers, mechanics, tailors, builders, printers, gardeners, shoemakers, and cooks. It was entirely self-supporting. There was a sawmill, carpentry shop, dairy equipment, and a repair shop for farm machinery, bicycles, watches, and many other items. The friars grew their own food, raised livestock, kept chickens, produced cheese, and managed beehives.

Father Kolbe founded the City of the Immaculata not as a great center of productivity, but as a fraternity united in unconditional self-giving to the Immaculata. Its members were knights of love, seeking to conquer the world, not to capture it but to free it. Here is part of a recruiting ad:

> The gates of the city of Mary Immaculate are always open! Enter by those gates all young men who seek to serve Mary without counting the cost! In work without end, in abandoning self, in penance — this is the way to that peace which the world cannot give.[20]

The original wooden chapel and small statue of Mary Immaculata at Niepokalanów.

The friars lived in a spirit of poverty and simplicity, but they sought to acquire the most modern equipment and techniques to better "win the world for Christ through the Immaculata." They obtained three machines which could produce 16,000 copies of the *Knight* in an hour. They adopted new methods of type, photogravure, and binding. In addition to the monthly magazine, they produced other publications as well. In 1935 they began to produce a daily Catholic newspaper, *The Little Daily*, of which 137,000 copies were printed on weekdays and 225,000 on Sundays.

Father Maximilian was not content with only written publications. In 1938, he installed a radio station, and before the war set back his plans, he intended to build a motion picture studio. And since there was so much valuable equipment around, some of the brothers were trained as firemen and Niepokalanów established its own fire brigade. With all this evangelizing activity reaching every corner of Poland, the nation was spiritually prepared to endure and survive the horrors of the coming war.

The Museum of St. Maximilian Kolbe, called "There Was a Man," is dedicated to the saint's life and work. The visitor is greeted by a bronze sculpture of the saint by Italian sculptor Roberto Joppolo of Viterbo. The statue was blessed by Pope John Paul II in October 1982 during the canonization of St. Maximilian Kolbe in Rome. In a second part of the museum, visitors can view prewar photographs and exhibits with explanations concerning the life and activity of St. Maximilian — his childhood and youth, his studies in Rome, the mission to Japan, and the building of Niepokalanów and its publications. The third section presents the missions of the Franciscans throughout the world.

Just before the outbreak of the war, Fr. Maximilian spoke to his friars about the suffering that would come upon them. He urged them not to fear, but to accept their suffering with love, as a way to draw closer to the Immaculata. During the war, Niepokalanów served as a shelter for wounded soldiers and about 3,000 refugees, among whom were 2,000 Jews. All the services of the friary were brought into use to house, feed, and clothe them. Closely watched by the Gestapo, Kolbe and four other friars were arrested on February 7, 1941, and charged with aiding the Jews as well as the Polish underground. They were held in Warsaw for three months, but Kolbe was then transferred to Auschwitz, where he gave up his life for a fellow prisoner.

In the cemetery of Niepokalanów rests the grave of Franciszek Gajowniczek, a Polish soldier imprisoned at Auschwitz, whose life was saved when St. Maximilian Kolbe offered to die in his place. Gajowniczek survived over five years of internment at Auschwitz and Sachsenhausen concentration camps, then spent the rest of his life telling the world about the heroic act of love that spared him. Living a long life, he was present at St. Maximilian's canonization in Rome in 1982, and he died in 1995. He was buried in a grave in Niepokalanów that had been reserved for Kolbe had he survived the death camp and returned.

MEDITATION

- What are the characteristics of knighthood? How can I direct these qualities to my own Christian service?
- Which attribute of St. Maximilian Kolbe do I most want to imitate?

Reading: Ephesians 6:11-17
Put on the whole armor of God, so that you may be able to stand against the wiles of the devil...

Response: "St. Maximilian Kolbe, pray for us."

Faithful follower of St. Francis of Assisi, teach us your zeal for Christ and total dedication to the gospel. R.

Courageous knight of the Immaculata, help us give our lives in her service and become her instruments in the world. R.

Apostle of the Miraculous Medal, give us confidence in the Sacred Heart of Jesus and the Immaculate Heart of Mary. R.

Model of poverty, chastity, and obedience, show us how to be rich in generosity, fruitful in compassion, and discerning in response to God's will. R.

Evangelist of Nagasaki, Japan, guide our efforts to plant the seeds of God's word in the midst of the diverse cultures of our world. R.

Apostle of the communications media, inspire us to use today's instruments of journalism, broadcasting, and social media to spread the good news of God's kingdom. R.

Prayer: O God, You filled St. Maximilian Kolbe with burning love for the Immaculate Virgin Mary, zeal for the salvation of souls, and a merciful love of neighbor. May his radical discipleship lead us to a deep desire to know Your will and to strive for Your glory by eagerly serving others.

2. Basilica of the Blessed Virgin Mary the Immaculata

Plans for a new church at Niepokalanów were approved in 1938, and a cross was blessed on the site in 1939, but all was put on hold until after the war. In 1948, the first brick was laid for the structure designed by Zygmunt Gawlik, and finally in 1954, the church was consecrated by Bishop Wacław Majewski, who replaced the imprisoned Cardinal Stefan Wyszyński. Pope John Paul II honored the church with the title of "basilica" in 1980.

The church is exceptional because it was built by the friars of Niepokalanów with the help of the local people, for whom the basilica is their parish church. Three massive double-winged doors hold symbols of the most famous places of Marian apparitions around the world. At the end of the long nave, the visitor can see the white statue of Our Lady Immaculata above the main altar. Evoking biblical imagery, she is standing on the serpent and her head is crowned with 12 stars.

The chapel on the left side of the church is dedicated to St. Maximilian Kolbe. A marble statue of the saint is offering the entire globe to Mary our Mother. On the chapel walls are hung many votive offerings, in

*Basilica of the Blessed Virgin Mary
the Immaculata.*

*Our Lady Immaculata above the
main altar.*

thanksgiving for graces received. A round mosaic next to these offerings presents St. Maximilian speaking to the other prisoners at Auschwitz. The chapel on the right side of the church displays a statue of St. Joseph holding the child Jesus. The mosaic features the Merciful Heart of Jesus and the Immaculate Heart of Our Lady. The round mosaic to the left commemorates the baptism of Poland. The Latin inscription reads: *"Mesco dux baptizatur — Polonia semper fidelis — 966-1966"* (Prince Mieszko baptized — Poland is always faithful — 966-1966).

A passageway on the left leads to the Chapel of Perpetual Adoration of the Blessed Sacrament, inaugurated in 2018. At the altar a silver figure of Mary serves as a monstrance for the Blessed Sacrament under her heart. She was indeed the first monstrance, teaching us how to adore Jesus. The figure is surrounded by a wreath of silver lilies and golden rays. This World Center of Prayer for Peace is one of 12 international prayer centers for peace that are being established on all continents of the world. In these twelve locations — represented by the 12 stars in the crown of Mary, Queen of Peace — there is constant prayer for peace before the Blessed Sacrament.

The figure of Mary in the adoration chapel and the image of the Immaculata on the main altar contain elements of the Miraculous Medal of Mary Immaculata, which was so beloved by St. Maximilian. The saint called the Miraculous Medal the spiritual "bullet" of his Militia in its war on all the powers that prevent a soul from embracing God wholeheartedly.

The Miraculous Medal is a devotional medallion based on the apparitions of the Blessed Virgin Mary to St. Catherine Labouré in Paris in 1830. In the image, Mary appears as if standing on a globe with rays of light emitting from her fingers. The figure is in an oval frame bearing the words "O Mary, conceived without sin, pray for us who have recourse to thee." On the reverse side is a circle of 12 stars, a large letter M surmounted by a cross, and underneath are the Sacred Heart of Jesus and the Immaculate Heart of Mary, the former surrounded by a crown of thorns and the latter pierced by a sword.

Side altar dedicated to St. Maximilian, showing the saint offering the entire globe to Mary our Mother.

Many conversions are associated with the medal, including that of the wealthy agnostic Jew, Alphonse Ratisbonne, who became a Jesuit priest and missionary, cofounding the Congregation of Our Lady of Sion in Jerusalem. The account deeply influenced Maximilian Kolbe, who thought that if Our Lady could do that with one soul, she could do it with the entire world to bring them to Jesus. Kolbe adopted the Miraculous Medal for his Militia of the Immaculata, and for the rest of his life he carried a pocketful of these medals. After meeting someone and exhorting them to live as a faithful Christian, he would hand them a Miraculous Medal and let the Blessed Mother take care of the rest. Throughout his life many souls were brought back to Christ through the handing out of these silver "bullets."

In this Basilica of the Immaculata, we honor the woman who was not only sinless but most completely filled with the love of God. As beloved daughter of the Father, mother of the Son, and spouse of the Holy Spirit, she is one with God in an incomparably more perfect way than any other creature. Kolbe knew that because Mary belongs to God, everyone who is united with her belongs to God in a much more perfect way than would have been possible without her. With her and through her, they will understand and love the Sacred Heart, the Cross of Jesus, and the Eucharist better than ever before.

Saint Maximilian expresses the mystical significance of the Immaculata as the spouse of the Holy Spirit:

> In the union of the Holy Spirit with Mary, love unites not only these two Persons, but the first love [that of the Holy Spirit] is all the love of the Most Holy Trinity, while the second, that of Mary, is all the love of creation and so in that union Heaven is united to earth, the whole of Uncreated Love with the whole of created love … This is the vertex of love.[21]

MEDITATION

• Why does Marian spirituality draw me more ardently to the Heart of Jesus?

• How does Mary's title, Spouse of the Holy Spirit, offer me a richer understanding of her role in God's saving plan for the world?

> Reading: John 19:26-27
> *He said to his mother, "Woman, here is your son."…*
>
> Response: "Blessed are you among women, and blessed is the fruit of your womb" (Lk 1:42).
>
> The LORD God said to the serpent…
> I will put enmity between you and the woman,
>   and between your offspring and hers;
> he will strike your head,
>   and you will strike his heel (Gen 3:14-15). R.
>
> Therefore the Lord himself will give you a sign. Look, the young woman is with child and shall bear a son, and shall name him Immanuel (Is 7:14). R.
>
> The angel said to her, "The Holy Spirit will come upon you, and the power of the Most High will overshadow you; therefore the child to be born will be holy; he will be called Son of God" (Lk 1:35). R.

Then Mary said, "Here I am, the servant of the Lord; let it be [done] with me according to your word" (Lk 1:38). R.

A great portent appeared in heaven: a woman clothed with the sun, with the moon under her feet, and on her head a crown of twelve stars (Rev 12:1). R.

Prayer: Risen Lord Jesus, at the foot of Your Cross you presented Mary as the mother of your disciples and mother of your Church. As we give ourselves totally into her merciful hands, make us instruments for leading many strayed and indifferent lives to the grace of conversion and sanctification. May our words and deeds, our prayers and sufferings, help extend as far as possible the blessed kingdom of your most Sacred Heart.

3. Auschwitz, Cell of St. Maximilian Kolbe

Nazi persecution of the Catholic Church was intense, and thousands of priests were imprisoned and executed in an attempt to eradicate the Church. The Polish clergy were considered the foremost challenge to the Nazi administration, and over 3,000 priests were martyred between 1939 and 1945.

On May 28, 1941, Fr. Maximilian was deported with 300 others from the Pawiak prison to Auschwitz, where he became prisoner number 16670. There he received his striped convict's garments and was put to work immediately, carrying blocks of stone for the construction of a crematorium wall. On the last day of May he was assigned with other priests to the Babice subcamp, which was under the direction of a ruthless ex-criminal called "Bloody Krott." The work went on all day without stop as Krott forced the priests to cut and carry huge tree trunks. He seemed to harbor a relentless hatred against the Franciscan and gave him heavier tasks than the others.

On one particular day, as witnesses remembered, Krott gathered some of the heaviest timbers and personally loaded them on Kolbe's back, ordering him to run. When he collapsed, Krott kicked him in the stomach and face and had his men give him 50 lashes. When the priest lost consciousness, Krott threw him in the mud and left him for dead. However, his companions managed to smuggle him to the camp hospital. Although Fr. Maximilian was suffering greatly, he secretly heard confessions in the hospital and spoke to the other inmates of the love of God. In this place where hunger and hatred reigned and faith evaporated, this man opened his heart to others and spoke of God's infinite mercy.

Maximilian Kolbe, beatified as a Confessor and canonized as a Martyr.

Father Maximilian always considered the needs of others first. When food was brought and everyone struggled to get their place in line, he stood aside, and frequently there was none left for him. At other times he shared his meager ration of soup or bread with others. Men gathered in secret to hear his words of love and encouragement, but it was his example that inspired most. Father Zygmunt Rusczak remembers: "Each time I saw Father Kolbe in the courtyard I felt within myself an extraordinary effusion of his goodness. Although he wore the same ragged clothes as the rest of us, with the same tin can hanging from his belt, one forgot this wretched exterior and was conscious only of the charm of his inspired countenance and of his radiant holiness."[22]

At the end of July 1941, the camp siren announced that there had been an escape from among the prisoners of Block 14. This prompted *SS-Hauptsturmführer* Karl Fritzsch, the deputy camp commander, to pick 10 men to be starved to death in an underground bunker to deter further escape attempts. As the men were chosen and the sentence of doom pronounced, a noncommissioned officer named Franciszek Gajowniczek cried out in despair, "O my wife, my poor children. I shall never see them again." Then, from among the ranks of those temporarily reprieved, prisoner 16670 stepped forward and offered himself in the other man's place.

Fritzsch's expression revealed his surprise at Fr. Kolbe's action. The stark difference between these two men is one that the witnesses would always remember: the contrast between the man who rejected God and the man who dared to love God totally. Eventually Fritzsch gave a sign and

Kolbe joined the group of the doomed, while Gajowniczek left the doomed and resumed his place in the ranks. A little later, the condemned men were marched off in the direction of the dreaded Block 13, to the airless underground cells where men died slowly without food or water.

The Nazi jailers soon realized that this caging would be different. "Whereas, in the past, howling and curses reverberated from the starvation bunkers like a scene of the damned in hell, this time the condemned prisoners did not curse and tear at each other, but sang and prayed. Soon the condemned in the other cells joined in the singing of hymns to Our Lady. What had formerly been a place of torment and bedlam became a place of divine worship."[23]

Bruno Borgowiec, prisoner number 1192, was an eyewitness of what followed, for he was an interpreter in the underground bunker. He tells us what happened:

> When no SS men were in the Block, I went to the Bunker to talk to the men and comfort them. Fervent prayers and songs to the Holy Mother resounded in all the corridors of the Bunker. I had the impression I was in a church. Fr Kolbe was leading and the prisoners responded in unison. They were often so deep in prayer that they did not even hear that inspecting SS men had descended to the Bunker; and the voices fell silent only at the loud yelling of their visitors. When the cells were opened the poor wretches cried loudly and begged for a piece of bread and for water, which they did not receive, however. If any of the stronger ones approached the door he was immediately kicked in the stomach by the SS men, so that falling backwards on the cement floor he was instantly killed; or he was shot to death....
>
> The ten condemned to death went through terrible days. ... The man in charge of emptying the buckets of urine always found them empty. Thirst drove the prisoners to drink the contents. Since they had grown very weak, prayers were now only whispered. At every inspection, when almost all the others were now lying on the floor, Fr. Kolbe was seen kneeling or standing in the center as he looked cheerfully in the face of the SS men....
>
> Fr. Kolbe never asked for anything and did not complain, rather he encouraged the others, saying that the fugitive might be found and then they would all be freed. One of the SS guards remarked: "This priest is really a great man. We have never seen anyone like him....

Two weeks passed in this way. Meanwhile one after another they died, until only Fr. Kolbe was left. This the authorities felt was too long. The cell was needed for new victims. So one day they brought in the head of the sick quarters, a German, a common criminal named Bock, who gave Fr. Kolbe an injection of carbolic acid in the vein of his left arm. Fr. Kolbe, with a prayer on his lips, himself gave his arm to the executioner. Unable to watch this, I left under the pretext of work to be done. Immediately after the SS men with the executioner had left I returned to the cell, where I found Fr Kolbe leaning in a sitting position against the back wall with his eyes open and his head drooping sideways. His face was calm and radiant.[24]

Maximilian Kolbe died on the eve of the Feast of the Assumption of Our Lady and was cremated on the day of the feast, a fitting date for one who had dedicated his life so completely to Christ and to His Blessed Mother. News of his heroic self-sacrifice spread through the camp like a powerful shaft of light in the darkness. After the war, newspapers throughout the world ran stories, and biographies were written about this saint for our times. "The life and death of this one man alone," wrote the Polish bishops, "can be proof and witness of the fact that the love of God can overcome the greatest hatred, the greatest injustice, even death itself."[25]

Proceedings for Kolbe's beatification began soon after, and in 1960 the papal decree introducing his cause began with these words from John's Gospel: "No one has greater love than this, to lay down one's life for his friends" (Jn 15:13). He was beatified as a Confessor of the Faith in 1971 and canonized by Pope John Paul II in 1982. At the end of his homily, the Polish pope declared, "In virtue of my apostolic authority, I have decreed that Maximilian Maria Kolbe — who after his Beatification was venerated as a Confessor — shall henceforward be venerated also as a Martyr!"[26] Thus, he confirmed the two crowns promised by Our Lady to the Church's new saint, the white crown of heroic virtue and the red crown of martyrdom.

Because the body of Maximilian Kolbe was cremated, some mistakenly believe there are no first-class relics of the saint. However, two friars at Niepokalanów, who served as barbers between 1930 and 1941, preserved hairs from his head and beard without his knowledge. Since his beatification and canonization, more than 1,000 of these relics have been distributed around the world for public veneration.

The man saved by the martyr of Auschwitz, Franciszek Gajowniczek, survived the war and spent much of his life traveling, speaking about the clutches of totalitarianism and telling the world about the heroic act of love performed by Maximilian Kolbe. When Pope John Paul II declared Kolbe a saint, Gajowniczek was present with his large family, including his children and grandchildren. Afterward he summed up his feelings: "For years I suffered remorse over the part I played in contributing to Fr. Kolbe's death. This great day has put an end to my doubts forever. Today is the happiest day of my life." Gajowniczek died in 1995 at the age of 93. At his request, he was buried in the cemetery at Niepokalanów.

The cell where Fr. Kolbe died at Auschwitz.

MEDITATION

- Why is love only credible and authentic when it is lived in sacrifice?
- What enabled Maximilian Kolbe to be so merciful to others while undergoing such great suffering?

Reading: John 15:12-16
No one has greater love than this, to lay down one's life for one's friends...

Response: "St. Maximilian Kolbe, pray for us."

You united your suffering with the Cross of Jesus Christ. Show us how to make our suffering a sacrificial offering for the good of others. R.

You prayed for your persecutors. Teach us how to love our enemies and forgive the wrongs done to us. R.

You volunteered to die for another. Help us to be grateful for those who have given of their life for us and lead us to give of our life for others. R.

You died for a husband and father of a family. Restore the dignity of marriage and the value of family life. **R.**

You cared for the dying prisoners by giving them comfort and hope. Stand by us and pray for us at the hour of our death. **R.**

You surrendered your life as a martyr of charity at Auschwitz. Show us how to be witnesses of Christ's love in our families, our communities, and our world. **R.**

Prayer: O God, You gave St. Maximilian Kolbe the white crown of heroic virtue and the red crown of martyrdom. Show us how to unite our hearts with the Immaculate Heart of Mary so that she may direct our lives in the way of Your divine will for us. May we, through our living faith and our apostolic works, witness Christ to those around us and draw many souls to You.

IV. Saint John Paul II

Cardinal Karol Wojtyła, the 58-year-old archbishop of Kraków, returned to Rome in October of 1978 for the second papal funeral and second papal election since August in that "year of three popes." Elected on the conclave's eighth ballot, the new Bishop of Rome took the name John Paul II, the first non-Italian pope in 455 years. Coming out on the loggia of St. Peter's Basilica to address the enormous crowd that had gathered within the colonnades, he said that the cardinal-electors had called him from "a faraway land."

The distinct history and culture of that distant country had formed the new Pope throughout his life. Born in 1920, he was part of the first generation of Poles born in an independent Polish state since the late 18th century. But it was the century and a quarter of Polish resistance to its elimination from the map of Europe — a struggle for national survival through its culture, literature, and especially its Catholic faith — that was most decisive in shaping the thought and action of John Paul II. Polish national identity had survived the hostile eradication of the state, indicating that what a people honors and cherishes is more potent and lasting than political subjugation. With firm convictions about human possibility formed from these experiences, Pope John Paul II would guide the Catholic Church through the final years of the turbulent 20th century and into the third millennium.

On the day of his papal inauguration, Pope John Paul gazed out at the multitude gathered in St. Peter's Square and preached a rousing homily, the climax of which was this: "Do not be afraid. Open wide the doors for Christ. To his saving power open the boundaries of States, economic and political systems, the vast fields of culture, civilization and development. Do not be afraid."[27] The words became his rallying cry, and he returned to them repeatedly in his preaching and writing: "Do not be afraid. Open your hearts to Christ."

Of course these words did not mean that Pope John Paul had no fears or that he expected others to live without them. Rather, in the face of fear, he drew on his faith to give him courage, and he lived beyond fear, teaching others to do the same. Over the course of his life he had to face most people's worst fears. When he was 8 years old, his mother died. When he was 12, his only sibling, Edmund, died of scarlet fever. At 19, just as he was beginning his university career, the Nazis rolled through Poland and began a reign of terror. At 20, he lost his father and was left without a family. During the war years, the Nazis decapitated Polish society, killing the intelligentsia outright or sending them to concentration camps.

But the young Karol Wojtyła was part of the resistance, taking an active part in underground religious and cultural activities. As he watched his parish priests being deported and killed and all distinctive forms of Polish culture cruelly suppressed, he displayed heroic courage by joining the underground seminary run by the cardinal of Kraków and by forming a small company of players who kept Polish literature and drama alive. Many of his colleagues in both of these endeavors were arrested or killed during those terrible years of occupation. When the Nazi tyranny was replaced immediately by the Soviet oppression, he lived for decades as a priest and bishop under constant surveillance. He watched as members of the clergy and hierarchy were imprisoned on fabricated charges, accused by false witnesses, assassinated, or "disappeared." So, as the Pope, when he urged his global flock of more than a billion members not to be afraid, he was speaking with the authority of his own experiences in Poland.

Because Pope John Paul spoke with an appeal to the human yearning for the noble and heroic, he appealed to the best instincts of young people all over the world. At a time when pandering to the young was the norm, John Paul II did not pander: he challenged. He did not ask young people to accept any challenge he had not accepted, take any risk he had not taken, or bear any burden he had not borne. In the face of the relativism and indifferentism of the age, he urged them to pursue truth and goodness with

Holy ground from the places visited on the worldwide pilgrimages of Pope John Paul II.

courage. Never settle, he would tell them, for anything less than the spiritual and moral greatness that the grace of God makes possible in your life. And when you fail, as we all do, then get up, seek forgiveness, be reconciled to God and others, and then continue the adventure of life in Jesus Christ. Live your life in this way, he suggested, and you will live wholeheartedly, with exhilarating purpose. As Pope, he was a demanding leader, but young people knew he loved them — which caused them to shout with joy at World Youth Days on every continent, "JP2, we love you!"

When he returned to Poland for a nine-day pilgrimage in 1979, two massive gatherings marked the beginning and end of those momentous days that changed the world. He began his pilgrimage in Warsaw, with an open-air Mass at Victory Square (today's Piłsudski Square). To the gathered throngs and with the whole nation of Poland watching and listening, he declared: "Man is incapable of understanding himself fully without Christ. He cannot understand who he is, nor what his true dignity is, nor what his vocation is, nor what his final end is. ... Therefore Christ cannot be kept out of the history of man in any part of the globe."[28] Responding spontaneously, the massive crowd began to chant in unison: "We want God! We want God! We want God!" Throughout the following days, he continued to lift up his voice for family, for freedom, for country, and for God.

On the ninth and final day of his pilgrimage, Pope John Paul celebrated another outdoor Mass at Błonia Krakówskie, the Kraków Commons. In his masterful homily addressed to a congregation of over a million of his countrymen, he concluded with these words:

Before going away, I beg you once again to accept the whole of the spiritual legacy which goes by the name of "Poland," with the faith, hope and charity that Christ poured into us at our holy Baptism. I beg you: Never lose your trust, do not be defeated, do not be discouraged; do not on your own *cut* yourselves off from the roots from which we had our origins. I beg you: Have trust, and notwithstanding all your weakness, always *seek* spiritual power from him from whom countless generations of our fathers and mothers have found it. *Never detach yourselves* from him.[29]

Those nine days began the greatest nonviolent revolution of the 20th century. And as John Paul II brought the Church into the third millennium, the world looked radically different than it had at the beginning of his papacy. He proved himself one of the most courageous figures of our time. Up against the face of communist totalitarianism, he spoke eloquently for religious freedom and human rights. Facing Western materialism and consumerism, he spoke persistently for the poor, the common good, and transcendent values. Through his transformative papacy, the Church and the world could look with confident hope to whatever the new century might hold.

1. Wadowice, Town of John Paul II's Birth and Youth

On his visit in 1999, Pope John Paul II said, "Here, in this town, in Wadowice, everything started. My life started, my school started, my studies started, theater started, and my priesthood started..." Today, pilgrims travel here from around the world to see those places that formed the saint's first 18 years of life. The city is centered on the market square, which has been renovated and named for John Paul II. Its granite surface holds 167 engravings commemorating the Pope's pilgrimages to the various cities of Poland and over 100 countries throughout the world. At the head of the square stands a bronze statue of the Pope from Poland.

The building to the right of the statue holds the John Paul II Family Home Museum. In 1919, Emilia and Karol Wojtyła with their 12-year-old son Edmund moved into apartment number 4. It was a modest size at about 540 square feet, consisting of a living room, bedroom, and kitchen. On the ground floor were several shops, and on the floor above were the apartments of the Wojtyłas and five other families, including the owners of the building. A few months after the family's move, Karol Józef, known fondly as Lolek, was born. The neighbors would later tell this future pope that during the final labor and delivery, from 5 p.m. to 6 p.m., the sound of the church organ

"Everything was given birth here in Wadowice"
- Karol Wojtyła.
Touring the Museum of the Family Home
of John Paul II.

and the singing of the May Vespers could be heard in the family bedroom where he was born. Praying among the congregation in the church at that time were his father and elder brother Edmund.[30]

The museum was opened in 1984, managed by the Archdiocese of Kraków and entrusted to the Sisters of the Holy Family of Nazareth. In the family apartment and a few additional rooms, they gathered mementos of their Polish Pope, especially of his childhood and youth: photographs, books, kitchen utensils, and sporting gear. In 2010 the entire building was purchased and renovated through a partnership of the archdiocese and several government ministries. With the cellars deepened and the attic developed, four stories were created for the museum's exhibition. As a result, the museum, which opened in 2014, portrays Karol Wojtyła's pilgrimage through life as it unfolded from Wadowice and eventually reached the whole world.

The heart of the exhibit is, of course, the three rooms that served as the Wojtyła family home. They have been reconstructed to the style of the 1920s, and artifacts of the saint include his parents' wedding portrait, a Carmelite scapular, First Communion mementos, articles of clothing, his mother's silver handbag and clover medallion, photographs of his early days in drama, and documents such as his secondary school graduation certificate. Larger exhibits throughout the museum include the cassocks worn in each period of his life, the Browning pistol used in the 1981 assassination attempt, a replica of the cross from Warsaw's Victory Square, Solidarity banners, earth from the places he visited on his worldwide pilgrimages, and

Basilica of the Presentation of the Virgin Mary, parish church of St. John Paul's childhood and youth; Karol Wojtyła's beloved image of Our Lady of Perpetual Help.

a model of the Holy Door from St. Peter's Basilica accompanied by a presentation of the Pope's encyclicals.

The church on the other side of the bronze statue of Pope John Paul is the Basilica of the Presentation of the Virgin Mary, the parish church of St. John Paul during his childhood and youth. The church was built in 1792-1798 in Baroque style with a tall clock tower and large spire. A stone figure of Mary, with a crown of 12 stars and treading on a serpent, stands above the entrance. On the right and left sides of the façade are statues of Sts. Peter and Paul. On the wall of the church seen from the Wojtyła home, a sundial is inscribed in Polish: "Time flies, eternity waits." Young Karol would have seen this reminder out of his window every day. Today it is marked with the precise date and time of St. John Paul II's death.

At the church's high altar stands a silver-clad image of the Blessed Virgin with the infant Jesus. On the left side of the church is seen the Chapel of the Holy Family, within which stands the Baroque stone font at which Karol Wojtyła was baptized on June 20, 1920. On the right side of the church is the Chapel of the Crucifixion, with the figures of Our Lady, St. Mary Magdalene, and St. John placed under the cross. The altar contains reliquaries of St. Maximilian Kolbe, St. Szymon of Lipnica, St. Padre Pio, and St. Stanisław Kazimierczyk (canonized in 2010).

At the rear of the church, the Chapel of Our Lady of Perpetual Help is separated by a black grille. Beneath the miraculous image are the Latin words, "*S. Maria de Perpetuo Succursu*" (Our Lady of Perpetual Help). The painting is in the center of the neo-Gothic altar built in 1903. Young Karol Wojtyła prayed here every day before going to school, and as Pope, he crowned the image during his visit in 1999. On the other side at the church's rear, the Chapel of St. John Paul contains a relic of the saint. It is symbolically protected from above by statues of Swiss Guards. The ceiling of the basilica features frescoes honoring the papal encyclicals of Pope John Paul.

In this church, Karol made his first Confession, received his first Communion in 1929, attended the priests as an altar server, and was confirmed in 1938. Among the priests who shaped his early life, Pope John Paul named Fr. Kazimierz Figlewicz, a vicar in Wadowice from 1930 to 1933 who was his catechist and confessor, and Fr. Edward Zacher, catechist at the secondary school from 1932 to 1939 and prefect of the Marian Sodality. Later Fr. Zacher served as pastor of the parish from 1965 to 1984 and gave talks at Karol's first celebrations in Wadowice on becoming bishop, archbishop, and cardinal, and spoke again at the Pope's visit to his hometown.

Looking from the church toward the John Paul II Square, the municipal building stands on the right side. Today it is the seat of the mayor and city council, but in the interwar period it held the primary school attended by young Karol. On the far end of the square, at the corner of Adam Mickiewicz Street and under an arcade, stood the confectionary of Karol Hagenhuber, who brought a recipe from Vienna for cream cakes (*kremówki* in Polish). Pope John Paul fondly recalled how the high school students would celebrate passing their comprehensive exams with this delicacy. Although that shop was closed in 1945, the cream cakes can be enjoyed at all Wadowice confectioneries. Further down Adam Mickiewicz Street stands the Marcin Wadowita High School. In this building, Karol Wojtyła was a student in the years 1930-1938. He was an excellent student, earning very good grades, two of which were noted "with exceptional performance." Since his childhood, he was taught Polish literature by his father, and his school offered him a classical education. He had an exceptional way of reciting poetry and he played in several dramatic productions.

Many personal experiences formed the young life of Karol Wojtyła in his hometown of Wadowice. His mother Emilia, who suffered from poor health for many years, died when Karol was 9 years old. His elder brother, Edmund, left home to study at the faculty of medicine at the Jagiellonian University in Kraków when Karol was four, but he could always find time to visit and make trips with Lolek. When Edmund became a doctor in 1930, he served at hospitals, caught scarlet fever, and died in 1932. At the age of 12, from the time of his brother's death, Karol lived alone with his father, who dedicated the rest of his life to raising his son, focusing his life on the church, the school, and the theater.

Wadowice was a town in which Jews and Catholics living together was the most ordinary thing in the world. Of the 10,000 inhabitants, about 3,000 were Jewish. Many of young Karol's closest friendships were with Jews, including his well-documented, lifelong camaraderie with Jerzy Kluger. The first memory shared between "Lolek and Jurek," as they called each other, was being chased around the town square by an irate policeman. Sitting side by side in the elementary school, they shared a great curiosity about the single police officer in Wadowice: whether the ceremonial sword he wore was real or not. One day they caught the officer napping, so they drew the sword partially out of its scabbard and were caught in the act as the policeman awoke. The sword was real, but fortunately for the two 6-year-old conspirators, the punishment was mostly symbolic.[31]

The Wojtyła family landlord was Jewish, as were many of the shop owners on the square. Ginka Beer, who lived on the floor above, was the first to introduce Karol to the theater. Young Jerzy and Karol, along with other Jews and Catholics, played soccer in the fields, did their homework in one another's homes, and went to school together throughout high school. Jerzy's grandmother, Mrs. Huppert, would often stroll through the square with the parish priest, Msgr. Prochownik. This was everyday life in Wadowice until the war swept everything away.

Karol grew up understanding the Jewish tradition from the inside, and at the end of the war, as he learned of the Nazi camps and the extermination of the Jewish people, the tragedy caused him deep grief. It is no wonder that he became the first pope in two thousand years to enter and pray in a synagogue. No other pope did more to purify Catholic teaching about Judaism and to denounce anti-Semitism. Although Jerzy Kluger's mother, grandmother, and younger sister all died in the extermination camps, Jerzy lived to fight with the Polish army in Italy, get married, and settle in Rome. Decades later, Mr. Kluger and Pope John Paul II renewed their friendship and became partners in a pursuit far more delicate than sword-snatching. The Pope quietly enlisted Mr. Kluger to serve as an informal intermediary

Carmelite Monastery founded by St. Raphael Kalinowski.

between Israeli and Vatican officials in the sensitive negotiations that eventually led to the formal diplomatic relationship between the Vatican and the State of Israel.[32]

Another nearby sanctuary important to young Karol Wojtyła was the monastery of the Discalced Carmelites "on the hill," where he would go with his father. At the front of the red brick monastery stands a statue of St. Rafał Kalinowski, founder of the monastery. The younger Kalinowski was a leader of the January Uprising in 1863 against the Russian oppressors and a member of the underground Polish National Government, for which he was exiled to 10 years of hard labor in Siberia. After his return, he joined the Carmelite Order in 1877. After founding this Carmel in Wadowice, he served as its long-term prior and died here. He was beatified in 1983 and canonized in 1991 by Pope John Paul. The patron of the monastery is St. Joseph, whose statue with the child Jesus stands in the monastery's window niche.

Inside the church, at the high altar, a painting of St. Joseph is flanked by wooden figures of St. Teresa of Avila and St. John of the Cross. At a side altar, a painting of Our Lady of Mount Carmel is flanked by statues of St. Simon Stock, a 13th-century Carmelite reformer, and Bl. Joan of Toulouse, the first Third Order Carmelite. At this altar the young Karol Wojtyła received the scapular, which he wore throughout his life. A plaque is inscribed

Altar with the relics of St. Rafał Kalinowski.

with the words Pope John Paul spoke in 1999 about receiving his scapular here. Below the plaque is one of the saint's last scapulars, which he bequeathed to the Carmelites. Here too is the tomb of Blessed Alfons Maria Mazurek, a Carmelite priest and head of the seminary, shot by the Gestapo in 1944. He is among the 108 Martyrs of World War II — bishops, priests, consecrated men and women, and laity, killed by Nazi Germany — beatified in 1999 by Pope John Paul II.

Another side altar is dedicated to St. Rafał Kalinowski and another to St. Thérèse of Lisieux, containing a wax figure of the saint made in Italy and installed in 1930, a few years after her canonization. To the left side of the main altar, a chapel is dedicated to Fr. Rudolf Warzecha, a Carmelite educator who died in this monastery in 1999. A small museum displays mementos and objects associated with his life while his cause for beatification is underway.

MEDITATION

- What memories most influenced my first 18 years of life? How do they compare with those of St. John Paul?

- What experiences of his youth seemed to be most formative for the future pope and saint?

Reading: Galatians 4:1-7
As long as they are minors ... they remain under guardians and trustees until the date set by the father...

Response: "St. John Paul, pray for us."

Here, in Wadowice, you were born of loving parents and experienced the joys of family life. Show us the way to love and strengthen our families. R.

Here, you were born from above in the waters of baptism. Show us how to renew the grace of our baptism and become more mindful of our dignity as children of God. R.

Here you were taught the Catholic faith by your catechists and educated by good teachers. Show us how to support and encourage the gifts of catechists and teachers among us. R.

Here you served at the altar and received Holy Communion. Show us how to be transformed through the offering of the Mass and become the living Body of Christ for others. R.

Here you shared your life with Jewish friends and families. Show us how to honor our elder brothers and sisters in the faith and denounce anti-Jewish attitudes and behaviors among us. R.

Here you experienced the death of your beloved mother and your dear brother. Show us how grief and suffering can refine our soul and deepen our love. R.

Prayer: Loving Father, as we experience the beginnings of the life of St. John Paul, we turn to You with gratitude for the people, places, and events that have shaped our lives from their small beginnings. Help us continue seeking Your will in all things as You guide our way through life. Show us how to trust in You as You direct us, prod us, encourage us, forgive us, and carry us during our earthly pilgrimage.

Our Lady of the Angels Basilica at Kalwaria.

2. Kalwaria Zebrzydowska

Located in the rolling hills a few miles east of Wadowice, Kalwaria Zebrzy-dowska is a pilgrimage sanctuary comprising the baroque basilica of Our Lady of the Angels, a Franciscan monastery, and a series of over 40 small churches and chapels laid out along a picturesque landscape. Commissioned in the early 1600s by Mikołaj Zebrzydowski, the governor of Kraków, the stations are modeled on Jerusalem and placed on the hills of the area, which represent Golgotha, the Mount of Olives, Mount Zion, and Mount Moriah, with the Skawinka River representing the Kidron Valley. On the death of Zebrzydowski in 1620, the construction continued with his son Jan, who ordered additional stations as well as eight Marian chapels. Walking the paths connecting these oratories provides an experience of the Passion of Jesus in one direction, while walking in the other direction offers an entry into the Sorrows of Mary, leading to her death and her glorious Assumption.

The guardians of this "Polish Jerusalem" are the Franciscan Order of Friars Minor, who are informally called "Bernardines" in Poland. For over 400 years they have made these grounds a place of pilgrimage. During the public commemoration of Holy Week, the grounds serve as the setting for a series of mystery plays. Rather than watching the action as a theater performance, the audience takes part and enters deeply and personally into the mysteries of redemption. The largest celebration at Kalwaria takes place around the Feast of the Assumption, focusing on Mary's burial on Friday and her triumph on Sunday. The processions draw large crowds and include musical groups in regional costumes.

Saint John Paul visited Kalwaria many times, first as a young boy with his father, then as the archbishop of Kraków. He organized pilgrimages for men in 1968 and added pilgrimages for women in 1973. Men and boys carried the cross while women and girls carried an image of Our Lady of Kalwaria. Later, the sanctuary developed a Pilgrimage of Families in September and of youth in June. Other pilgrimages for priests, seminarians, altar servers, and other groups take place throughout the year. Wojtyła also came here privately, as a priest and a bishop, to walk and contemplate the mysteries. When he returned in 1979 as Pope, he said in his homily:

> The whole of this, well laid out in time and space and covered with the prayer of so many hearts, of so many generations, constitutes a unique living treasury of the faith, hope, and charity of the People of God in this land. Every time that I came here I was aware of drawing from that treasury. And I was always aware that the mysteries of Jesus and Mary on which we meditate while praying for the living and the dead are truly inscrutable.[33]

Our Lady of the Angels Basilica is entered through Paradise Square, at the entrance of which is an iron balustrade with stone posts, each supporting stone figures including eight Franciscan saints: from left to right, St. Szymon of Lipnica (a Polish Franciscan canonized in 2007), St. Anthony of Padua, St. Bonaventure, St. Francis, Jesus Christ, Blessed Mary, St. Clare, St. Louis, St. Bernard of Siena, and St. Jan of Dukla (a Polish Franciscan canonized in 1997). The church façade includes four niches that feature statues of Matthew, Mark, Luke, and John, with Our Lady in the center.

The basilica's main nave is high and wide, separated by a rood arch from the narrower original church. On the left and right sides of the arch are altars dedicated to St. Mary Magdalene and St. Francis of Assisi. Above the arch is a crucifix surrounded by a fresco of a procession in Kalwaria. The paintings in the vaulted ceilings are of the birth of Mary, her Annunciation, Assumption, and Coronation in Heaven. Altars on the right side include St. John Capistrano, St. Michael the Archangel, and St. Joseph. On the opposite wall stand altars to St. Didacus (a Spanish Franciscan canonized in 1588) and St. Catherine of Alexandria. Above the organ, the stained glass presents Blessed Mary among the angels, St. Francis, and St. Anthony. Adjoining the nave on the left is the Chapel of the Immaculate Conception of the Blessed Virgin Mary.

(Clockwise from top) One of dozens of chapels commemorating the Passion of Jesus and the sorrows of Mary; Paradise Square with figures of Franciscan saints; Chapel of Our Lady of Kalwaria with its miraculous image and votive offerings; Basilica and monastery of Kalwaria.

Entering through the arch, the visitor approaches the high altar with the image of Our Lady of the Angels. The stained-glass windows on the left depict St. Stanisław and St. Maximilian Kolbe. On the wall is a painting honoring Pope John Paul's pilgrimage to Kalwaria in 1979 and a plaque remembering his request for prayer here. Behind the altar are the carved wooden stalls of the monastic choir, and above is a baroque crucifix on a silver background depicting the outdoor pilgrimage way of Kalwaria.

A monumental doorway leads to the Chapel of Our Lady of Kalwaria. The walls of the chapel are divided by eight pairs of pilasters, which support a lantern topped with an elliptical dome. The image was brought to Kalwaria in 1641, after it miraculously wept tears of blood, and in 1667 the image was placed in this special chapel built to honor it. In four frames on both sides of the image are votive offerings for healings and favors received.

The corridors of the monastery contain a gallery of portraits and other interesting paintings, along with displays with liturgical vessels and vestments from the 17th and 18th centuries. The papal rooms are the apartment where the Pope stayed on his final visit. On display are his white cassock, his chasuble, chalice, and the bed where he slept. On the wall is the 16th-century "Ecce Homo," the image of Christ the Sufferer. During his last visit in 2002, the Pope expressed his sentiments about this place:

> This place wondrously helps the heart and mind to gain deeper insight into the mystery of that bond *which united the suffering Savior and his co-suffering Mother.* At the center of this mystery of love everyone who comes here rediscovers himself, his life, his daily existence, his weakness and, at the same time, the power of faith and hope: that power which springs up from the assurance that the Mother does not abandon her children at times of trouble, but leads them to her Son and entrusts them to his mercy.[34]

MEDITATION

• What is the value of imaginatively entering into Christ's Passion?

• Pope John Paul said that what attracts people here is "that mystery of uniting the Mother with the Son and the Son with the Mother." How do I experience this mystery?

Reading: John 19:1-16
Then Pilate took Jesus and had him flogged. And the soldiers wove a crown

of thorns and put it on his head...

Response: "Most Holy Mother, Our Lady of Calvary, turn your eyes of mercy toward us."

Carrying the cross by himself, [Jesus] went out to what is called The Place of the Skull, which in Hebrew is called Golgotha (Jn 19:17). R.

There they crucified him, and with him two others, one on either side, with Jesus between them (Jn 19:18). R.

Pilate had an inscription written and put on the cross. It read, "Jesus of Nazareth, the King of the Jews" (Jn 19:19). R.

When the soldiers had crucified Jesus they took his clothes and divided them into four parts, one for each soldier (Jn 19:23). R.

Standing near the cross of Jesus were his mother, and his mother's sister, Mary the wife of Clopas, and Mary Magdalene (Jn 19:25). R.

A jar full of sour wine was standing there. So they put a sponge full of the wine on a branch of hyssop and held it to his mouth (Jn 19:29). R.

When Jesus had received the wine, he said, "It is finished." Then he bowed his head and gave up his spirit (Jn 19:30). R.

Prayer: Hail, Holy Queen, Mother of Mercy, our life, our sweetness and our hope. To you do we cry, poor banished children of Eve. To you do we send up our sighs, mourning and weeping in this valley of tears. Turn then, most gracious advocate, your eyes of mercy toward us, and after this our exile show unto us the blessed fruit of your womb, Jesus. O clement, O loving, O sweet Virgin Mary. Pray for us, O Holy Mother of God, that we may be made worthy of the promises of Christ.

3. Kraków–Dębniki, Wojtyła Apartment and Church of St. Stanisław Kostka

After passing his final secondary school exam in Wadowice, Karol Wojtyła was accepted to study at the Jagiellonian University in Kraków, where he planned to study language and literature while also continuing his work in the theater. For this reason, in the summer of 1938 Karol Jr. and Karol Sr. moved to a modest apartment at 10 Tyniecka Street in Kraków's Dębniki district. Situated on the south side of the Vistula River, the apartment offered a view of the Old Town and was a short walk to the university. It was originally built by Lolek's uncle, and his mother's two surviving sisters lived on the top two floors. The father and son took up a basement suite consisting of two bedrooms, a kitchen, and a bath. Although the home is still within an inhabited tenement building, it is now a branch of the Archdiocesan Museum and is open for visitors at limited hours.

From here the young man threw himself into his studies at the Jagiellonian. Then a year later, on the morning of September 1, 1939, Hitler's army invaded Poland, beginning the Second World War. Because it was a First Friday, Karol walked across the Dębniki Bridge and up to Wawel Cathedral to serve the early morning Mass for his mentor from Wadowice, Fr. Figlewicz, who had been assigned there. The priest quickly concluded Mass as Luftwaffe bombs began to fall on the city. He hurried home to his aging father; then the two decided to travel with the mass migration of refugees fleeing the city toward the East in order to escape Hitler's onslaught. But after many days on the road, they found themselves confronted by Stalin's Red Army, advancing into Poland from the East. So father and son retraced their steps back to Kraków and their Dębniki apartment to live a life under German occupation.

To avoid being deported as slave labor and to scrounge enough food to sustain them both, young Karol got himself hired at the Zakrzówek Quarry and later at the Solvay chemical plant at Borek Fałęcki. Returning home from breaking rocks in February of 1941, he discovered that his father had died of a heart attack in his room. Weeping at his bedside, Karol realized that the last member of his close family had departed, and he felt a terrible loneliness. This was the end of what the Pope described years later as his "first seminary"— the formation he received from the inspiring example of his father's faith while experiencing weakness and hardship.

As Wojtyła's theatrical mentor in Wadowice, Mieczysław Kotlarczyk had a profound influence on him. In this apartment on Tyniecka Street, Kotlarczyk, Wojtyła, and several other young people formed an underground

Church of St. Stanisław Kostka, Wojtyła's parish church.

theatrical company called the *Teatr Rapsodyczny* (Rhapsodic Theater) as an act of resistance against the Nazi suppression of Poland's culture. A devout Catholic, Kotlarczyk believed that drama was a means of "transmitting the word of God" and that the actor, by opening up the realm of transcendent truth, "had a function not unlike a priest." They would rehearse in this basement apartment, which the group called "the catacombs," before going out to clandestinely perform throughout wartime Kraków. Performing the classics of Polish drama and poetry as a "theater of the word," freed from sets and props, the group risked their lives in defiance of the occupation's determination to erase Poland's cherished culture.

The Church of St. Stanisław Kostka, just a few blocks from Wojtyła's apartment, was his parish church from 1938 to 1944. Newly built when Karol began to worship there, the church is designed and decorated in a unique modernist and constructivist style. The high lantern is supported by four concrete pillars, each decorated with black and white images of numerous saints. The apse comprises a mosaic of the Risen Christ, greeted by heavenly angels. The church is named for a Polish saint of the 16th century, who died in Rome as a Jesuit novice. During his studies in Rome, Fr. Karol Wojtyła would often stop to pray at the tomb and the reconstructed rooms of the saint at Sant'Andrea al Quirinale. As a patron of students and novices, St. Stanisław Kostka is admired for his youthful determination and devotion.

Modernist interior of the church, staffed by the Salesians of St. John Bosco.

The parish is staffed by the Salesians of St. John Bosco, who are dedicated to the care and education of youth. In May of 1941, 12 Salesian priests were taken from the parish by the Gestapo, imprisoned at Auschwitz, and died there as martyrs. They include Bl. Józef Kowalski, 31 years of age, who ministered secretly to his fellow prisoners in Block 25. Discovered with a Rosary, he was ordered to trample on it during a roll call. When he refused, he was ridiculed and beaten, and eventually he was tortured to death. Giving his last slice of bread to his fellow prisoners, he asked them to pray for him—and for his persecutors.

On the left side of the church, a small altar is marked by a painting of Jan Tyranowski and a young Karol Wojtyła behind him. Beneath the altar is a sarcophagus with Tyranowski's remains. This simple tailor, who lived nearby at 11 Różana Street, was forever changed in 1935 when he heard a Salesian priest say in a sermon that "it is not difficult to become a saint." He then began a lifelong pursuit of prayer and personal holiness. After the Salesians were deported from the parish by the Nazis, the remaining priest asked Tyranowski to take responsibility for the young men of the parish, a work that also risked banishment or worse. The tailor accepted and organized the young men into what he called "Living Rosary" groups: 15 teenagers per group, with each group led by a more mature young man, an "animator" to

First stained glass window depicting events from the life of St. John Paul;
second stained glass window depicting the Salesian martyrs and later events of the
life of St. John Paul.

whom Tyranowski gave instructions and spiritual direction. This clandestine network was able to evade the Nazis' suspicion of larger organizations.

By 1943, Tyranowski had four such groups, and Karol Wojtyła, a manual laborer with intense literary interests, was the leader of one of them. In weekly meetings in his apartment, Tyranowski taught his group leaders both the fundamentals of the spiritual life and methods for steadily improving their lives. He met with the entire Living Rosary organization every third Sunday of the month and was also available to any member as needed. Once the Gestapo raided Tyranowski's apartment during one of these meetings, but they were persuaded that their activity was not subversive. Pope John Paul remembered particularly that Tyranowski introduced him to the Carmelite spirituality of Sts. Teresa of Avila and John of the Cross, an influence that would impact the rest of his life. And it was Tyranowski who showed Wojtyła the Marian theology of St. Louis de Montfort, a spiritual path that would even determine his episcopal and papal motto: *Totus Tuus* (Totally Yours).

These Carmelite and Marian paths to sanctity persuaded the young Karol Wojtyła that the path to fulfillment was not through self-assertion but through the gift of self in obedience to God's will, a conviction that moved him to recognize his call to the priesthood and to reject an acting career. Tyranowski showed him how, through contemplative prayer, he could not only inquire about God, but could live in God's presence, participating in God's life. In 1946, Wojtyła's mentor fell ill with tuberculosis and suffered great pain over the next several months. But he managed to see his favorite student attain the priesthood before he died in 1947.

Opposite the altar to Tyranowski, on the right side of the church, is an image of the Merciful Jesus. Adoring him are statues of St. Faustina, St. Padre Pio, Pope Francis, and Pope Benedict. Further on is found the Chapel of Mary Help of Christians. Cardinal Wojtyła said in 1972, "In front of this picture I prayed and I grew strong in my priestly vocation." The image is surrounded by votive offerings, and a sculpture of John Paul II serves as a reminder of Mary's intercession.

Two stained-glass windows depict the most important events of St. John Paul's life and his relationship with the parish. Reading upwards, the first window depicts young Lolek at his parish church in Wadowice; his family; the suffering Christ looking at the young boy at Kalwaria Zebrzydowska; his Carmelite scapular; and Our Lady of Kalwaria. Above we see Jan Tyranowski with Sts. John of the Cross and Teresa of Avila behind him; to the left is the young student with his confessor while German bombers fly over Kraków; and to the right is Karol the worker at the quarry. Further up is the young Wojtyła praying before the image of Mary Help of Christians; to the left is St. Brother Albert; and to the right is Cardinal Adam Stefan Sapieha, whose secret seminary Wojtyła joined. Continuing upward we see newly ordained Fr. Wojtyła offering his first public Mass in this church, flanked by St. Stanisław Kostka to the left and St. John Bosco to the right. At the top is the elderly Pope during his 2002 visit to the parish, the Divine Mercy Shrine in Łagiewniki, and the parish church here.

In the second window, we see the 1981 assassination attempt on Pope John Paul; his recovery in the hospital; Our Lady of Fatima, in whose crown he placed the bullet that wounded him; Our Lady of Częstochowa, to whom he offered his bloodstained sash; and the dying Pope clinging to the crucifix during his last Way of the Cross. On each side of the crucified Christ stand the martyred Salesians, with one anonymous saint looking toward Christ to represent all nameless Salesian martyrs. The top images show the book of Sacred Scripture on the Pope's coffin during his funeral, while the image of the Holy Spirit accompanies the words *"Santo Subito"* chanted by the immense multinational crowd gathered for the funeral. Finally, St. John Paul is blessing the people from his window, expressing the words of Cardinal Ratzinger during the funeral: "We can be sure that our beloved pope is standing today at the window of the Father's house, that he sees us and blesses us."

MEDITATION

• Why are spiritual mentors so critically important for young people?

• How have I discovered the truth that God's power is made perfect in my own weakness?

> **Reading:** 2 Corinthians 12:7b-10
> *To keep me from being too elated, a thorn was given me in the flesh...*
>
> **Response:** "Mary Help of Christians, in your mercy hear and answer us."
>
> Holy Mary, St. John Bosco taught the Salesian family and all young people to look to you for guidance and confidence. Teach us to trust in you like St. John Bosco and the Salesian martyrs of the 20th century as we continue our pilgrimage through life. **R.**
>
> Virgin Mary, you are the supreme model for a youthful church that seeks to follow Christ with acceptance and enthusiasm. As you led St. John Paul to this Church of St. Stanisław Kostka, give us a fresh zeal for following your Son and keep us young at heart. **R.**
>
> Hail Mary, you accepted the risky message of the angel and replied with an open heart to the mission given to you. As you guided St. John Paul to understand and accept his vocation to the priesthood, help us discern and follow the will of your Son for our own lives. **R.**
>
> Comforting Mary, when both of his parents died in his youth, you became a tender Mother to St. John Paul throughout the rest of his

life. We ask you to support and accompany us, to embrace and protect us, and to be the guardian of our hope. R.

Mother of the Church, your desire to serve Christ and His mission was stronger than any doubts or difficulties. As you led St. John Paul through the terrors of war, the dangers of occupation, and the perils of concealment, may we always flee to your protection, implore your help, and seek your intercession. R.

Mary Help of Christians, you helped defend the Christian faith over the course of history from all its enemies. As you led St. John Paul through totalitarian fascism and atheistic communism, guide us through the sinful systems that surround us today and guard our faith from deception. R.

Queen of Martyrs, you watched in agony the death of your Son. May we be inspired by the Salesian martyrs honored here and all the martyrs of this land. May we be witnesses to our Christian faith in all we say and do, and may we remain faithful now and at the hour of our death. R.

Prayer: Remember, O most gracious Virgin Mary, that never was it known that anyone who fled to thy protection, implored thy help, and sought thy intercession, was left unaided. Inspired with this confidence I fly unto thee, O Virgin of virgins, my Mother! To thee do I come, before thee I stand, sinful and sorrowful. O Mother of the Word Incarnate, despise not my petitions, but in thy mercy hear and answer me.

4. Jagiellonian University and Collegiate Church of St. Anne

Standing in the arcaded courtyard of the Collegium Maius, the visitor is surrounded by the oldest buildings of the Jagiellonian University. As a place of higher learning for over 600 years, the space exudes an atmosphere of academic tradition, worthy scholarship, and principled debate. In 1364, King Kazimierz III the Great issued the royal charter founding the university. In the same year, Pope Urban V issued the bull assuring that all degrees awarded would be honored throughout the whole of Catholic Europe. In the 1390s, Queen Jadwiga and her husband Władysław II Jagiełło established the university on a firm foundation with faculties of philosophy (liberal arts), law, medicine, and theology.

Courtyard of the Jagiellonian University's Collegium Maius; musical clock sounding the academic anthem.

The lecture halls are situated on the ground floor, while the library, rooms of the professors, and treasury are on the upper floors. Only the "Professors' Stairs" break the rhythm of the arches and the cloisters surrounding the courtyard. On the upper level is a musical clock which sounds at 9, 11, 1, 3, and 5 with the academic anthem *"Gaudeamus Igitur"* (On the Shortness of Life) accompanied by a procession of six figures, each representing people connected with the university's history: the bedel (university official) carrying the scepters, Queen Jadwiga, King Władysław Jagiełło, St. John Cantius, Hugo Kołłątaj, and Rector Stanisław of Skarbimierz. In the middle of the courtyard stands the reconstructed well, once famed for the purity of its water, made of black marble ornamented with the coats of arms of Poland, Kraków, King Jagiełło, and Queen Jadwiga. Other coats of arms adorn the courtyard, including that of the university's most famous 20th-century graduate, Pope John Paul II. Today the Collegium Maius houses the Jagiellonian University Museum, displaying priceless treasures, a rich collection of paintings, sculptures, globes, and scientific instruments, as well as an assembly of rare astronomical devices from the time when Copernicus was a student.

After the Nazi invasion, the Gestapo called a meeting of all the university professors in a secret operation. The 184 academics who showed up were immediately arrested and banished to the concentration camp at Sachsenhausen, a horrific example of the Nazi effort to eliminate the cultural leaders of Poland. But the university defiantly reconstituted itself during the war years as an underground institution. Karol Wojtyła, who had begun his studies in Polish literature before the war, studied in hiding during the war, then continued his theological studies at the university before ordination. Later, after completing his first doctorate in Rome, he earned a second doctorate from the Jagiellonian during the years 1951 to 1953, the last such degree conferred by its theology faculty before it was shut down again, this time by Poland's postwar communist government. The university's most

Tomb of St. Jan Kanty, patron of the university, professors, and students.

distinguished 20th-century graduate reflected the Jagiellonian's expansive tradition through his conviction about the ennobling capacities of faith purified by reason and reason amplified by faith. In the opening sentence of Pope John Paul's encyclical *Fides et Ratio* (*Faith and Reason*), he stated, "Faith and reason are like two wings on which the human spirit rises to the contemplation of truth."

Off a hallway leading from the Collegium Maius toward the entrance on St. Anne Street, the visitor may view the two-room apartment of St. Jan Kanty (St. John Cantius), which has been transformed into a chapel. Born in Kęty in 1390, he became a lecturer, priest, faculty dean, provost, and professor of theology at the university. Renowned for his great knowledge and oratory skills, he was beloved by his students and revered for his generosity and compassion toward the poor, especially needy university students. Next to the entrance of the chapel stands a statue of the saint under an ornamental canopy, both of which were carried in processions in the years after his canonization in 1767. Next to the altar is a sepulchral image of the saint and a marble sarcophagus in which his body rested until 1603. On the walls of the chapel hangs a painting entitled "*Felix saeculum Cracoviae*," honoring the 15th-century saints of the city.

Across St. Anne Street stands the 17th-century Collegiate Church of St. Anne. Its interior is a dynamic expression of late-Baroque, featuring a variety of picturesque stuccowork. The high altar features a painting of St. Anne with St. Mary and the Infant Jesus. Along with the two previous churches on this site, it has been the setting for the ceremonial inauguration of the academic year, meetings of professors, and promotions of doctors.

In the left transept, near the altar with the Pietà, is found the tomb of Bishop Jan Pietraszko. After his theological studies at the Jagiellonian, he was ordained by Archbishop Sapieha. From 1948 until his death in 1988, he served St. Anne Church. Even after being made an auxiliary bishop under Archbishop Karol Wojtyła, he chose to remain a parish priest. He was known as a popular preacher, a sought-after confessor, director of student ministries, and promoter of devotion to St. Jan Kanty, whose virtues were an inspiration for him.

In the right transept is found the tomb of St. Jan Kanty, patron of the university, professors, and students. The marble coffin containing his relics is supported by allegorical figures representing the university faculties. The altar is surrounded by four spiral columns and crowned with figures of four St. Johns — John the Baptist, John the Evangelist, St. John Chrysostom, and St. John of Damascus. In all of his activities — in scientific research, writing, educating young people, and preaching in this church, Jan Kanty loved the pursuit of truth, gained from both human reason and divine revelation. Each day after his round of duties, he would go straight from the lecture room to the church, where he would spend long hours in contemplative prayer before the Blessed Sacrament. He lived simply, taught humbly, worked for God's glory, and died in the odor of sanctity in 1473.

Near the tomb of the saint rest the ashes of Jerzy Ciesielski, a married man, father of three, civil engineer, and teacher. As a young adult, he came to know Fr. Karol Wojtyła while he was ministering to college students. Ciesielski was an avid sportsman who enjoyed rowing and camping, and even taught Wojtyła how to kayak. Throughout his life, he combined profound Catholic faith with family life and scientific work. In 1970 he died tragically along with two of his children in a shipwreck on the Nile River.

MEDITATION

- Why are both human reason and divine faith necessary when seeking the fullness of truth?

- What does St. Jan Kanty teach me about putting into practice what I preach and teach?

Reading: James 2:14-18
What good is it, my brothers and sisters, if you say you have faith but do not have works?...

Response: "St. John Cantius, come to our aid."

We pray for the grace of a living faith in imitation of St. John Cantius, a faith that is expressed in good works, humility of life, and generosity of spirit. R.

We ask for faith purified by reason and reason amplified by faith. May our work and study, like that of St. John Cantius, always be guided by the truth of the Gospel. R.

We beg for the gift of prayerful contemplation like St. John Cantius, so that our lives may be marked by the ability to discern your will and follow it always, giving praise to you in all we do. R.

We pray that we may always live the Gospel of mercy like St. John Cantius, seeking to care for others, especially those who are poor, lost, in prison, and abandoned. R.

We seek to always have a heart for students and young people, so that like St. John Cantius we may inspire them in the pursuit of truth and goodness, guiding them in the way of virtue and integrity. R.

We ask to be formed as Christian witnesses like St. John Cantius, so that with hearts open to the Spirit, we may be laborers sent out into the harvest to serve the human family. R.

Prayer: Grant us, O Lord, the gift of Christian wisdom in this place of the academic pursuit of truth. May Your gifts of reason and faith, the products of our minds and the grace of Your revelation, continue to lead the people of Poland to prosperity and peace. Guide us, through the intercession of St. John Cantius, to care for our children and youth, so that they may be enabled through our witness and prayer to hear the calling You have given to them.

*Collegiate Church of St. Florian marks
the beginning of the Royal Road;
St. Florian, early Christian martyr who
led a firefighting brigade in the
Roman army.*

5. The Basilica of St. Florian

The Royal Way, passing through the center of Kraków and terminating at the royal residence on Wawel Hill, began outside the northern flank of the old city walls at the Church of St. Florian. From here, coronation processions, parades for distinguished foreign visitors, and royal funerals passed through St. Florian's Gate, past St. Mary's Basilica, toward Wawel Cathedral. The church is identified by an image of St. Florian, which is found both at the center of the exterior façade and of the interior Baroque altar.

Saint Florian was an early Christian martyr in present day Austria, put to death in 304 A.D. for refusing to worship the Roman gods. In the Roman army, he was responsible for leading an elite group of soldiers as a firefighting brigade. The first church dedicated to St. Florian in Poland dates to the 12th century, when relics of the third-century martyr were brought to Kraków. Legend holds that the mules carrying the relics of St. Florian into Kraków stopped here — the relics miraculously grew too heavy to be taken any further — and it was decided that the church would be built at this exact spot. In the 16th century, the saint's intervention extinguished the fire that consumed a part of Kraków in 1528, enhancing his reputation as the patron saint of firefighters.

From 1949 to 1951, Fr. Karol Wojtyła was assigned to the parish. As a young curate, he was charged with establishing a second center of university chaplaincy to complement the work of Fr. Jan Pietraszko at the Church of St. Anne near the Jagiellonian University. He offered campus ministry for the many other academic institutions clustered around Jan Matejko Place, including the Academy of Fine Arts and the Kraków Polytechnic. Shepherding these students as they responded to the challenges of young adulthood — falling in love, beginning marriages, and raising young families — there began to emerge in his mind what would, many years later, crystallize into his teachings on the theology of the body.

To the left of the sanctuary stands an altar dedicated to St. John Paul. The painting shows the saint as a young priest during the days when he served in this parish. In the course of his ministry to university students, a group of friends gathered who would later be called his *środowisko*, a word that translates as "environment," the surrounding conditions that influence development and growth. The community created by Fr. Wojtyła with these college students offered them a setting of truth and authentic fellowship amidst the dreary propaganda of atheistic communism. This youthful community — which took Wojtyła trekking through mountains and kayaking rivers — was the beginning of St. John Paul II's signature outreach to young people. Here he grew to understand more deeply that young people want the full Gospel, with all of its challenges and opportunities for living a purposeful and heroic life.

Outside, on the façade of the rectory to the left of the church, a commemorative plaque is placed by the window of the room where Fr. Dr. Karol Wojtyła lived from 1949 to 1951. Whenever the priest would leave the rectory, a member of the Communist secret police would track his activities. Normally on trips out of the city on the train, the group did not call him "father" or "priest" out of caution. Once the students asked Wojtyła if they could call him *Wujek* (Uncle). To the delight of the group, Wojtyła agreed to the new pseudonym. This special group of students, while respecting him as priest and professor, the inspirer of their spiritual lives, would hereafter affectionately refer to him as *Wujek*. Through the years, he witnessed their marriages and baptized their children. In August of 2000, three generations of *środowisko*, including the grandchildren of the original group, came to Rome for a visit and spent several days with *Wujek*.

MEDITATION

- What was the reason for Fr. Wojtyła's magnetic appeal to youth and young adults?

- Why do we need teachers and mentors to more fully understand the work of the Holy Spirit within us?

Reading: 1 Corinthians 2:6-13
Among the mature we do speak wisdom, though it is not a wisdom of this age…

Response: "Come Holy Spirit, enkindle in us the fire of your love."

O Holy Spirit, we ask You for the gift of wisdom, so that we may come to know Your divine depths, what no eye has seen, nor ear heard, nor the human heart conceived. R.

O Holy Spirit, we ask You for the gift of understanding, so that we may better apprehend the mysteries of our holy faith. R.

O Holy Spirit, we ask You for the gift of knowledge, so that we may be guided in life by the principles of our faith. R.

O Holy Spirit, we ask You for the gift of counsel, so that we may seek and find Your guidance in all that we do. R.

O Holy Spirit, we ask You for the gift of fortitude, to keep us inseparable from You, undaunted by fear or worldly attachments. R.

O Holy Spirit, we ask You for the gift of piety, so that we may always serve Your divine majesty with the love of sons and daughters. R.

O Holy Spirit, we ask You for the gift of reverent fear of the Lord, so that we may dread sin and all offenses against You, and seek to live a life pleasing to You.[35] R.

Prayer: Come, Holy Spirit, lead us to eternal wisdom, planned for our glory before the world began. Give us the mind of Christ so that we may be able to interpret spiritual things and discern all things. Enlighten our minds with understanding and enkindle our hearts with love.

6. Residence on Kanonicza Street and the Metropolitan Curia

Father Dr. Karol Wojtyła lived on Kanonicza Street at the foot of Wawel Hill. From 1952 to 1958, he lived in a small room at ul. Kanonicza 19 ("ul." stands for *ulica*, or street). Today, we can view his bookcase, wardrobe, bed, desk, and typewriter. After receiving the episcopal consecration in 1958, Bishop Wojtyła moved to the neighboring Dziekańska tenement house at ul. Kanonicza 21, where he lived until the end of 1967. Today, both buildings have been restored and together they form the Archdiocesan Museum of Cardinal Karol Wojtyła. In these rooms, the visitor can still feel his presence and remember his many deeds during this important period of his life as a priest and bishop.

Archbishop's Chapel, where Karol Wojtyła was ordained a priest.

In addition to mementos of St. John Paul from 1952 to 1967, the museum showcases ecclesiastical art from the 13th to the 20th centuries, including painting, sculpture, fabrics, and liturgical crafts coming from the churches and monasteries of the Archdiocese of Kraków. The museum also houses a valuable collection of gifts received by Pope John Paul II during his pontificate. During his pilgrimage to Poland in 1997, he visited the museum and had breakfast. Today, in the room that used to be his library, his porcelain breakfast set, produced in Ćmielów, is displayed.

Upon first moving to Kanonicza Street, Fr. Wojtyła wrote his postdoctoral habilitation thesis, exploring a Catholic ethic based on the ethical system of phenomenologist Max Scheler. In 1954, he earned his second doctorate from the Jagiellonian University, and in addition to his pastoral work, began to teach ethics at the Catholic University of Lublin. Wojtyła wrote a series of articles in Kraków's Catholic newspaper, *Tygodnik Powszechny*, dealing with contemporary Church issues, and he continued to write poetry and plays.

Kanonicza Street residence of Karol Wojtyła, priest and professor, 1952-1967.

While teaching, he continued to gather his *środowisko* for hiking, skiing, bicycling, camping, and kayaking, accompanied by prayer, outdoor Masses, and theological discussions.

In 1958, when Wojtyła was named auxiliary bishop of Kraków and his friends expressed concern that his new position would cause him to change, he responded, *"Wujek* will remain *Wujek,"* and he continued to live a simple life, shunning the trappings that came with his new status. At the age of 38, Wojtyła became the youngest bishop in Poland. In 1960, he published his influential book *Love and Responsibility*, a defense of Catholic teaching on marriage from a personalistic rather than a utilitarian view. The former views marriage as an interpersonal relationship, in which the well-being and self-realization of each partner are of overriding importance to the other.

Beginning in 1962 and continuing until 1965, Bishop Wojtyła took part in the Second Vatican Council, where he contributed significantly to *Gaudium et Spes (Joy and Hope)*, the Pastoral Constitution on the Church in the Modern World. During the council when he was introduced to Cardinal Ottaviani, the prefect of the Holy Office was surprised that the bishop was so young. Wojtyła replied, "This is a defect that will pass quickly."[36]

In 1964, Pope Paul VI appointed Karol Wojtyła as Archbishop of Kraków, and in 1967, the Pope announced Archbishop Karol Wojtyła's promotion to the Sacred College of Cardinals. During these years and until his election as Pope in 1978, the residence and office of Archbishop Wojtyła was at ul. Franciszkańska 3, the Metropolitan Curia, also known as the Archbishop's Palace. From here, Wojtyła conducted his episcopal ministry under the watchful eye of the secret police, charged with counter-Church activities. In 1973, Independent Group D was given the mandate to "disintegrate" the Catholic Church in the Polish People's Republic. Cardinal Wojtyła, described as a "very dangerous ideological opponent," was one of its principal targets.[37] In the tradition of St. Stanisław, he defended the people's fundamental rights of faith and conscience and fought the battle for the soul of Poland.

After the Second Vatican Council, Archbishop Wojtyła participated with Cardinal Wyszyński in the 1966 millennial celebrations of the Church in Poland. He later summoned an archdiocesan synod, including laypeople as well as clergy, to study the documents of Vatican II and ponder their meaning for the pastoral life of the Church in Kraków. Wojtyła wrote a commentary on the council's documents, *Sources of Renewal*, to help guide the synod's deliberation. The discussions guided his pastoral priorities for his final years in Kraków.

When Archbishop Wojtyła moved into the Metropolitan Curia, he already knew it well. He had lived here in 1944, as a student of the clandestine Kraków Archdiocese Seminary. In the archbishops' chapel, he was ordained to the priesthood on November 1, 1946, by Cardinal Sapieha. The chapel today contains a memorial and relic of St. John Paul. Here Wojtyła would often bring his worktable in order to prepare his sermons, pastoral letters, and other writing in the presence of the Blessed Sacrament.

Here Pope John Paul would return on each of his pilgrimages to Kraków from 1979 to 2002. He stayed in his old rooms, which were kept as he left them in 1978. Outside the building from the street, just above the entrance, the iconic window can be seen from which the Pope would speak to the young people who would gather each evening. The people of Kraków came here immediately after hearing of his death on April 2, 2005. For weeks the area in front of the palace was filled with flowers, candles, and people at prayer.

MEDITATION

• What aspects of Karol Wojtyła's life demonstrate his pastoral love for the people of Kraków?

• What indicates to me that the love between two people is genuine?

Reading: 1 Corinthians 13:4-13
Love is patient; love is kind...

Response: "St. John Paul, teach us how to love."

Love is the fullest realization of the possibilities inherent in man. The potential inherent in the person is most fully actualized through love. The person finds in love the greatest possible fullness of being, of objective existence. Love is an activity, a deed which develops the existence of the person to its fullest. It must of course be genuine love.[38] R.

Love is never something readymade, something merely "given" to man and woman, it is always at the same time a "task" which they are set. Love should be seen as something which in a sense never "is" but is always only "becoming," and what it becomes depends up on the contribution of both persons and the depth of their commitment. R.

A woman is capable of truly making a gift of herself only if she fully believes in the value of her person and in the value as a person of the man to whom she gives herself. And a man is capable of fully accepting a woman's gift of herself only if he is fully conscious of the magnitude of the gift — which he cannot be unless he affirms the value of her person. R.

For this reason genuine human love, love "for" a person, and love "between" persons, must combine two elements: tenderness and a certain firmness. Otherwise, it will lose its inner soundness and resilience, and turn into sterile sloppiness and mawkishness. We must not forget that love for a human being must also contain certain elements of struggle. Struggle for the beloved human being, and his or her true good. R.

Love consists of a commitment which limits one's freedom — it is a giving of the self, and to give oneself means just that: to limit one's freedom on behalf of another. Limitation of one's freedom might seem to be something negative and unpleasant, but love makes it a positive, joyful, and creative thing. Freedom exists for the sake of love. R.

Prayer: God of love, we praise You for the deep joy, genuine freedom, and true fulfillment that committed love offers to us. Thank You for the crosses and blessings given to us through the vocation to married life. Through the intercession of St. John Paul, in whose pastoral care married couples and families held a special place, make our love authentic, mutual, sacrificial, and everlasting.

7. Basilica of St. Francis of Assisi

Across Franciszkańska Street from the Metropolitan Curia stands the Franciscan basilica and friary, one of the first Gothic brick-and-sandstone buildings in the city. To the left of the main entrance is a modern statue of Cardinal Adam Stefan Sapieha, the Archbishop of Kraków for 40 years, from 1911 until his death in 1951. The pleading figure is entitled "Prayer in the Dark Night of Occupation," and was placed here in 1976, on the 25th anniversary of his death. Sapieha was heroic and steadfast during the worst period of the previous century and a decisive influence on the century's great liberator, St. John Paul II. Archbishop Wojtyła would often cross the street from his office and come to this church to pray. A small, engraved plaque was placed on his preferred pew, which is on the left side in the second-to-last row.

Chapel of the Passion with relics of Franciscan martyrs.

Built after the Franciscans settled in Kraków in 1237, the church has been severely damaged by several fires and subsequently rebuilt in different styles. The austere Gothic exterior contrasts with the interior's gentle arches and the explosion of colors in the Art Nouveau polychrome wall decorations by Kraków artist Stanisław Wyspiański. Designing and executing the interior around 1900, the artist balanced geometric forms with unique floral patterns featuring lilies, poppies, pansies, mullein, forget-me-nots, dandelions, nasturtiums, roses,

Archbishop Wojtyła often crossed the street from his office to come here and pray.

Main altar of the Basilica of St. Francis and Wyspiański stained glass.

Tomb of Bl. Aniela Salawa, beatified by Pope John Paul II.

sunflowers, and other flowers of Poland. The church retains its 13th-century vault, which is decorated with stars on a blue sky.

Equally impressive are the series of eight windows, also designed by Wyspiański. The murals and glass together evoke the concept of God's creation. Above the church choir, the window depicts the powerful image of God the Father in the act of fashioning the world from chaos. Different colors dominate, depending on the sunlight at different times of the day. The other windows surround the main altar. Left of center, the window features Bl. Salomea, a 13th-century Polish princess who became the first of the Polish Poor Clares. She drops her crown as the Holy Spirit sends down mystical flames. To the right of center, St. Francis stands among the branches with his face raised to the sky. He is receiving the stigmata with a vision of Christ shown above him. The middle window, covered by the altar, displays floral motifs and the Holy Spirit in the form of a dove, placed in the window's finial. Two more windows to the left express the power of the element of fire, with one window showing burning logs with blue and yellow flames shooting up, and the other displaying fiery-red flowers. Two more windows on the right express the power of the element of water, symbolized by irises and water lilies amid lakes and rivers.

The cloisters integrate the church with the monastery buildings and are used for Eucharistic processions. They have retained their Gothic character, with several 15th-century frescoes remaining, including the well-known "Mystical Winepress." The cloisters also display a gallery of portraits of Kraków bishops from the 15th century to the present, including a painting of Pope John Paul II. Saint Maximilian Kolbe lived in this friary from 1919 to 1922, where he printed his first issues of *Knight of the Immaculata*. A venerated painting of him is found in a side altar on the right side of the church's nave. Also found in the nave are statues of five founders of religious orders: Basil the Great, Benedict, Augustine, Dominic, and Francis.

Of the three chapels connected with the church, the first is the 15th-century Chapel of the Blessed Salomea. It features a Baroque coffin containing the remains of the Polish princess who joined the order of St. Clare of Assisi. The chapel also contains the remains of her brother, Bolesław V the Chaste, the husband of St. Kinga and the great benefactor of the church and monastery. The second chapel is that of Our Lady of Sorrows, featuring a miraculous painting from the 15th century known as the Sorrowful Lady of Kraków, the "Beloved Benefactress," and crowned with papal diadems in 1908. Maximilian Kolbe, when he was worrying about how to pay his first printing bill, approached her altar to pray. As he was leaving, he noticed an envelope on the altar, addressed "To you, O Mother Immaculate." Since it contained the exact amount necessary to pay the printing bill, the superior allowed Kolbe to use it to pay the printer.[39]

Finally, there is the Chapel of the Passion, marked by a black marble altar containing a statue of Christ in Sorrow. Within the altar are relics of Bl. Michał Tomaszek and Bl. Zbigniew Strzałkowski, both murdered by Shining Path guerillas in Peru while serving as missionaries in 1991. As young Franciscans, aged 31 and 34, they dedicated themselves to serving the people with the gospel and charity, restoring their dignity and loving them to the point of giving their lives. The golden tomb-sarcophagus of Bl. Aniela Salawa is also featured in the chapel. Working for many years as a maid, she served with patience and shared everything she owned, making a great impression on others. In 1912, Aniela became a member of the Secular Franciscan Order, and when World War I broke out, she cared for soldiers in Kraków as her health deteriorated. After her death in 1922, she became known for interceding for those in need and was beatified by Pope John Paul II in 1991. The chapel also contains a certified copy of the Shroud of Turin, which many believe covered the deceased body of Jesus and remains an icon of His Passion. The Stations of the Cross were painted from 1933 to 1946 by Józef Mehoffer. Archbishop Wojtyła would often pray these 14 stations privately on Fridays.

MEDITATION

• What might Archbishop Wojtyła have looked upon as he prayed in this church?

• What do the stained glass and the polychrome wall decorations speak to me about God's creation?

Reading: Philippians 3:8-14
I regard everything as loss because of the surpassing value of knowing Christ Jesus my Lord…

Response: "All praise is yours, all glory, all honor, and all blessing."

Be praised, my Lord, through all your creatures, especially through my lord Brother Sun, who brings the day; and you give light through him. And he is beautiful and radiant in all his splendor! Of you, Most High, he bears the likeness. Be praised, my Lord, through Sister Moon and the stars; in the heavens you have made them, precious and beautiful.[40] R.

Be praised, my Lord, through Brothers Wind and Air, and clouds and storms, and all the weather, through which you give your creatures sustenance. Be praised, My Lord, through Sister Water; she is very useful, and humble, and precious, and pure. R.

Be praised, my Lord, through Brother Fire, through whom you brighten the night. He is beautiful and cheerful, and powerful and strong. Be praised, my Lord, through our sister Mother Earth, who feeds us and rules us, and produces various fruits with colored flowers and herbs. R.

Be praised, my Lord, through those who forgive for love of you; through those who endure sickness and trial. Happy those who endure in peace, for by you, Most High, they will be crowned. Be praised, my Lord, through our Sister Bodily Death, from whose embrace no living person can escape. Woe to those who die in mortal sin! Happy those she finds doing your most holy will. The second death can do no harm to them. R.

Prayer: We adore You, Lord Jesus Christ, here, and in all Your churches throughout the whole world, and we bless You, because by Your holy Cross, you have redeemed the world. Through these words of St. Francis of Assisi, grant to us a right faith, a certain hope, and perfect charity, so that we may be united with You in a spirit of joy and deep humility.

8. Nowa Huta, Ark of the Lord Church

Nowa Huta was built in the 1950s, a colossal center of heavy industry just east of Kraków. In 1954 the Vladimir Lenin Steelworks was opened along with other large factories. In response to the resistance of Kraków to the communist ideology, Nowa Huta was designed to replace the royal city's culture with a communist utopia where the "New Soviet Man" could be fabricated along with steel. Young people were recruited from all over Poland to live in this model workers' city, freed from the shackles of traditional Catholic culture. Its broad boulevards were built on a gargantuan, inhuman scale to facilitate mass parades of human robots on May Day and other Communist "holy days." The architecture was functional, comprising huge apartment blocks, and public art, such as it was, exhibited the crudest form of socialist

Ark of the Lord Church, consecrated in 1977 by Cardinal Wojtyła.

Bells ring out in Nova Huta with St. John Paul, "The Wind of Hope".

realism. Apartments were small to discourage large families, and there was no passage from one to another enabling neighbors to gather, thus impeding the formation of communities other than those under party control.

In keeping with the Communist Party's futile experiment in the remanufacture of the human person, Nowa Huta's most striking feature was its deliberate godlessness. It would be the first Polish city in its thousand-year history without a church. But it was not long before people erected a high cross in an empty field, a reminder of the church they hoped to build there one day. Government attempts to remove the cross were met with street demonstrations and a violent response by the police, then it would be replaced within a matter of days. On Christmas Eve of 1959, Bishop Karol

Twenty-seven-foot-tall figure of the crucified Christ, entitled "From Life to Life," forged at the Lenin steel mill.

Wojtyła, the auxiliary bishop of Kraków, began celebrating an open-air Midnight Mass on the site, attended by thousands in subzero weather, a tradition he would continue as archbishop. The battle continued for 20 years, shaping Wojtyła's pastoral program as archbishop, and defining the future Pope as an unyielding defender of the human rights to freedom of conscience and religion.[41]

Ultimately the struggle was won, as the Ark of the Lord Church was consecrated in 1977 by Cardinal Wojtyła in the heart of Nowa Huta. Built by the people, using picks, shovels, and wagons, the church is strikingly modern in style, with the darker upper parts reminiscent of Noah's ark saving creation from destruction and the boat of Jesus sailing through stormy winds and rough seas. Its asymmetry and rounded edges form a glaring contrast to the rectangular functionalism of the surrounding buildings and streets. A steel cross, forming the mast of the boat, towers above the church, a reminder of the cross erected in the field decades before. The eight bells in front of the entrance ring every hour and can electronically play dozens of traditional songs. The statue of St. John Paul is entitled "The Wind of Hope."

The interior is dominated by the 27-foot-tall figure of the crucified Christ, entitled "From Life to Life" and forged by the workers at the Lenin steel mill. The bronze tabernacle expresses the cosmos and is embedded with a stone brought back from the moon by the Apollo astronauts. The altar symbolizes an open hand, offering the Bread of Life to the world. An image of Our Lady Queen of Poland, to whom the church is dedicated, is suspended from above. The ceiling resembles the hull of a boat, while the patterned blue-green marble of the floor evokes the churning sea. A unique Way of the Cross shows Christ carrying the Cross through Poland.

Two chapels are found on the church's lower level. A cave chapel is dedicated to Our Lady of Fatima and features adoration of the Blessed Sacrament. The Reconciliation Chapel evokes the tragedy of the Polish people during World War II. At the entrance stand several images of the Pietà. On the left in the chapel is a wall of confessionals, and on the right a sandstone wall representing the "Death Wall" in Auschwitz. By the wall is a sculpture presenting St. Maximilian Maria Kolbe, entitled "A Tormented Man." On the table stands a figure called "Our Lady the Armored," which is made entirely of pieces of shrapnel removed from Polish soldiers wounded at the Battle of Monte Cassino during World War II.

During the 1980s, most of the workers of the Lenin Steelworks joined the Solidarity trade union, and Nowa Huta became a stronghold of Kraków's Solidarity. The church became a focal point of anti-communist protests, which was a perilous undertaking during the period of martial law (which lasted from December 13, 1981 to July 22, 1982), as proven by the monument dedicated to Bogdan Włosik opposite the church. Włosik was shot in the chest by security services, and his death and funeral was a critical moment in the resistance. The monument commemorating the site of his death stands as a tribute to all those who died during this period.

MEDITATION

- Why is atheistic communism's understanding of the human person so inadequate?
- In what ways does a boat on the sea symbolize the besieged church of Poland?

Reading: Matthew 8:23-27
And when [Jesus] got into the boat, his disciples followed him...

Response: "Give thanks to the Lord, his love is everlasting."

The flood continued forty days on the earth; and the waters increased, and bore up the ark, and it rose high above the earth. The waters swelled and increased greatly on the earth; and the ark floated on the face of the waters (Gen 7:17-18). R.

And God made a wind blow over the earth, and the waters subsided; the fountains of the deep and the windows of the heavens were closed, the rain from the heavens was restrained, and the waters gradually receded from the earth (Gen 8:1-3). R.

[Noah] sent out the dove from the ark; and the dove came back to him in the evening, and there in its beak was a freshly plucked olive leaf; so Noah knew that the waters had subsided from the earth (Gen 8:10-11). R.

God said, "This is the sign of the covenant that I make between me and you and every living creature that is with you, for all future generations: I have set my bow in the clouds, and it shall be a sign of the covenant between me and the earth (Gen 9:12-13). R.

Who is as mighty as you, O LORD?
Your faithfulness surrounds you.
You rule the raging of the sea;
when its waves rise, you still them (Ps 89:8-9). R.

They cried to the LORD in their trouble,
and he brought them out from their distress;
he made the storm be still,
and the waves of the sea were hushed (Ps 107:28-29). R.

Prayer: Lord God, the people of Poland experienced the torrent of war and the deluge of oppression, but in the midst of their struggles they trusted in You to rescue them. During the storms of life, give us the courage to rise above the threatening waters and remember Your everlasting covenant.

9. The "Be Not Afraid!" Saint John Paul II Center

The White Seas area of Kraków's Łagiewniki and Borek Fałęcki districts, which is now the home of the Saint John Paul II Center, was formerly an industrial area dominated by the Solvay chemical factory. "White Seas" was the name given to the dunes of white by-product left from the production of soda ash. Karol Wojtyła toiled as a laborer at the Solvay plant during the years of the Nazi occupation, often stopping to visit the nearby chapel of the Sisters of Our Lady of Mercy and the grave of Sr. Faustina. Since Solvay's closure in 1990, the postindustrial landscape has been reclaimed for green space, and in 2006 part of the area was allotted for the construction of the "Be Not Afraid!" Center to honor John Paul II. Today the Divine Mercy Shrine and the Saint John Paul II Center are joined not only by the bridge across the Wilga River, but by the sacred history that unites these two apostles of mercy, St. Faustina and St. John Paul.

"Do not be afraid! Open the doors for Christ."

The "Be Not Afraid!" Center focuses on the octagonal Shrine of St. John Paul, but also incorporates the John Paul II Museum; the John Paul II Institute of Intercultural Dialogue; a conference center; observation tower; and open-air chapels in the meditation park. All of this is subsumed under the theme of John Paul's rousing homily on the day of his papal inauguration: "Do not be afraid. Open wide the doors for Christ." The decree establishing the Center, signed by Archbishop Stanisław Dziwisz, states that its purpose is "to commemorate the great legacy and pontificate of God's servant, Pope John Paul II, so that his example and words are passed on to future generations."

The octagonal space on the lower level, the Church of the Relics, focuses on an ampoule holding the blood of St. John Paul, encased in a glass casket, and placed within the marble altar. Behind the main altar there is a painting of John Paul II surrounded by Polish saints whom he canonized. They include, from left to right, Jan of Dukla, Rafał Kalinowski, Princess (later, Sister) Kinga, Brother Albert Chmielowski, Queen Jadwiga, Faustina Kowalska, Edith Stein, Maximilian Kolbe, Bishop Józef Pelczar, and Sister Urszula Ledóchowska. On the walls surrounding the altar there are paintings portraying John Paul visiting the most famous Marian shrines around the world: Fatima, Lourdes, Mariazell, Altötting, Częstochowa and Kalwaria Zebrzydowska. The ceiling beams are arranged in the form of an eight-pointed star, symbolizing Mary under the title of Stella Maris, Star of the Sea.

Around this central space are various chapels honoring the legacy of St. John Paul. One of these chapels contains the original marble slab

Blood-stained cassock worn by Pope John Paul on the day of his attempted assassination; chapel containing the original marble slab that covered the first burial space of John Paul in the grotto of St. Peter's Basilica.

that covered the first burial space of John Paul in the grottos of St. Peter's Basilica. The chapel is made to resemble the Crypt of St. Leonard in Wawel Cathedral, where the newly ordained Karol Wojtyła celebrated his first Mass. On the slab there is a reliquary modeled on the open Book of the Gospels, the pages of which were turned by the wind during the Pope's funeral in St. Peter's Square. Displays around the chapel include a papal pastoral cross, a chasuble with a miter, and the cross before which John Paul prayed in his private chapel during his last Stations of the Cross in the Roman Colosseum in 2005. Another chapel honors St. Kinga, containing a statue of the saint and reliefs of other Gospel scenes made from salt. Others are dedicated to St. Queen Jadwiga, Mary of Loreto, and St. James.

The upper level of the shrine, also built on an octagonal plan, is decorated with mosaics designed by a Slovenian Jesuit, Fr. Marko Rupnik. Around the nave there are four main chapels dedicated to four themes: Eucharistic Adoration, Baptism, Our Lady of Częstochowa, and Our Lady of Fatima. In addition, behind the sanctuary are chapels depicting Nazareth, Bethlehem, and the Cross. Another chapel holds a priceless relic, the bloodstained white cassock worn by Pope John Paul on the day of his attempted assassination. In the

Octagonal upper church decorated with mosaics.

chapel stands an image of Our Lady of Fatima, on whose feast the Pope was shot by the assassin Mehmet Ali Agca on May 13, 1981.

Leading from the outdoor plaza into the shrine is a bronze door depicting the figure of St. John Paul, accompanied by many of those he elevated to be saints and blessed. These include St. Faustina, Jerzy Ciesielski, St. Gianna Beretta Molla, Bl. Pier Giorgio Frassati, Bl. Jerzy Popiełuszko, and St. Br. Albert Chmielowski. Above the door on the outside, the words of St. John Paul are engraved in Latin: "Do not be afraid! Open the doors for Christ."

MEDITATION

• What did St. John Paul do for the Church when he proclaimed, "Do not be afraid. Open wide the doors for Christ"?

• What would happen in my life if I were able to rid myself of fear?

Reading: Romans 8:31-39
If God is for us, who is against us?...

Response: "Do not be afraid. Open wide the doors for Christ."

Those who wait for the LORD shall renew their strength,
   they shall mount up with wings like eagles,
they shall run and not be weary,
   they shall walk and not faint (Is 40:31). R.

Do not fear, for I am with you,
 do not be afraid, for I am your God;
I will strengthen you, I will help you,
 I will uphold you with my victorious right hand (Is 41:10). R.

For I, the LORD your God,
 hold your right hand;
it is I who say to you, "Do not fear,
 I will help you" (Is 41:13). R.

But now thus says the LORD,
he who created you, O Jacob,
 he who formed you, O Israel:
Do not fear, for I have redeemed you;
 I have called you by name, you are mine (Is 43:1). R.

When you pass through the waters, I will be with you;
 and through the rivers, they shall not overwhelm you;
when you walk through fire you shall not be burned,
 and the flame shall not consume you.
For I am the LORD your God,
 the Holy One of Israel, your Savior (Is 43:2-3). R.

Prayer: Mighty God, You have called us by name and are with us
always. When Your people experienced hardship, distress, persecution, and famine, You were with them and made them conquerors.
Give us courage in our trials, for we believe that nothing can separate
us from Your love, O God, in Jesus Christ our Lord.

10. Zakopane, Tatra Mountains and Shrine of Our Lady of Fatima

Nestled at the foot of the Tatra Mountains, Zakopane is a resort town and a
popular departure point for winter skiing and summertime hiking into the
Tatra National Park. Karol Wojtyła was a frequent visitor here: as a child,
with his father and his brother, and later as a priest and bishop, often with
the students to whom he was chaplain. He returned to Zakopane in 1997 as
Pope, offering an outdoor Mass in the stadium under the Wielka Krokiew
ski jump. Gubałówka is a mountain above Zakopane that offers sweeping
mountain views which visitors may reach by funicular.

The Tatra Mountains are the home of the Polish highlanders, who
possess their own traditional attire, cuisine, music, and dances. On formal

Chapel of the Sacred Heart of Jesus built by highlanders in the Zakopane style.

occasions, the men are distinguished by their white felt cape and dark felt hat, while the women wear flowing skirts with colorful floral patterns and a scarf worn on the head or over the shoulders. As an outdoor people, they eat large amounts of cheese and meat-based dishes. Guests may try their popular salty smoked cheese *oscypek*, made with sheep milk, and *kwaśnica*, a soup made from sauerkraut and meat with a side dish of potatoes or bread.

The area is known for its traditional wooden architecture in chalets and churches. The Chapel of the Sacred Heart of Jesus (Jaszczurówka Chapel), consecrated in 1907, was designed by Stanisław Witkiewicz, built by highlander carpenters, and is a perfect example of the famous wooden Zakopane-style architecture. The wooden façade is topped with a small bell tower, while the interior is decorated with carved figures. The stained-glass window on the left contains the image of Our Lady of Ostra Brama with the emblem of Lithuania, and on the right, Our Lady of Częstochowa with the emblem of Poland. This chapel was visited many times by the young Karol Wojtyła during his outings to the mountains. He used the walking paths surrounding the chapel for prayer and reflection.

The nearby Shrine of Our Lady of Fatima was built by the highlanders as an expression of gratitude to God for saving the life of Pope John Paul II in

Stained glass of the assassination attempt on Pope John Paul II in St. Peter's Square; him crowning the image of Our Lady of Fatima.

the assassination attempt of May 13, 1981. Since the two gunshot wounds were inflicted on the Feast of Our Lady of Fatima, the Pope realized that his life had been spared from certain death: "One hand pulled the trigger, another guided the bullet."

This beautiful church, whose architecture reflects the traditional folk architecture of the region, was completed in 1992 and consecrated by Pope John Paul in 1997. The interior features a statue of the Blessed Virgin Mary of Fatima, crowned by the Pope. Stained-glass windows express the story of Fatima: the revelation of the angel to the children in 1916; the consecration of the world by Pope Pius XII in 1942; Pope John Paul II; Pope Paul VI's pilgrimage to Fatima in 1967; the assassination attempt in St. Peter's Square in 1981; Mary's first apparition at Fatima on May 13, 1917; Primate Wyszyński handing over the statue of Our Lady of Fatima to the Shrine in 1961; Pope John Paul II crowning the image of Our Lady. Notice, too, the Stations of the Cross and the incorporation of Pope John Paul into the fifth station, helping Jesus carry his Cross, and in the 12th station, standing at the foot of the Cross.

Behind the church, in the Park of Fatima, the altar at which Pope John Paul II celebrated the outdoor Mass in 1997 has been preserved in a stained-glass covering. The image, called "Homage of the Polish Highlanders," memorializes the historical event. The multilayer altar is topped by openwork tracery with eight biblical scenes carved from lime wood. The papal altar is made of stone and supported by two bronze rams. Above the altar are the words *Sursum Corda* (Lift up your hearts), part of the opening dialogue to the Eucharistic Prayer, dating back to at least the third century.

Statue of St. John Paul looking toward the Giewont massif in the Polish Tatras.

From this altar, at its original location in 1997, Pope John Paul could see the most iconic massif in the Polish Tatras, divided into three distinctive peaks: Small Giewont, Great Giewont, and Long Giewont. The silhouette, according to local legend, evokes the image of a sleeping knight, who will awake when Poland is in danger to raise the spirit of the nation. On the highest peak of Giewont, a 50-foot-high iron cross was erected in 1900, the site of many pilgrimages. After the Mass, Pope John Paul declared:

> That cross speaks to us saying, "Lift up your hearts!" I pray that all of Poland will look toward that cross and hear that invitation. "Let us lift up our hearts!"[42]

The Old Chapel of the Shrine of Our Lady of Fatima, built by the highlanders in gratitude for the life of Pope John Paul II.

Pilgrims enjoying the cuisine of the Polish highlanders.

The popular salty smoked cheese oscypek, made by the Polish highlanders.

In front of the Shrine of Our Lady of Fatima, a statue of St. John Paul with hands uplifted looks toward the Giewont massif. There also stands a replica of the cross that rests on the peak of Giewont. Saint John Paul, as an avid outdoorsman, knew that the beauty of creation is a revelation of the Creator. The Tatra Mountains offer a splendid canvas on which to discern the brushstrokes of God.

MEDITATION

• In what way do the mountains and the faith of the highlanders invite us to "Lift up our hearts"?

• For what do I wish to pray through the intercession of Our Lady of Fatima?

Reading: Isaiah 61:10-11
I will greatly rejoice in the LORD...

Response: "Blessed are you among women, and blessed is the fruit of your womb, Jesus."

Blessed Virgin Mary of Fatima, with renewed gratitude for your motherly presence, we join in the voice of all generations that call you blessed. We celebrate in you the great works of God, who never tires of lowering Himself in mercy over humanity, afflicted by evil and wounded by sin, to heal and to save it. R.

Accept with the benevolence of a Mother this act of entrustment that we make in faith today, before this your image, beloved to us. We are certain that each one of us is precious in your eyes and that nothing in our hearts has estranged you. May we allow your sweet gaze to reach us and the perpetual warmth of your smile. R.

Guard our life with your embrace: bless and strengthen every desire for good; give new life and nourishment to faith; sustain and enlighten hope; awaken and animate charity; guide us all on the path to holiness. R.

Teach us your own special love for the little and the poor, for the excluded and the suffering, for sinners and the wounded of heart: gather all people under your protection and give us all to your beloved Son, our Lord Jesus.[43] R.

Prayer: O my God, who chose the Mother of your Son to be our Mother also, grant that we may further each day the reign of Christ through our penance and prayer for the world. We believe, we adore, we hope, and we love You. We ask pardon for those who do not believe, do not adore, do not hope, and do not love You.

V. THE PATRONAL SAINTS OF POLAND

The well-known 20th-century saints are just the most recent holy men and women of Poland canonized by the Church. Throughout its history, the national identity of Poland has rested on its saints. This devotion to the saints has fortified the Polish people during times of trial and revitalized their hope in periods of peace. The constellation of holy ones in Poland includes over 30 who have been proclaimed as saints by the Church and over 50 who have been pronounced as Blessed. This does not include those raised to the altar as a group, such as the Five Holy Martyrs from Poland's first known monastic foundation who were martyred in the year 1003, or the 108 Blessed Polish Martyrs killed by the Nazis during World War II. This most recent group of martyrs comprises three bishops, 79 priests, seven male religious, eight female religious, and 11 lay people beatified by Pope John Paul II at Warsaw in 1999.

Poland's first patron saint is St. Wojciech (Adalbert), honored at Gniezno Cathedral from Poland's earliest history. His primacy was gradually challenged by St. Stanisław, a native son, whose patronage benefited from its location in Kraków, Poland's second royal capital. The ranks of Poles venerated as saints expanded over the 12th and 13th centuries, with Poland's mendicant communities as particularly zealous promoters of devotion to the saints. The Dominicans focused their fervor on the holy mendicant

Jacek (Hyacinth), who died in 1257. Meanwhile the Franciscans promoted the cause of Kinga, who died in 1292 after a holy life and gradually came to be identified as the patroness of salt miners. Kraków has been called the "Rome of the North" because of the number of its saints and churches. The 15th century, in particular, was a unique and blessed period, known as the "happy century of Kraków," a period when a number of mystics lived there who were later beatified or canonized.

The Polish faithful have always flocked to the shrines of the saints, both to honor their lives and seek their intercession, and their homeland is one of the most saint-rich countries of Europe. They honor the remains of the saints as relics because of Catholicism's incarnational view of the world, the belief that the created body has an innate dignity because the Son of God has taken on our flesh. In response to cures and favors from the saints, the faithful deposit votive offerings of various sorts at the shrines as an expression of thanksgiving. The accumulation of these offerings witnesses to the power of the saints' intercession and strengthens the popular devotion to them. In coming to know these holy men and women better and honoring them in their shrines, we join with them in Holy Mass to worship our God. Our faith is fortified by their courage, our hope is heartened by their deeds, and our love enflamed by their passion for God's kingdom.

1. Gniezno, Royal Cathedral and Shrine of St. Wojciech-Adalbert

The ancient Lech Hill, on which Gniezno's cathedral was built, is a sacred site in the founding mythology of the Polish people. According to legend, three Slavic brothers on a hunting trip sought different prey, which took them in different directions: Lech to the north, Czech to the west, and Rus to the east. Lech, the precursor of the Polish people, followed his arrow and found himself face-to-face with a white eagle, fiercely guarding its nest from intruders. Seeing the eagle against the red of the setting sun, Lech took this as a good omen and decided to establish his settlement there, naming it Gniezno (from Polish *gniazdo*, meaning "nest"). Because Lech adopted the white eagle as his coat of arms, the eagle remains a symbol of Poland to this day, and the colors of the eagle and the setting sun are depicted in Poland's coat of arms as well as its flag.

Gniezno's Primatial Cathedral Basilica of the Assumption of the Blessed Virgin Mary honors the beginnings of the Church in Poland, the nation's first patron saint, and its first royal dynasty. It was built first as a chapel in the ninth century by Mieszko I, Poland's first Christian ruler, who

Gniezno's cathedral built on Lech Hill; Primatial Cathedral Basilica honors the beginnings of the Church in Poland.

extended the church on a cruciform plan; there in 977 he buried his wife Dąbrówka (Dobrawa). His son, Bolesław I the Brave, rebuilt it into the rectangular plan that would be designated as the first cathedral of Gniezno. Because of its early history, Gniezno holds the status of "capital of Christianity in Poland" and the archbishops of Gniezno hold the title of Primate of Poland.

Saint Adalbert is known in Poland by his birth name, Wojciech (Vojtěch, in Czech). As bishop of Prague, he opposed the slave trade, polygamy, and idolatry, and so was forced into exile. As an itinerant missionary, Wojciech traveled to Poland where he was welcomed by Bolesław I the Brave. With the support of Bolesław, he set out on mission to the Prussians, traveling along the coast of the Baltic Sea to the area near Gdańsk. At the instigation of one of the pagan priests, Wojciech was martyred and beheaded on April 23, 997. Bolesław the Brave ransomed his body — purchasing it, as it is said, for its weight in gold — and brought it back to the church in Gniezno. Two years later, the Pope canonized Wojciech, and Poland gained its first patron saint. Having the bones of St. Wojciech in his capital city assisted Bolesław in increasing Polish political and diplomatic power in Europe.

In the year 1000, Emperor Otto III came to Gniezno to pray at the tomb of St. Wojciech (Adalbert) and called the Congress of Gniezno, which

12th century bronze doors with eighteen scenes from the life of St. Wojciech.

initiated the Archdiocese of Gniezno, charged with overseeing new dioceses throughout Poland. The Metropolitanate of Gniezno served as the essential source of unity and continuity for the Polish state throughout its first two centuries. In 1025 Bolesław the Brave became the first Polish king to be crowned in the Gniezno Cathedral. He was followed by his son and three other Polish kings of the Piast dynasty.

At the entrance to the Gothic cathedral stand a pair of ancient bronze doors, made and installed in 1175 to honor St. Wojciech. They are decorated with 18 bas-relief scenes from the saint's life, with nine panels on each door. The sequence starts from the bottom of the left door (or the right door when viewed open from inside the cathedral), going upwards: the saint is born and baptized; as a sick child he is saved by being placed on an altar dedicated to the Virgin Mary; his parents place him in the monastery at Magdeburg at his request; he prays before a shrine (with doorknob); Emperor Otto II gives him his bishop's crozier; he expels a demon from a possessed man; he has a vision of Christ telling him to save Christians from slave traders; he pleads with the Duke of Bohemia for the release of Christians slaves by their masters; and he drops a pitcher but the vessel does not break and the wine is not spilt. The sequence continues, beginning at the top of the right door, going downward: the saint lands in Gdańsk by ship; he converts many to the faith; he preaches; he offers Mass on the morning of his death; he is martyred; his body is exposed with his severed head on a stake as an eagle guards it (with doorknob); his remains are purchased by Bolesław from the Prussians; his remains are taken back to Gniezno; and his remains are buried in Gniezno's cathedral.

The cathedral has suffered the ravages of fire and war throughout the centuries. The great fire of 1760 damaged the towers and consumed the roof, leading to the collapse of the vaults and significant damage to the interior. The resulting rebuilding and renovation led to the present Neoclassical, Baroque, and Rococo architectural elements. But above the contemporary

Silver sarcophagus of St. Wojciech carried on the figures of a priest, peasant, townsperson, and knight.

central altar is placed a wooden beam with a precious Gothic crucifix made from linden wood, dating from around 1430. In the crypt of the cathedral is found the oldest sepulchral stone inscription in the country. Other aspects of the crypt include the remaining fragments of the walls of the first church funded by Mieszko I, Poland's first king.

At the center of the cathedral's chancel stands an 18th-century golden baldachin, based on the design of Bernini's altar in St. Peter's Basilica in Rome. Beneath the canopy, the Baroque silver sarcophagus of St. Wojciech (Adalbert) is carried on the figures of a priest, peasant, townsperson, and knight. The entire silver memorial was designed by Gdańsk master crafts-man Peter van der Rennen in 1662. The black altar beneath is engraved with a prayer in Latin: "Christ hear us, through the intercession of St. Adalbert: and through his prayers hasten to help us the wretched ones." Behind the shrine rests a red-marble medieval tombstone dating from 1480, commem-orating the patron.

In 1979 and 1997, Pope John Paul II visited Gniezno and its cathe-dral. During the second visit, celebrations took place on the thousand-year anniversary of the martyrdom of St. Wojciech. Outside the cathedral, mon-uments honor these visits and also King Bolesław I the Brave. Other art and artifacts from the cathedral treasury can be seen at the nearby Museum of the Archdiocese in Gniezno.

MEDITATION

- What does it mean to me to be at the "nest" (Gniezno) or the cradle of the Polish nation?
- Why is hardship and suffering necessary to share in the Church's mission?

Reading: 2 Corinthians 6:1-10
We urge you not to accept the grace of God in vain…

Response: "Through the merits of St. Wojciech, hear us Lord."[44]

Almighty God, through the gift of faith sown by St. Wojciech and fertilized with his martyr's blood, You united and strengthened the Polish nation in all the difficult and painful moments of its history. At this moment, like the Polish forebears who stood before the tomb of Your holy martyr to forge the foundations of Polish national identity, we raise our prayer and cry out. R.

Lord God, because Gniezno, the nest of Poland, has always expressed the beginnings of the nation, you remind us through the words of St. John Paul: "If we were to detach ourselves from our roots, if we forgot about our Nest, we would also lose ourselves among the complicated paths of history." May we never lose our spiritual roots, but build our future on the solid foundation of Gospel values. R.

Holy God, through Your faithful witness St. Wojciech, You show how the truth of the Gospel is indispensable for the harmonious development of society, and You have placed responsibility for the heritage of our Catholic culture in the fragile hands of each of us. May we prove ourselves worthy of the great spiritual heritage we have inherited and bear a living witness of faith. R.

Living God, in St. Wojciech, apostle to the Slavic people, You give us a model of missionary service because he proclaimed the Gospel and gave his life for it. May we support the evangelizing ministry of the Church with our work, prayer, and sacrifice, and may we take up our call to missionary discipleship as we proclaim the Gospel through our words and deeds. R.

Merciful God, as the legacy of St. Wojciech crosses human boundaries of nationality, race, and culture, You call us to conversion of heart, the work of justice, and the ministry of reconciliation. Unite Your Church from east to west, from north to south, and make us fearless and faithful followers of Jesus Christ our Lord. R.

Prayer: Hear us Lord, who bestowed the crown of martyrdom on the bishop, St. Wojciech, as he burned with zeal for souls. We pray, through his intercession, that the obedience of the flock may never fail the shepherds, nor the care of the shepherds be ever lacking to the flock. May we be faithful to the faith, the Gospel, the Cross, and the Church handed down to us through Your saints.

Kraków's Cathedral on Wawel Hill.

2. Kraków, Wawel Cathedral and Shrines of St. Stanisław and St. Jadwiga

Although Gniezno represents the inauguration of the Church and state in Poland, Kraków expresses the heart of Poland's ecclesial and royal traditions. Kraków's "Old Town" begins at Wawel Hill, a limestone mount overlooking a bend in the Wistula River, home to Kraków's cathedral and its royal castle. Kraków's renown as the repository of Poland's identity began with King Kazimierz I the Restorer, great-grandson of Mieszko I, when he reunited the kingdom of Poland, moved its capital to Kraków in 1042, and erected the new Wawel Cathedral.

Considered the most important single building in all of Poland, the cathedral of Kraków contains the sacred relics of two of the nation's patron saints, the martyred bishop Stanisław and the virtuous queen Jadwiga. The first cathedral, from the 11th century, was made of wood and destroyed by fire. A second one, a Romanesque design constructed in the 12th century, was also destroyed by fire. Władysław the Short, the first of many rulers to be crowned at Wawel, was made king among the charred rubble. He ordered the construction of the present Gothic cathedral, which was consecrated in 1364.

Shrine and remains of Kraków's early bishop, St. Stanisław of Szczepanów.

At the center of the church stands the imposing tomb of Kraków's early bishop, St. Stanisław of Szczepanów, to whom the cathedral is dedicated. His remains are venerated in a silver coffin supported by four angels and adorned at the top by the arms of the saint and the bishop's insignia held by a pair of cherubs. The reliquary is adorned with 12 relief scenes from the life, martyrdom, and posthumous miracles of Stanisław. The sarcophagus was designed by Gdańsk master craftsman Peter van der Rennen and completed in 1671.

As the bishop of Kraków, Stanisław stood up to King Bolesław II the Bold when the faithful suffered oppression and were too heavily punished by the king. The conflict between the bishop and the king resulted in a bloody tragedy on May 8, 1079. Bishop Stanisław was killed by order of the king while offering the Mass at St Michael's Church in Skałka. The king was forced to flee the country, but the body of Bishop Stanisław was transferred to the cathedral and devotion to the saintly bishop continued to grow.

The grave of Bishop Stanisław became a primary destination for pilgrims, and his memory played an enormous role in the growing national awareness and strength of the Church among Poles. He has been called the "conscience of the nation," the first to express the sovereignty of Church authority as differentiated from state authority. His martyrdom continues to express the Church's mission to serve the people in an autonomous way, not serving on behalf of the state, but with it. Visitors to his tomb are reminded that he gave his life defending human rights and freedom of conscience, a beacon of hope in every age of oppression for the Polish people.

The altar of St. Stanisław has functioned for centuries as the "Altar of the Homeland," the place where prayers have been offered for the prosperity of the nation and thanksgiving made for success in war and peace. Silver lamps are always burning at the martyr's tomb. The dignity of this shrine is expressed through the baldachin and canopy, made of black and pink marble with gilded bronze and wood. Around the cupola are figures of the four evangelists, and at the top of the four pillars are statues of Sts. Stanisław, Wojciech (Adalbert), Wenceslas, Florian, Kazimierz, Jacek (Hyacinth), Zygmunt, and Ignatius of Loyola.

The cathedral's monumental high altar holds a painting of the crucified Christ. This was the coronation altar for Poland's kings for 400 years as well as the site for royal weddings, baptisms, and funerals. Today, it is the site for many state and ecclesial ceremonies and the most important Liturgies of the Church's year. The "chair" of the archbishop is to the right of the altar and covered with a canopy.

Altar of Christ Crucified, with its miracle-working Black Crucifix and the tomb of St. Jadwiga below.

The other particularly sacred shrine in the cathedral is the Altar of Christ Crucified, with its miracle-working black crucifix from the 14th century, often called "St. Jadwiga's cross," which stands against the background of a silver sheet. Jadwiga often prayed before this crucifix during her reign as Queen of Poland, and she had a mystical vision during which the image of Christ spoke to her. After her beatification in 1986 by Pope John Paul II, her relics were placed in a small bronze coffin and inserted beneath this altar. She was canonized on her feast, June 8, 1997.

Saint Jadwiga (Hedwig) became the first female monarch of Poland in 1384, at the tender age of 11. With her mother's consent, Jadwiga's advisors opened negotiations with Lithuanian prince Jogaila concerning his potential marriage to Jadwiga. Because he was still a pagan, Jogaila signed the Union of Krewo, pledging to convert to Catholicism and to promote the faith among his pagan subjects. After lengthy prayer, seeking divine guidance, Jadwiga agreed to marry him. After being baptized in this cathedral and taking the Christian name Władysław, he married Jadwiga in 1386, becoming King Władysław II Jagiełło of Poland and coruler with Queen Jadwiga. The marriage formed a Polish-Lithuanian union, bringing vast territories into Poland's sphere of influence, proving beneficial for both the Polish and Lithuanian people.

Throughout her reign, Queen Jadwiga became famous for her unwavering faith, kindness, and generosity. She was a benefactor for the construction of monasteries, churches, hospitals, and dormitories for students. She was a fierce propagator of education and played a large role in converting pagan Lithuanians to Christianity. She was well versed in music and the fine arts, and she was the first monarch to order a translation of parts of the Bible into the Polish language. She donated all her personal jewelry to expand the University of Kraków, which was later named the Jagiellonian University. She died tragically at age 25 after giving birth to a premature daughter, who also died.

The sarcophagus of St. Jadwiga, made of white Carrara marble, is found on the opposite side of the cathedral. On the top of the tomb lies the recumbent figure of the queen, her hands folded in prayer, dressed in a long sweeping gown with a laced bodice and a cloak decorated with lilies. Her head rests on a cushion and her feet rest on a sleeping dog to symbolize fidelity. The inscription around the top of the tomb reads *"HEDVIGIS REGINA POLONIAE"* (Jadwiga Queen of Poland) with the year of her birth, 1374, on the left, and the year of her death, 1399, on the right. The queen's scepter and orb, which were originally gilded, are displayed nearby.

Near St. Jadwiga's sarcophagus rests that of her husband, Władysław II Jagiełło, who reigned another 35 years after her death. His reign laid the foundation for the centuries-long Polish-Lithuanian union and is often considered the beginning of Poland's golden age. His red marble tomb depicts his effigy lying supine, with two lions under his head symbolizing his power and a dragon at his feet signifying the evil he defeated. Many other tombs and chapels are nearby, the most famous of which is the Zygmunt Chapel, with its elaborate Renaissance decor. Here are found the tombs of the last kings of the Jagiellonian dynasty: Zygmunt I the Old and his son Zygmunt II Augustus. The Zygmunt Bell is the cathedral's largest bell and may be viewed by climbing the Zygmunt Tower. Weighing over 12 tons, it is rung on special occasions and feasts.

The cathedral crypt harbors the mortal remains of many heroes of Polish history: King Jan III Sobieski, victor over the Ottomans and savior of Europe at the 1683 Battle of Vienna; Marshal Józef Piłsudski, founder of the Second Polish Republic in the aftermath of World War I; General Władysław Sikorski, leader of the Polish government-in-exile in World War II; and Tadeusz Kościuszko, friend of Thomas Jefferson, who fought for both American and Polish freedom. Here, in St. Leonard's Crypt, Fr. Karol Wojtyła chose to celebrate his first Mass following his ordination as a priest. In this way he wished to express his spiritual bond with the history of Poland and to pay tribute to the Polish heroes buried nearby who were so influential in his education as a Catholic and a patriot.

Wawel Cathedral was the seat of Karol Wojtyła's ministry as archbishop of Kraków from 1964 to 1978. He had a great devotion to his predecessor, St. Stanisław, whose martyrdom set the pattern for the Catholic Church in Poland as the *defensor civitatis*, the defender of the nation and its liberties. That tradition was embodied in a particularly powerful way by St. John Paul, during both his years as archbishop and his years as Pope, as he fought for the rights of the Church against the oppressive hand of the communist government. In 2008, Cardinal Stanisław Dziwisz blessed a 10-foot-high outdoor memorial near the cathedral entrance to honor the life of St. John Paul II.

MEDITATION

• For what do I wish to pray as I stand within the heart of Poland's national identity?

• Why is freedom of conscience so precious to me?

Reading: Colossians 2:6-10
Continue to live your lives in him, rooted and built up in him…

Response: "Through the intercession of your saints, hear us Lord."

Holy God, hear our prayer through the intercession of Your bishop St. Stanisław, who proclaimed the gospel and taught that Christ is the head of every earthly authority. Guide us on our pilgrimage and give us a burning desire to choose Your kingdom over the values of the world. R.

Merciful God, hear us through the merits of St. Stanisław, the conscience of the Polish nation, who gave his life defending human rights and freedom. Give us courage in the face of opposition and zeal to work for human dignity. R.

Living God, hear our prayer through the grace offered through Your martyr St. Stanisław, who laid down his life in sacrificial love. Make us faithful witnesses, speaking truth in charity, to the whole human family. R.

Almighty God, hear our prayer through the intercession of Poland's young queen St. Jadwiga, who used the gifts of wisdom and judgment to surrender her life to your divine will. Guide us as we seek to discern what You desire in all things. R.

Lord God, hear our prayer through the merits of St. Jadwiga, who prayed so often before the image of the crucified Christ and learned that she was created for things greater than earthly joy. Teach us to gaze upon the Cross and draw us to personal intimacy with Him. R.

Compassionate God, hear our prayer through the holy example of St. Jadwiga, whose wonder at Christ's Passion led her to a purified love for the people of her nation. Grant us a desire like hers to devote our personal treasure to the benefit of Your suffering people. R.

Prayer: Hear us Lord, who bestowed the crown of martyrdom on the bishop St. Stanisław, and the crown of life on the beautiful queen St. Jadwiga. At their tombs, we pray for all leaders of church and state, that they may follow the shining example of Your saints and guide their people with courage, faithfulness, and generosity.

Basilica of St. Michael the Archangel and the Sanctuary of the Martyrdom of St. Stanisław on Skałka.

3. The Skałka Sanctuary and Altar of Three Millennia

Every year on the first Sunday following May 8 (Feast of St. Stanisław), a great procession is held in Kraków, attended by bishops, priests, monks, and nuns from all the religious houses in the city, as well as representatives of guilds, trade unions, and other historical groups in their gala uniforms and costumes. Following a tradition that reaches back to the days of the bishop's canonization in 1253, they carry the relics of St. Stanisław and other saints from Wawel Cathedral to the Skałka Sanctuary, the site of his martyrdom, walking to the sound of brass instruments playing the religious hymns of Poland. In times past, on the eve of their coronation the Polish kings would make a similar pilgrimage to "Skałka" in reparation for the notorious deed of their predecessor, King Bolesław II the Bold.

Today's white church "on the Rock" (Skałka) has replaced the original Romanesque rotunda of St. Michael the Archangel, where Bishop Stanisław was murdered while offering the Mass. In 1472 the church was entrusted to the care of the Order of Pauline Fathers, the monastic community whose first Polish settlement was in Częstochowa at Jasna Góra. The current 18th-century Baroque church is named the "Basilica of Saint Michael the Archangel and the Sanctuary of the Martyrdom of Saint Stanisław on Skałka."

The high altar is marked by six columns of blue marble and images of angels surrounding a painting of St. Michael. The first chapel to the left contains a jeweled image of St. Stanisław with his miter and crozier. This altar preserves the site of his murder and original tomb. Ten years after his death, his coffin was transferred to Wawel Cathedral. At the foot of the altar, the timeworn piece of wood is saturated with the blood of the saint. Differing traditions describe this wood as the medieval altar step onto which the blood of St. Stanisław spilled or the tree trunk on which his body was dismembered. Located beneath the silver eagle, the glass case preserves the pectoral cross donated by St. John Paul as a votive offering to express his episcopal unity with St. Stanisław.

Other side altars within the church are dedicated to St. Paul the First Hermit, the Holy Family, St. John of Nepomuk, Our Lady of Jasna Góra, and St. Barbara. Situated beneath the church, the crypt has been designed as one of Poland's national pantheons, housing the tombs of outstanding representatives of modern Polish culture. Set in the wall opposite the crypt entrance there is a stained-glass window of Our Lady of Jasna Góra, and the crypt's tombs contain the remains of poets, writers, artists, composers, scientists, and other distinguished Poles.

During his papal visit to Skałka in 1979, commemorating the 900th anniversary of the death of St. Stanisław, Pope John Paul II delivered two memorable speeches: one addressed to representatives of the world of science and the other to the crowd of young people who filled the outdoor spaces of the property. These encounters are commemorated with a bronze monument of the Pope outside the church.

Next to the church stands the monastery and theological seminary of the Pauline Fathers. Named for their patron, the third-century hermit St. Paul of Thebes, they follow the Rule of St. Augustine. They join the contemplative life of their patron with the apostolic life of service. In front

High altar marked by columns of blue marble and dedicated to St. Michael.

of the monastery complex sits the spring and pond of St. Stanisław, which became an important place for the saint's veneration. The pool was used for baptisms when the country converted to the Christian faith at the turn of the millennium. It is said that the king discarded the dismembered body parts of the slain bishop into this pond, where they were guarded by eagles. When the people of Kraków were attracted by a strange light and reached the site, they found his body had miraculously grown whole again without any mark. The pool has been adorned with a 17th-century sculpture of the saint engaged in a healing miracle. The mineral-rich water is drinkable and is said to have healing properties.

In 2008, the Pauline Fathers added the open-air Altar of Three Millennia, to be used for the procession and Mass associated with the Feast of St. Stanisław as well as for other musical and theatrical performances. At the front of the contemporary shrine stands a high three-sided monolith representing three millennia, with each side devoted to one of the three Sacraments of Initiation. On each of the three surfaces, the upper section refers to a biblical scene and the lower refers to the history of Poland. The Baptism scenes depict the baptism of Christ followed by the baptism of the Polish nation at the end of the first millennium. Water

Chapel of St. Stanisław at the place of his murder and original tomb, with wood saturated with the saint's blood.

Spring and pond of St. Stanisław, used for baptisms when the country became Christian at the turn of the millennium.

Outdoor Altar of Three Millennia.

from the hand of St. Wojciech-Adalbert becomes water from the nearby pond, referred to as the "baptistery of Poland." The Confirmation scenes portray the descent of the Holy Spirit at Pentecost followed by the second-millennium confirmation of Poland with the martyrdom of St. Stanisław. The image is enhanced with many other figures of Church and State, expressing the unity of the nation. The Eucharistic scenes show the sacrifice of Christ for the world, which is then expressed in the Mass and distribution of Communion by St. John Paul, representing the third millennium. The image is enriched with the presence of other contemporary witnesses such as Cardinal Stefan Sapieha, Cardinal Stefan Wyszyński, St. Rafał Kalinowski, St. Brother Albert Chmielowski, and Cardinal Stanisław Dziwisz.[45]

On the opposite side stand seven high pillars, and in front of the pillars are seven bronze statues of figures representing three millennia of faith in Poland. The central statue depicts St. Stanisław, and to the left and right of him stand St. Wojciech and St. John Paul II. These three figures, representing three millennia, stand before pillars made of pink stone, representing the blood they shed for the faith. To their left and right are St. Jadwiga and St. Faustina, holy women from the 14th and the 20th centuries. And on the left and right ends stand Fr. Augustyn Kordecki, 17th-century prior at Jasna Góra during the Swedish invasion, and St. John Cantius, the holy university professor of the 15th century.

MEDITATION

• What does it mean to me to be surrounded by these holy witnesses of three millennia?

• What are my hopes for the third millennium of Christianity in my own land?

Reading: Hebrews 12:1-13
Since we are surrounded by so great a cloud of witnesses, let us also lay aside every weight...

Response: "Make us holy as you are holy."

Saint Stanisław, you suffered a martyr's death in defense of the human dignity of your people against their oppressive ruler. Inspire us to defend human rights against lawless power. R.

Saint Wojciech, you died as a martyr while evangelizing in pagan lands. Give us a missionary heart so that we may witness to the Gospel in word and deed. R.

Saint John Paul II, your blood was shed through a deadly wound, but God desired your witness to continue into the third millennium. Protect our Church and give us hope in the unknown future. R.

Saint Jadwiga, you are a model of holy rule and sacrificial generosity. Guide us to discern God's will and to live wholeheartedly in following God's way. R.

Saint Faustina, your mystical intimacy with God reminds the Church of Divine Mercy. Teach us to contemplate Christ's Passion and invoke his compassion upon the world. R.

Father Augustyn Kordecki, you believed, loved, fought, and won, when all others were in despair at the invasion of the Pauline monastery of Jasna Góra. Inspire our efforts to defend the honor of Our Lady and to follow her as our queen. R.

Saint John Cantius, as university professor you combined your deep theological knowledge with your sensitivity to the needs of the poor. Guide educators and students to the fullness of truth through the paths of human reason and divine faith. R.

Prayer: God of the ages, may we lift up our drooping hands and hearts, as we receive our trials with joy. Surrounded by the witnesses of past centuries, help us to follow their example and seek their intercession as we become the saints of Your Church's third millennium.

4. Saint Albert Chmielowski Ecce Homo Sanctuary

Kraków's Ecce Homo Sanctuary has become the center of the growing devotion to St. Br. Albert Chmielowski since his relics were transferred here in 1985. Built next to the convent of the Albertine Sisters, the shrine owes its name to the saint's painting above the high altar, entitled "Ecce Homo" ("Behold the Man!"), the words of Pilate when he showed Jesus to the crowd before the Crucifixion (see Jn 19:5). Working on this painting changed the artist's life, and he subsequently decided to serve God.

Ecce Homo Sanctuary honoring St. Brother Albert Chmielowski.

Born Adam Chmielowski into an aristocratic family in 1845, he joined the January Uprising of 1863 against Russian rule over Polish lands. During battle a Russian grenade killed his horse and damaged his leg to the extent that it had to be amputated. He suffered greatly as his leg was removed without anesthesia, then eventually he was fitted with a permanent wooden prosthesis. During the next phase of his life, he discovered he had a talent for painting, which he developed by joining the Munich Art Academy. Returning to Poland, he became a popular artist in Kraków. His extant artistic output includes about one hundred oils, watercolors, and drawings.

His strong political convictions inspired his interest in the human condition, developing a gentle and compassionate spirit that made him aware of the suffering of the poor. While working on his painting "Ecce Homo," the artist discovered the Creator of all beauty and goodness, which brought him to the Savior's Cross where he found his ultimate place and mission. Years of deep reflection led Chmielowski to abandon his painting career in order to live among the poor and to accept a beggar's life. At the age of 35, this man from a wealthy family left his bohemian lifestyle and began to help alcoholics, the poor, and the homeless.

Albertine Sisters in front of their convent at Ecce Home Sanctuary.

Although he first entered the novitiate of the Jesuits, he soon discovered the Rule of St. Francis of Assisi, which inspired him to seek out the Franciscans. In 1887 he joined the Third Order of St. Francis and took their habit and the religious name Br. Albert. He took up residence in the homeless shelter where he had been volunteering and devoted himself to caring for the poor and homeless of Kraków. The next year he founded the Servants of the Poor, later known as the Albertines, selling his paintings to raise money for his work. In 1891, alongside Maria Jabłońska, he founded a parallel women's congregation known as the Albertine Sisters, who organized food and shelter for the homeless and destitute. The Albertines established homes for the poor across Poland, including shelter for homeless children and teenagers, as well as facilities for people with disabilities, the elderly, and the incurable.

Brother Albert died due to stomach cancer at noon on Christmas Day, 1916, in the shelter that he had established. Pope John Paul II — whom Chmielowski's example had influenced to a significant degree — beatified him in 1983 while in Kraków and later canonized him in 1989 in Rome. The life of Br. Albert had so moved the young Karol Wojtyła that in 1949 he wrote a play about him entitled *Our God's Brother*, which was later made into a film with the same title. As Pope John Paul II, he said that he had found in him a real spiritual support and example in leaving behind the world of art, literature, and the theater, and in making the radical choice of a vocation in God's service. The Pope said that anyone who wanted to understand his views on the topic of social justice should study *Our God's Brother*. The tension in the film isn't just between art and God, but also between the many poor and the wealthy few, and between the two forms of solidarity, Christianity and Marxism. The former argues that poverty can be overcome by seeing God's image in the individual, while the latter argues that the rich must be violently overthrown through class struggle.

Paintings of St. Brother Albert.

In the Ecce Homo Sanctuary, the earthly remains of St. Br. Albert rest under the altar. Next to his lie the remains of Bl. Sr. Bernardyna Jabłońska. She was well-known for her all-embracing love for poor and sick people. After the death of Br. Albert, she preserved and continued his spirituality, being particularly devoted to Jesus present in the Eucharist. The Poles compare their lives to those of St. Francis and St. Claire. In the lower church, visitors can view an exhibition on the life and activity of St. Br. Albert and Bl. Sr. Bernardyna and the work of the Albertine congregations.

Brother Albert attributed great importance to bread, and nearly every image of the saint depicts him with a loaf of bread in his hands. "You should be good like bread," he said, "which rests on the table for everyone and from which everyone, if hungry, may cut himself a piece, and so be nourished." The Albertines adopted as their motto, "Be good like bread." The symbol of bread's goodness is for Br. Albert indispensable to the essence and meaning of the Eucharist: "I look at Jesus in the Eucharist; could his love have provided anything more beautiful? He becomes bread, so let us be bread too; let us give of our very selves."

MEDITATION

- In what ways does the painful beauty of St. Br. Albert's "Ecce Homo" move my heart?

- What questions does the image present to me?

Reading: John 19:1-6
Then Pilate took Jesus and had him flogged. And the soldiers wove a crown of thorns and put it on his head...

Response: "May we become good like bread for others."

The fresh wounds of scourging are on Christ's exposed breast. When the sin of humanity strikes, God's heart does not stop loving. As Christ responded to hatred with mercy and overcame evil with good, may we defend people who are misunderstood, harmed, and beaten through the power of forgiving love. R.

The head of Christ is crowned with thorns and a purple robe is on His soldiers. When the sin of humanity mocks Christ's royal dignity, God takes the form of a suffering servant. As the Lord Jesus reigned in suffering and gave us salvation in humiliation, may we offer hope to the helpless and not be afraid of selfless service. R.

Christ's face is disgraced and disfigured with blood and bruises. When the sin of humanity attacks, His downcast eyes do not condemn the torturers. As Christ was flogged and ridiculed, may we offer strength of spirit to the rejected and respect each person in the light of God's love. R.

When the chief priests and police saw Jesus, they shouted, "Crucify him! Crucify him!" In the darkness ruled by hatred and violence, Christ stands in the light. As He stood alone and steadfast, may we have the conviction to stand for the truth with inner conviction. R.

When Jesus came out to the crowd, Pilate said to them, "Behold the man!" Despite the sinfulness of humanity, Christ shows us the beauty of our humanity. As the world's true king stood defenseless, may we foster His loving reign in every human heart. R.

Christ knows His dignity and ours, a nobility that no one can take away. Although St. Brother Albert was unable to paint Christ's image as he wanted, he perfected it with the beauty of his own life. May each of us achieve the fullness that God desires for us through the work of divine grace. R.

Prayer: Lord Jesus, Your image is engraved in every human heart. As St. Brother Albert taught us, "The more one is abandoned, the greater the love with which we must serve that person, since it is the wounded Lord Jesus himself whom we rescue in the person of the poor." O King of Heaven, crowned with thorns, scourged, and clothed in purple, O King, insulted and spat upon, be our King and Lord here and in eternity.

5. Wieliczka Salt Mine and Chapel of St. Kinga

The Wieliczka salt mine began to be excavated in the 13th century, and today displays a fascinating underground museum of shafts, labyrinthine passage-ways, displays of historic salt-mining technology, an underground lake, and numerous chambers and chapels containing statues and reliefs carved by miners out of the rock salt. The mine ceased to operate as an extraction facility in 1996, and has since focused on developing tourism. The visitors' route, over two miles in length, covers less than two percent of the total length of the mine's passages.

Over the centuries of the mine's operation, various technologies were used for hauling salt to the surface, some of which are demonstrated today. The 14th-century King Kazimierz III the Great contributed significantly to the development of salt mining, which produced a third of the income of the Polish treasury at the time. In 1368, King Kazimierz issued the Statute of the Kraków Saltworks, which specified the principles of mine organi-zation, production and sale of salt, and regulations for hiring and firing employees. While the king used the "white gold" to maintain his court and finance his building projects, he also cared for the mines and their several thousand workers.

The Catholic workers adopted the custom of erecting wooden memo-rials for workers who perished in the mine, but in 1697, when a wooden chapel was consumed by fire, it was forbidden to construct anything flam-mable underground. So the miners turned to the available material and began to carve statues and chapels out of the rock salt. The dedication and perseverance of these unsung heroes is truly amazing.

The beautiful story of St. Kinga is illustrated by a group of sculptures located in the Janowice Chamber, depicting the moment when a worker finds her ring in a piece of salt. It is said that when Kinga was a young girl in Hungary, she received an engagement ring from Duke Bolesław of Poland (Bolesław V the Chaste). When her father offered her a dowry of gold and silver, she told him it would not be what her future subjects needed, since Bolesław was rich, and his country prosperous. After considering the matter, she requested a dowry of rock salt since there were no salt mines in Poland. So her father brought her to the largest Hungarian mine and told her, "Here you will find the richest deposits of salt." But not knowing how to transport the salt to Poland, she prayed to God for discernment. Then she removed her engagement ring and cast it into the mine shaft.

So Kinga traveled toward the court of Bolesław in Kraków, but approaching the city, she stopped at Wieliczka and ordered her attendants to

Chapel of St. Kinga, Poland's underground salt cathedral.

Altar of St. Kinga.

Altar of St. Kinga.

dig in the place she indicated. When they hit rock and could dig no further, Kinga asked them to chip off a piece of the rock. She immediately recognized that it was rock salt, and she directed them to break it open. To everyone's delighted surprise, her engagement ring was inside the rock, and she knew that her dowry had been miraculously brought to Poland, the gift of the princess to her new country.

After her wedding to Duke Bolesław, Kinga ruled wisely over the Polish people who loved her greatly. She was merciful, generous, saintly, and performed several miracles during her lifetime. After the death of her husband, she sold her possessions, gave the money to the poor, and spent the rest of her days in a convent of the Poor Clares. Then after her own death in 1292, people began to honor her, especially miners, who began to believe she brought them good fortune in their search for salt and watched over them in their hazardous daily work. As the patron saint of salt miners, she is still honored as one of Poland's most beloved saints. At the end of the 17th century, Kinga was beatified, and in 1999, she was canonized by Pope John Paul II.

The Chapel of St. Kinga is the most magnificent in the mine, often called Poland's "underground salt cathedral." Visitors first view the vast chamber by looking down from a balcony as the chapel is lit with five mammoth chandeliers, creating a magical atmosphere. All around the walls are bas relief and sculptures, a veritable art gallery filled with works by talented sculptor-miners. Everything — floor, ceilings, the chandeliers, the staircases — is carved from salt.

Two wide staircases lead down to the chapel floor and to the main altar at the other end. Here the figures of St. Joseph and St. Clement stand on the sides, with the luminous image of St. Kinga in the center. Relics of the saint have been deposited under the altar. Two brothers, Józef and Tomasz Markowski, and a third man, Antoni Wyrodek, are generally credited with being the main sculptors, working one after the other for seven decades. In reality, however, newer generations of miners are continually adding to their work. On the opposite side of the chapel stands a new statue of St. John Paul, installed in 1999, the only image of the saint made entirely of salt.

When canonizing St. Kinga in 1999, Pope John Paul spoke these words:

> In speaking today of sanctity, of the desire for and the pursuit of holiness, we need to ask ourselves how we can create environments which favor the aspiration to holiness. What can be done to make the family, the school, the workplace, the office, the villages and the cities, and finally the whole country a dwelling-place of saints, who can influence others by their goodness, their fidelity to Christ's teaching and the witness of their everyday lives, and thus foster the spiritual growth of all people? Saint Kinga and all the Saints and Blessed of the thirteenth century reply: it requires witness. It requires courage not to put your faith under a bushel-basket. And in the end it requires that in the hearts of believers there should abound that desire for holiness which not only shapes one's private life but also influences society as a whole. ... Brothers and Sisters, do not be afraid to aspire to holiness! Do not be afraid to be saints! Make of this century now drawing to a close and of the new millennium an era of saintly men and women![46]

MEDITATION

• What does it mean to me when Jesus challenges me to be the salt of the earth?

• How can my life become luminous like that of St. Kinga?

Reading: Matthew 5:13-16
You are the salt of the earth; but if salt has lost its taste, how can its saltiness be restored?...

Response: "Saint Kinga, obtain for us the grace of holiness."

Saint Kinga, caring mother of the people entrusted to you, concerned for the salvation of every person, pray for us. R.

Saint Kinga, exemplary disciple of St. Francis and spiritual daughter of St. Clare, pray for us. R.

Saint Kinga, patron of the salt miners and powerful patron of Poland, pray for us. R.

Saint Kinga, may we trust in God's Providence in our daily experiences and glorify the goodness of our merciful God. R.

Saint Kinga, may we open our hearts to the needs of our neighbors and live a truly Christian life. R.

Saint Kinga, may we live with forgiveness, in the joy of true unity and peace. R.

Prayer: Lord God, who destined St. Kinga to be a special patroness of the Polish nation, we pray with confidence through her intercession in our present needs. As she had a passionate love for You and affectionate compassion for those in need, help us aspire to holiness and not be afraid to be saints.

6. Dominican Basilica of the Holy Trinity and Shrine of St. Jacek-Hyacinth

The Basilica of the Holy Trinity and its adjoining friary has been the stronghold of the Dominican Order in Kraków since the 13th century. What began as a small church was soon built into a fine example of the Polish Gothic style. Visitors may visit its numerous altars and shrines, its chapel of Our Lady of the Rosary, and the monastery cloister.

The church is most noted for its beautiful Shrine of St. Jacek-Hyacinth, which is found at the end of the left aisle at the top of stairs. The chapel was originally the monastery cell where St. Jacek lived in the 13th century as the founder of the community. Its present form dates to the 17th century. A magnificent Baroque altar and tomb of the saint stands in the middle of the richly decorated shrine to one of Poland's patron saints. The space is decorated with attractive stuccos and covered by a splendid dome.

Saint Jacek Odrowąż, better known outside of Poland as St. Hyacinth, was born into a noble family of Poland in 1185. He earned a doctorate in law and divinity at Bologna and returned to Kraków. While traveling in Rome with Bishop Iwon Odrowąż of Kraków in 1220, he met St. Dominic. He soon received the religious habit from him, becoming one of the early members of the Order of Preachers. During his novitiate, he lived at the Roman basilica of Santa Sabina, which the Pope had given to the burgeoning community. Sent back to Poland, Jacek returned to Kraków and established the first Dominican friary in Poland at Holy Trinity Church.

Called the "Apostle of the North," St. Jacek carried out missionary work that took him through Poland, Prussia, Scandinavia, Lithuania, and other regions of Eastern Europe. He is particularly noted for spreading devotion to the Blessed Sacrament and Our Lady. One of the stories told about him happened during a Mongol attack on Kiev. As the friars prepared to flee the invading forces, Jacek went to save the ciborium containing the Blessed Sacrament from the monastery chapel, when he heard the voice of Our Lady asking, "Jacek, do you take the Son and leave the Mother?" So Jacek lifted the large, stone statue of Mary as well as the ciborium, despite the fact that the statue weighed far more than he could normally lift. This scene of Jacek

Dominican Basilica of the Holy Trinity.

Shrine of St. Jacek-Hyacinth.

Holy Trinity high altar.

carrying the Blessed Sacrament and a statue of Mary is often depicted in art of the saint.

The Polish exclamation *Święty Jacku z pierogami!* (St. Jacek and his pierogi!) is used as a call for help in some difficult circumstance. It is derived from the legend of the saint's visit to Kościelec. During his visit a hailstorm broke out, destroying crops and leaving people with the terrible prospect of poverty and famine. The saint urged the people to pray, and the next day the crops were miraculously restored. As an expression of gratitude, the people used their restored grain to treat the saint to pierogi, the famous dish of stuffed dumplings that the saint then brought to Kraków.

Saint Jacek teaches the Church to evangelize even in times of great tribulation, while holding fast to the Church's great treasures, the Eucharist and the Mother of Jesus. In 1243, St. Jacek returned to Kraków's Holy Trinity monastery, where he died on August 15, 1257. The saint's grave became a place of veneration as soon as he was entombed. He was proclaimed blessed in 1527 and canonized a saint in 1594 by Pope Clement VIII.

MEDITATION

- How does St. Jacek inspire me to missionary discipleship?
- In what way would I like to ask St. Jacek to encourage me in faith?

Reading: Luke 9:57-62
As they were going along the road, someone said to him, "I will follow you wherever you go…"

Response: "Come to our aid, O saint of God."

Saint Jacek, inspired apostle of the Slavs, we pray for a strong faith, so that we understand that God is the highest value of our lives and the goal we are striving for. R.

Saint Jacek, tireless preacher of God's Word, we ask for a courageous faith, so that it will not fail in the difficulties of life and the struggles that face us. R.

Saint Jacek, father of Polish Dominicans, we beg for a living faith, so that our hearts are drawn to the zealous service of God. R.

Saint Jacek, priceless stone on the Polish crown, we plead for a joyful faith, so that we may live gladly for the glory of God and the reign of

His Son. R.

Saint Jacek, faithful guardian of Christ in the Eucharist, we ask for a persistent faith, so that we may cultivate a deep reverence for the Blessed Sacrament through frequent Communion and prayer at the tabernacle. R.

Saint Jacek, devoted son of the Blessed Virgin Mary, we ask for a fervent faith, so that we may be always united with the Mother of Christ and of His Church. R.

Prayer: Lord God, Who has exalted St. Jacek throughout this land for his sanctity of life and his missionary fervor, we pray that we receive his help in the face of our adversities and his guidance to contribute effectively to the mission of our Church. May we grow in trust and witness the flowering of our holy faith among Your people.

7. Warsaw, Sanctuary of St. Andrzej Bobola

Entering the contemporary church of St. Andrzej Bobola in Warsaw's Mokotów district, one can see the body of the holy martyr resting in a silver coffin between two rows of steps leading to the altar. On the left side of the wall behind the altar is a painting of the saint, standing with his hands tied in front of the crucified Christ. Saint Andrzej is surrounded by three angels, representing three nations: the angels of Lithuania and Russia weep in captivity, while the angel of Poland holds a burning candle to enlighten those who have been restricted from practicing their faith. The design of the national shrine expresses Poland's devotion to this Jesuit priest, missionary martyr, and patron saint of Warsaw and Poland.

In 1935 the Writers' House of the Society of Jesus was opened on this property. In 1938, the relics of St. Andrzej Bobola were placed in its chapel. In 1944, in the basement of the Writers' House, the Nazis murdered 16 Jesuit priests and brothers and 28 laypeople. After the war, the room in which the massacre was carried out was transformed into a chapel, and the remains of the victims were buried beneath it. In 1953, Cardinal Stefan Wyszyński established a parish here, but the agreement to build a church was canceled by the government authorities. Only in 1980 was permission received to erect the church, and in 1988 the first Mass in the upper church was celebrated by the Primate of Poland, Cardinal Józef Glemp.

Church of St. Andrzej Bobola.

The sanctuary has the shape of an octagonal tent. The dominant elements of the interior decor are the stained-glass windows, made to resemble enormous fabrics. At the top of the four large stained-glass windows are medallions, from which the eye falls downward. Two of these windows surround the altar, and two mark the entrance. The four narrow windows on each side of the church resemble Slutsk belts, a unique kind of handwoven craft typical of the Belarusian people. The details of these eight windows cannot be distinguished from afar and at first glance, so as to allow the worshiper to be enveloped in the colors, forms, and dynamism of the light, as if in God's presence, unhindered by any narrative. Nevertheless, each window contains at least secondary content, symbols of the connection between the visible and the invisible world as expressed in the vision of the New Jerusalem from the Book of Revelation. Saint Andrzej is presented with signs of his torment, but in a glorified form, his eyes raised to the throne of God, with blowing hair and robe, wrapped in God's Spirit.

Born in 1591, St. Andrzej entered the Jesuit novitiate in Vilnius, where he received a solid spiritual and intellectual formation in the dynamically developing order. After his ordination in 1622, he worked as an educator and chaplain in many places of Poland, but in 1652 he began evangelization work in Pinsk on the outskirts of the Polish-Lithuanian Commonwealth, which is today in Belarus. He did not get discouraged by the difficulties of his increasingly difficult missions, regardless of the dangers that faced him.

He was known as "God's hunter of souls," despite the tightening circle of enemies around him and the increasing threats to his life. Following St. Paul, full of trust, he repeated: "Whether we live or whether we die, we are the Lord's" (Rom 14:8).

On May 16, 1657, caught up in the conflict between the Polish and Russian forces, Andrzej Bobola was captured by the Cossacks for preaching the Catholic faith without compromise and bringing many back to the Church. All his life of service had been a preparation for this final victorious fight. Brought to a slaughterhouse in Janów Poleski, he was inflicted with the cruelest tortures, but he refused to deny his faith. He was martyred, com-

Saint Andrzej surrounded by three angels, representing three nations.

pletely devoted to God in sacrificial love. After a vain attempt to rescue him, a band of Poles took his body back to Pinsk, where they placed it in the crypt beneath the Jesuit church.

In the midst of war with the Cossacks, when the Jesuit college and church were attacked numerous times with plunder and arson, the body of Andrzej was forgotten. But in 1702, the saint appeared to the rector of the Jesuit college in Pinsk, who then searched for the body of St. Andrzej and found it buried in the damp crypt of the church. The corpse was preserved totally incorrupt, making it possible to learn the cruel details of the martyr's death. The body was then placed in a new coffin and positioned in a prominent place in the church. Crowds began to come to his tomb, devotion to the saint grew, and miracles occurred due to his intercession. Both Catholics and Orthodox made pilgrimages to his relics, uniting in common prayer.

In 1853, Andrzej Bobola was beatified in Rome by Pope Pius IX, and efforts began toward his canonization. In 1922, the Bolsheviks took away the body from its shrine and brought it to Moscow, where they put the corpse on public display at the Museum of Hygiene, a move that outraged

Stained glass windows made to resemble enormous fabrics.

Body of the holy martyr St. Andrzej Bobola.

the Poles. After two years, a Jesuit mission from Rome regained the relics of the martyr and transported them to Rome. There the body was placed in the Jesuit church of the Gesù. Confirmed miracles contributed to the canonization of St. Andrzej by Pope Pius XI in 1938.

The relics of the canonized saint then traveled in procession through Slovenia, Hungary, and Czechoslovakia to Poland. Everywhere the body of St. Andrzej Bobola was greeted with great joy and devotion. The relics then journeyed through many cities and towns of Poland on the route to Warsaw. Millions of faithful Poles paid homage to the holy martyr along the way. The processed relics were transported to the Warsaw Cathedral of St. John, where a solemn Mass was offered attended by Church and state authorities, clergy, military, and crowds of the faithful. After the Mass, the relics were brought in solemn procession to the chapel of the Jesuits at the present location of the sanctuary. On the eve of the Second World War, God wanted to strengthen the Polish people, through his example and intercession, for the trials that awaited them in the war and during the communist occupation that followed.

The martyrdom of St. Andrzej was like a seed that fell to the ground during a very difficult period of Poland's history and only bore its mature fruit centuries later. Because of his zeal for the gospel regardless of the hardships he had to undertake, the saint is the patron of evangelization in difficult times. His intercession is needed today because Poland's regained political and social freedom requires vigilance through ongoing religious and moral renewal. In 2002 the Bishops' Conference of Poland declared St.

Andrzej Bobola to be a patron saint of Poland, and in 2007, the episcopate gave the Church of St. Andrzej Bobola the status of a national shrine. Our secularized culture today needs the memory of his martyrdom, because in the lives of the martyrs, love is written in blood, in the most convincing and indisputable way.

The shrine also contains a museum dedicated to Poland's patron. It collects exhibits related to the life, pastoral activity, and martyrdom of the saint, as well as the long saga of his relics and the growing devotion to him. Display cases show remembrances related to St. Andrzej's canonization, publications devoted to him, votive offerings, and many paintings and images of him.

MEDITATION

• What were the losses and gains of St. Andrzej Bobola because of his faith in Christ?

• What do I wish to request from St. Andrzej Bobola at his tomb?

Reading: Philippians 3:7-11
Whatever gains I had, these I have come to regard as loss because of Christ…

Response: "May the blood of the martyrs be the seed of the Church."

Saint Andrew Bobola, you spurned the vanities of the world and earnestly strove after "the greater gifts," offering yourself as a youth to service in the Society of Jesus. Teach us to deny ourselves, take up the Cross daily, and follow Jesus. R.

Saint Andrew Bobola, you were on fire with love for God and neighbor, and you desired to spend hours before the sacred tabernacle and assisted the poor and lost in every possible way. Show us how to humble ourselves and seek the glory of God in all things. R.

Saint Andrew Bobola, you fervently sought to preserve, extend, and defend the Catholic faith by teaching Christian doctrine, encouraging devotion to the Eucharist, and inspiring an ardent love for the Blessed Virgin Mary. Give us a passionate desire to share the joy of the gospel and the beauty of Christ's Church. R.

Saint Andrew Bobola, through your holiness of life and burning zeal for Christ's mission, you invited those of wavering faith in cities, towns, and villages to return to the one fold of Jesus Christ. Form us as missionary disciples, desiring to enrich your Church with new souls and to transcend the shallow deviations of secularism and consumerism that plague us today. R.

Saint Andrew Bobola, you endured unimaginable tortures with unconquerable fortitude and with a resolute and unbroken trust in God. Instill in us a spirit of repentance for our carelessness, sluggishness, and procrastination in doing the will of our God and seeking first the Kingdom. R.

Saint Andrew Bobola, you shed your blood and gave your life in sacrificial service and witness to the faith. Inspire us to offer courageous and constant resistance to the lure of evil and to give complete and generous dedication to our Redeemer and Lord. R.

Prayer: Saint Andrew Bobola, stand with us in faithful union with the Sacred Heart of Jesus, under the protection of his Immaculate Mother. Help us to trust always in the infinitely merciful love of God, so that our faith does not waiver in the midst of persecution, and so that we are given the grace to accept God's will, whatever it may be.

VI. Shrines to the Blessed Virgin Mary

Devotion to the saints in Poland has always reserved the place of honor to the Blessed Virgin Mary. Over the course of the Middle Ages, the Church in Poland followed the other nations of Europe in cultivating an increasingly intense, empathic connection with Mary, recognizing her as the ultimate heavenly intercessor and a paradigm of perfect devotion to Christ.[47]

The oldest known hymn in the Polish language is "*Bogurodzica*" ("Theotokos/God-Bearer"). The origin of the song is unknown, but it was composed somewhere between the 10th and 14th centuries. Those who hold for an early date of composition speculate that its composer was St. Wojciech. The hymn begins with expressions of acclaim for Mary as Virgin, Bearer of God, praised by God. It then requests that she ask her Son to have mercy on His people. The *Bogurodzica* was initially connected with the Mass and processions, but it soon also became an anthem sung by Polish knights before going into battle and performed at the coronation ceremonies of Poland's early rulers. For this reason, Jan Długosz, Poland's 15th-century historian called it Poland's *carmen patrium* (hymn of the fatherland). Sung in times of war and peace, the anthem reminds the listeners to turn to the Blessed Virgin Mary in all the struggles of life.

Throughout Poland one of the Blessed Virgin's most widespread titles is Our Lady Queen of Poland. The designation dates to the second half of the 16ᵗʰ century when she was first given this title by the Polish Renaissance poet Grzegorz of Sambor. In 1656, King Jan Kazimierz, in a grand ceremony in Lwów's cathedral, proclaimed the Blessed Virgin Mary as the queen of his realm, placing his subjects under her maternal care. He then petitioned for her assistance in the Commonwealth's "present affliction" in which Cossack, Muscovite, and Swedish armies were ravaging the land.

Throughout the centuries, the Virgin Mary has been considered the first among the nation's patron saints and the Queen of Poland. She is believed to have protected Poland in troubled times and to have miraculously saved the nation during the Swedish Deluge, the Battle of Vienna, the Partitions of Poland, the Polish-Soviet War, World War II, and the communist oppression of the Polish People's Republic. On May 3, the Church in Poland celebrates the liturgical feast of the Blessed Virgin Mary, Queen of Poland.

Shrine of the Black Madonna of Częstochowa.

1. Częstochowa, Shrine of Our Lady of Jasna Góra

The Shrine of the Black Madonna at Częstochowa is unquestionably the spiritual heart of Poland. The way between Kraków and Częstochowa forms the Trail of the Eagles' Nests, named for the many castles and watchtowers built along the limestone hills. Because the sanctuary is built on a hill and includes a soaring steeple, it can be seen from quite a distance. Several million pilgrims travel to the shrine each year, including several hundred thousand coming on foot.

Shrine of Our Lady of Jasna Góra.

The name "Jasna Góra" (Bright Mountain) was given to the site in the 14th century by the Pauline Fathers, a community originally from Hungary. Officially named the Order of Saint Paul the First Hermit, they were brought to Poland by Prince Władysław Opolski from the Piast Dynasty and were given the small Church of the Blessed Virgin Mary at Jasna Góra. In 1382, they placed there the miraculous painting of Our Lady, which has become Poland's foremost national treasure.

The compact architectural complex, which is today's Shrine of Our Lady of Jasna Góra, has developed over more than six centuries. At its heart is the Shrine of the Mother of God, containing the priceless icon of Our Lady. Next in importance is the Basilica of the Assumption of the Blessed Virgin Mary and the Finding of the Holy Cross. The sumptuously rich decor centers on the scene of Mary being carried by angels into heaven, while witnessed by the four evangelists. Above her the Holy Trinity waits for Mary's arrival to crown her. The basilica also features a beautiful ambo for the proclamation of Scripture, a splendid organ in the choir loft, and numerous side altars. The sacristy contains several works of art, including seven large paintings depicting the lives of hermits: Sts. Martinianus, Sophronia, Anthony the Abbot, Mary of Egypt, Thaïs, Dymphna, and Romuald.

Visitors may also explore the several museums on the grounds, including the Votive Treasury of the Blessed Virgin Mary, which displays the votive offerings given to Our Lady over six centuries. Pilgrims may also visit the Perpetual Adoration Chapel above the Shrine of the Mother of God; the Chapel of the Sacrament of Penance; the bronze outdoor Stations of the Cross; the 20 Stations of the Mysteries of the Rosary; and the contemporary indoor stations, which consist of 18 large paintings by the Polish painter Jerzy Duda-Gracz. The striking images were consecrated in 2001 and entitled "Golgotha of Jasna Góra of the Third Millennium."

The miraculous icon of Our Lady of Jasna Góra, also known as Our Lady of Częstochowa, depicts the Blessed Virgin Mary holding the child Jesus in her left hand while gesturing toward him as the source of salvation with her right. The image is classified as a Byzantine *Hodegetria*, meaning "She who shows the way." The Child Jesus is holding the Scriptures in His left hand and His right is extended in blessing. Normally only the face and hands of the original icon are seen. In the 17th century, the practice began of making robes adorned with jewels for the Mother and Child. Several unique robes have been created over the centuries, which are periodically changed as royal attire for the image.

The origin of the icon is shrouded in mystery. According to legend, its origin is traced to St. Luke, who painted it on a tabletop from the home of the Holy Family, and its discovery to St. Helena, who brought it back from Jerusalem and presented it to her son in Constantinople. Historians date the origin of the original icon from the sixth century or later, but the age of the painting is difficult to determine, due to extensive repainting after the image was slashed and severely damaged in 1430 by Hussite iconoclasts from Bohemia. Mary's cheek is marked by two parallel scratches, with several others less noticeable extending to her neck, as the result of the assault. The present form of the icon is a harmonious combination of the Byzantine art of the East and the Latin imagery of the West.

The Black Madonna is credited with miraculously saving the Jasna Góra Monastery during the Siege of Jasna Góra at the time of the 17th-century Swedish invasion, turning the course of the war. Shortly thereafter King Jan Kazimierz solemnly pronounced his vows to consecrate the country to the protection of the Mother of God and proclaimed her Patron and Queen of his kingdom. Events of the 20th century confirmed and intensified the unity between the Polish nation and its Queen. On the 300th anniversary of King Kazimierz' vows in 1956, the Polish Episcopate, on the initiative of the imprisoned Primate, Stefan Wyszyński, gathered about a million of the faithful at Jasna Góra to pronounce the Vows of the Polish Nation and re-entrust the whole nation to Mary. This event began the great nine-year novena in preparation for the Millennium of the Baptism of Poland. In

Shrine of the Black Madonna of Częstochowa.

that year, on May 3, 1966, Cardinal Wyszyński pronounced the act of total servitude to the Mother of God for the freedom of the Church in Poland and throughout the world.

When St. John Paul visited Jasna Góra on his first papal trip to his homeland in 1979, he urged the Polish people to "listen in this holy place in order to hear the beating of the heart of the nation in the heart of the Mother."[48] His words echo here today as he calls upon us to heed the invitation of Poland's royal mother:

> The history of Poland can be written in different ways; especially in the case of the history of the last centuries, it can be interpreted along different lines. But if we want to know how this history is interpreted by the heart of the Poles, we must come here, we must listen to this shrine, we must hear the echo of the life of the whole nation in the heart of its Mother and Queen. And if her heart beats with a tone of disquiet, if it echoes with solicitude and the cry for the conversion and strengthening of consciences, this invitation must be accepted. It is an invitation springing from maternal love, which in its own way is shaping the historical processes in the land of Poland.[49]

MEDITATION

- What strikes me most about the icon of Our Lady?
- What invitation is my royal mother Mary offering me today?

> Reading: Luke 1:46-55
> *And Mary said, "My soul magnifies the Lord, and my spirit rejoices in God my Savior...*
>
> Response: "Holy Virgin Mary, we entrust our lives to you."
>
> Spouse of the Holy Spirit and Seat of Wisdom, it is to your intercession that we owe the magnificent vision and the program of renewal of the Church in our age that found expression in the teaching of the Second Vatican Council. Grant that we may make this vision and program the object of our activity, our service, our teaching, our pastoral care, our apostolate — in the same truth, simplicity, and fortitude with which the Holy Spirit has made them known through our humble service.[50] R.

Mother of Unity, help us in this great endeavor to meet in an increasingly mature way our separated brothers and sisters in faith. Through all the means of knowledge, of mutual respect, of love, of shared collaboration in various fields, may we be able to rediscover gradually the divine plan for the unity into which we should enter and bring everybody to the one fold of Christ. R.

You, who were the first to reveal your Son at Bethlehem, not only to the faithful shepherds but also to the wise men from distant lands, exhort us to go out to meet all peoples who are seeking God and wishing to serve Him on the way of different religions. Help us all to proclaim Christ and reveal "the power of God and the Wisdom of God" (1 Cor 1:24) hidden in His Cross. R.

Mother of Good Counsel, show us always how we are to serve the individual and humanity in every nation, how we are to lead them along the ways of salvation, and how we are to protect justice and peace in a world continually threatened on many sides. We entrust to you all the difficult problems of the societies, systems and states — problems that cannot be solved with hatred, war, and self-destruction but only by peace, justice, and respect for the rights of people and of nations. R.

Mother of the Church, grant that the Church may enjoy freedom in fulfilling her saving mission and that to this end she may come to a new maturity of faith and inner unity. Help us to rediscover all the simplicity and dignity of the Christian vocation. Grant that there may be no lack of laborers in the Lord's vineyard. Sanctify families; watch over the souls of the young and the hearts of the children. Help us to overcome the great moral threats against the fundamental spheres of life and love. Obtain for us the grace to be continually renewed through all the beauty of witness given to the Cross and Resurrection of your Son. R.

Prayer: We entrust to you, Mother of the Church, all the problems of the Church, the whole of her mission, and all of her service, in this third millennium of the history of Christianity on earth. Grant that the whole Church may be renewed by drawing from the eternal spring of her ancient wisdom, and not from the poisoned cisterns of deceptive ideology.

2. Licheń Stary, Basilica of Our Lady of Licheń

The beautiful account of Our Lady of Licheń, the Sorrowful Mother of Poland, begins with the story of two visionaries in the 19th century. The first was a Polish soldier, Tomasz Klossowski, one of the horrendous casualties of the bloody battle of Lipsk (Leipzig) in 1813. Gravely injured and lying on the battlefield among the dead, he sought the help of Our Holy Mother and asked her for safe deliverance. He then saw an apparition of Mary, which he described in this way:

> She was moving across the battlefield in a long amaranth [rose-colored] dress, floating above the ground and hugging a white eagle at her breast, Virgin Mary! She was slowly coming toward me. She stopped and leant over me and then I saw her face, most beautiful, but full of indescribable sorrow.[51]

She promised that he would recover and return to Poland, and she committed him to search in his homeland for an image most faithfully representing her so that "my nation may pray to it and take graces from my hands in most difficult times." Tomasz settled in the village of Izabelin, located near Licheń, and took up his profession as a blacksmith. After many years of searching, he found the small image of the Sorrowful Mother while on a pilgrimage. He brought it to his home, housed it in a small shrine, and hung it on an old pine tree in Grablin Forest.

After the death of this first visionary, the Sorrowful Mother appeared three times in 1850 to Mikołaj Sikatka, a white-haired shepherd of estate cattle, while he was grazing his herd in Grablin Forest. Because he often prayed at the small shrine hanging in the forest, he recognized the Virgin Mary with her rose-colored dress and the white eagle at her breast. Through this pious shepherd, Mary called all people to conversion, penance, and prayer in preparation for a coming plague and difficult times. She promised that she would clasp the nation of Poland to her heart as she did with the white eagle.

When a cholera epidemic broke out in 1852, the ill and endangered people of the nearby villages began to gather at the apparition site and the small shrine in the forest. As health and graces were experienced by the local people, a chapel was built in the forest for the image. As devotion to the Sorrowful Mother continued to grow more widely, the miraculous image was brought to the parish church in Licheń. The image was housed at the main altar of the Church of St. Dorothy, until in 2006 it was solemnly transferred to the new Basilica of Our Lady of Licheń.

The image of the Licheń Madonna depicts the upper part of the figure of Mary, with her head slightly turned and tilting downwards. Her young and delicate face expresses a disposition of melancholy reflection. The elements of her attire are dominated by two guiding themes: the royal dignity of Mary and the consideration of her Son's Passion. The first is expressed by a crown, held up by angels. The sign of the white eagle, the emblem of Poland, indicates that Mary is the Queen Mother of her Son's realm. The second theme is expressed by her sorrowful expression and the symbols of Christ's Passion on each side of the robe that flows down from her shoulders. Symbols of the Passion include nails, thorns, a spear, cross, whips, a sacrificial lamb, a rooster, a ladder, and a chalice. Our Sorrowful Queen knows the suffering of her children.

Jubilee Chapel with monuments of the two visionaries.

Pilgrims may spend quiet time in Grablin Forest to prepare for their visit to the basilica, which is about one-and-a-half miles north of the forest. The peaceful wooded area contains several chapels honoring the apparitions and the miraculous image. The Biała Chapel (White Chapel) was first built in 1852 at the place where Our Lady first appeared to the shepherd Mikołaj on August 15, 1850. The miraculous image

Miraculous image of Our Lady of Licheń.

Church of the Ten Evangelical Virtues of the Blessed Virgin Mary.

was removed from the pine tree and placed in this chapel for a short time before being moved to Licheń. After the image was moved from the forest, pilgrims often chipped off pieces of bark from the tree on which the image once hung. Because the tree gradually withered and broke, the parish priest wanted to save the trunk from destruction, so he built the Pine Chapel in 1903 to house and honor it. Both of these chapels had to be rebuilt after being destroyed by German soldiers during World War II. The Jubilee Chapel was erected in memory of the 150th anniversary of the apparitions. In front of it are monuments to the two visionaries, the soldier Tomasz Kłossowski and the shepherd Mikołaj Sikatka. Leading from the Pine Chapel are four paths honoring the Joyful, Luminous, Sorrowful, and Glorious Mysteries of the Rosary, and around the entire forest are 15 images of the Stations of the Cross and the Resurrection. At the edge of the forest stands the uniquely modern Church of the Ten Evangelical Virtues of the Blessed Virgin Mary, built in 2010 as the convent chapel of the Sisters of the Annunciation. These virtues may be prayed as a chaplet or litany honoring Mary most pure, most prudent, most humble, most faithful, most devout, most obedient, most poor, most patient, most merciful, and most sorrowful.

In 1857 the new stone church of St. Dorothy was completed in Licheń. The miraculous image was transferred to its main altar and attracted increasing numbers of pilgrims. Deep faith and prayer to Poland's Sorrowful Queen made the ill recover, the addicted give up their compulsions, and the lost find their way. In 1940, Nazis transported the parish priest to Dachau concentration camp, looted the church, destroyed its furnishings, and whitewashed its walls. They burned all the parish books and documents, including the Book of Graces, which contained nearly 3,000 records of healing miracles and graces received through the miraculous image of Our

Lady of Licheń. The church and its grounds were converted to a training camp for Nazi youth, hosting 200 boys aged 16 to 18.

Crucifix with several bullet marks from the Hitlerjugend camp.

The miraculous image itself, however, was hidden during the war and returned to the badly damaged church in 1945. A few years later, in 1949, the Marian Fathers came to Licheń to care for the parish. The village was one of the poorest in Poland, the houses made of clay and thatch and the road unpaved and often muddy. It took many years to slowly restore the church to its previous state. In 1965, Fr. Eugeniusz Makulski came to Licheń at age 37 to prepare the parish for the coronation of the miraculous image, a papal honor and recognition of the image's benevolent and miraculous nature. The coronation was performed by Cardinal Stefan Wyszyński on August 15, 1967, as part of the celebration of Poland's Millennium.

The parish Church of St. Dorothy is a high neo-Gothic brick structure. On the high altar, where the image of Our Lady of Licheń was honored for nearly 150 years, there is today a picture of the church's patron, the third-century martyr St. Dorothy. The altar table, consisting of figures of two angels, and the pulpit, symbolizing the breath of the Holy Spirit, are made of Carrara marble. The side chapels are dedicated to St. Stanisław Papczyński, the 17th-century founder of the Marian Fathers, and to Our Lady of Licheń, featuring a copy of the miraculous image.

Next to the parish church stands the smaller Church of Our Lady of Częstochowa. In the lower church, pilgrims visit the Chapel of the Holy Cross, featuring a crucifix with an extraordinary history. When the parish church was being used as a Hitler Youth (*Hitlerjugend*) camp for boys in 1944, one of the instructors, Berta Bauer, gathered her pupils in front of the cemetery chapel, aimed her pistol, and fired several shots at the crucifix above the chapel's entrance. "If God existed," she said, "he should punish me immediately." A few hours later, when she was going to the train station

Basilica of Our Lady of Licheń.

in Konin, a passing plane shelled her car and she died instantly. On the crucifix today, several clear bullet marks can be seen. Outside the chapel, the path leads to the rocky hill called "Golgotha," a labyrinth of grottoes, chapels, and stations of Christ's Passion connected by passages made of rock and concrete, complemented by small mountain stones, blocks of colored glass, and pebbles from the Holy Land. Dominated by the cross and figures of the Blessed Virgin and St. John, the hill was created as a work of atonement for the sacrilege committed by Berta Bauer and for the sacrilege of removing the crucifix from Polish schools, offices, and hospitals. Coming down from the top, pilgrims enter the crystal grotto of Jesus's tomb, the cave of Mary's Assumption, and a cave commemorating the Lord's Resurrection.

The construction of the Basilica of Our Lady of Licheń extended from the blessing of the site in 1994, through the visit of Pope John Paul II in 1999, to the consecration of the church in 2004. Under the leadership of the Marian Fathers and the long-time parish custodian Fr. Eugeniusz Makulski, Poland's largest church was built as a cross with a dome over the intersection of the nave and the transept, according to the design of Polish architect Barbara Bielecka. The Madonna and Child, accompanied by six archangels, loom over the main portico.

To the left of the main entrance stands a high tower, with viewing terraces on two levels. To the right of the basilica is the belfry, which hosts the 14-ton bell, dedicated in 2000 and named "Mary the Mother of God." There are 33 steps leading to the church, referring to the years of Jesus Christ's life on earth. The basilica has 365 windows and 52 doors, which symbolize the days and weeks of the calendar year. The large windows are made of amber-colored glass, divided with aluminum slats in such a way that the windows resemble ears of grain. The sun's rays create a unique play of colors within the church.

In 2006, the miraculous image of Our Lady of Licheń was solemnly transferred from the Church of St. Dorothy to the new basilica. Today it is honored at the central altar, above the tabernacle, with the papal crown above it, surrounded in royal red and contained in a richly decorated golden frame. High above the image, at the level of the columns' capitals, are the words *"Jestem który Jestem"* ("I Am Who I Am"), from Exodus 3:14. Below are the words of the oldest Polish Marian hymn, *"Bogurodzica."* The remarkable organ, the largest in Poland, saturates the basilica with sound. It consists of three separate instruments located in the west and east aisles and in the main choir, containing a total of over 12,000 pipes.

In the left transept stands the altar of Golgotha. The cross is made of black oak and the figure of Christ is made of Carrara marble. Within the altar is a stone from Golgotha, offered by the Franciscans of the Holy Land. To the left of the cross is a fresco depicting the coronation of the miraculous image in 1967. To the right is a fresco of the baptism of Mieszko I, Poland's first ruler, in 966. The Rosary Chapel contains a fresco of the apparition of Our Lady to Mikołaj Sikatka in Grablin Forest. In the right transept are numerous images to the saints and heroes of Poland and a series of side chapels dedicated to St. Jadwiga the Queen, the Holy Family, the Marian Fathers, the Souls in Purgatory, St. Francis of Assisi, St. Michael the Archangel, and the Sacred Heart of Jesus.

In the lower part of the basilica, the oldest and largest chapel honors the Holy Trinity. Dedicated in 1996, it has a unique rotunda shape and a remarkable marble floor constructed using natural shades of marble from

White eagle and observation tower of the basilica.

green to violet. Next to it is the St. John Paul Chapel, containing the altar and papal throne used during his visit in 1999. Other memories on display are his skullcaps as Cardinal and as Pope, the chalice he donated, and a fragment of his white sash. Another large chapel honors the 108 Martyrs of the Second World War, the Poles who died during the years 1939-1945 for their faith in God, their faithfulness to the Church, and their sacrificial love of the homeland. In the altar there is an image of the Risen Christ among the 108 Martyrs, the image used in the Mass of beatification in Warsaw in 1999. Portraits of each of the martyrs are on the walls of the chapel, including two Marian Fathers, George Kaszyra and Antoni Leszczewicz, martyred in 1943.

The Chapel of St. Stanisław Papczyński, the founder of the Congregation of Marian Fathers of the Immaculate Conception of the Most Blessed Virgin Mary, features a painting and relics of the saint. The beginning of the Marians in 1670, the first Polish congregation of men, is interwoven with a period of Polish history best illustrated by the images of clashing weapons and thousands of war casualties: the Cossack wars, the Swedish invasion, the defense of the Jasna Góra monastery, and the Polish victory over the invading Turks. For over 350 years, the Marians have valiantly served the needs of the Church in the midst of history's most tumultuous events. After centuries of patient waiting on the part of the Marian Fathers, their founder was beatified at this basilica in 2007. The altar and pulpit in the chapel, both made of oak, were those used at that event. He was then canonized by Pope Francis in 2016 in St. Peter's Square.

Chapel of St. Stanisław Papczyński, founder of the Congregation of Marian Fathers.

In thanksgiving for the visit of Pope John Paul II, the Marians created the Licheń Center for Assistance to Families and Addicted People in 2000. A few years later, in gratitude for honoring St. Stanisław Papczyński, the Marians opened in 2009 a hospice for those who are terminally ill. Serving people's physical, emotional, and spiritual needs, the Marians honor the Sorrowful Mother of Licheń and continue to plead for her consolation.

MEDITATION

• Why is Mary, Our Lady of Sorrows, such a comfort for those who are lost and grieving?

• In what parts of my heart do I need the healing consolation of Our Sorrowful Queen?

Reading: Luke 2:33-35
And the child's father and mother were amazed at what was being said about him...

Response: "Holy Virgin Mary, unite our hearts to yours."

Sorrowful Mother, when you offered your infant Son at the temple, your heart was filled with grief as Holy Simeon foretold that a sword would pierce your soul. Unite our sorrowful hearts with yours so that we may know the hope and consolation that comes from offering our sufferings in union with those of your Son. R.

Sorrowful Mother, when you fled into Egypt, your maternal heart brimmed over with sorrow at the hatred of Herod for your innocent Son. Unite our sorrowful hearts with yours so that we may avoid evil and temptation and so join our sufferings with those of your Son. R.

Sorrowful Mother, when you discovered your 12-year-old Son was missing during your pilgrimage to Jerusalem, your heart was filled with fear as you and your holy spouse desperately searched for him for three days. Unite our sorrowful hearts with yours so that when we are separated from Jesus, we will return to Him with repentance and renewed commitment. R.

Sorrowful Mother, when you saw your Son fall, wounded and bleeding under the crushing weight of the Cross, your heart was filled with anguish as you sought to comfort Him on the way to Calvary. Unite our sorrowful hearts with yours so that we may obtain the grace to bear whatever cross life brings to us. R.

Sorrowful Mother, when you stood by the Cross of Jesus, your heart was breaking in torment as you watched Him die out of love for the whole world. Unite our sorrowful hearts with yours so that we may fight against sin and die in His holy grace. R.

Sorrowful Mother, when your Son's body was lowered from the Cross and laid in your arms, your heart was flooded with grief as you looked upon His battered and lifeless body. Unite our sorrowful hearts with yours so that we may receive Jesus in our souls and be united with Him forever. R.

Sorrowful Mother, when the sacred body of your Son was taken from your arms and placed in the tomb, your heart was filled with faith that He would rise again. Unite our sorrowful hearts with yours so that our confident trust in the resurrection may be renewed. R.

Prayer: Most holy Virgin, Mother of our Lord Jesus Christ, by the sufferings of your life, by the sword of pain that pierced your soul, and by your perfect joy in Heaven, look upon us with your tender mercy. Take us under your protection and be our guide along the road to our Father's house in Paradise.

St. Mary's Basilica at Kraków's Main Market Square.

3. Kraków, Basilica of Our Lady Assumed into Heaven

The brick Gothic church, best known as St. Mary's Basilica, lies at one corner of the Main Market Square in Kraków. Seen from the square, the church is marked by two asymmetrical towers. The taller north tower was the city's watchtower in the Middle Ages. A bugle call from the tower announced the opening and closing of the city gates, outbreaks of fire in the city, or enemy attacks. According to an ancient legend, in the 12th century the city's watchman started to play the bugle to warn the townspeople that the city was being attacked by the Tatars. As he was playing, he was shot through the throat by a Tatar arrow. To this day, a bugle sounds the *Hejnał mariacki* (meaning "St. Mary's dawn") every hour on the hour from the watchtower, but cuts off at the same note in memory of the heroic bugler, thanks to whom Kraków was able to rise to battle with the invaders.

The shorter south tower serves as the bell tower, housing four liturgical bells that are rung regularly. Like the taller tower, it is built on a square plan and its stories are clearly marked out with ledges and windows. Another legend tells of two brothers, known as Kraków's best builders, who were hired to supervise the construction of each tower. After a while, the south tower began to grow taller than the north tower. In a fit of jealous rage, the younger brother killed his older sibling and ordered that the unfinished south tower be crowned with a cupola. He then proceeded to complete his

15ᵗʰ century masterpiece dedicated to the role of the Virgin Mary in God's plan of salvation.

north tower to its soaring height. On the day of the church's consecration, the younger brother, consumed with guilt, climbed to the top of his watchtower holding the knife he used to murder his brother, publicly confessed to the murder, and jumped. To commemorate the murder, an ancient knife hangs to this day in an arch near one of the entry gates of the Cloth Hall in the center of the Main Market Square.

Saint Mary's Basilica was founded in the 13ᵗʰ century by the Bishop of Kraków. The original Romanesque church was destroyed during the Mongol invasion, and the early Gothic church was built on its foundations and consecrated in 1320. Over the centuries, the church underwent numerous reconstructions and renovations. Only three of the original medieval stained-glass windows were preserved. The other windows and new painted decorations were created in the 19ᵗʰ century by Jan Matejko, Stanisław Wyspiański, and Józef Mehoffer. The vault imitates a star-studded sky, and the walls are covered by paintings with ornamental and heraldic themes, prayers to Our Lady, and images of angels playing instruments or holding banderoles (banners) inscribed with the Litany of the Blessed Virgin Mary.

The main altar is a late Gothic masterpiece, sculpted from 1477 until 1489 by Veit Stoss. The retable is a pentaptych (having five panels), composed of the central part, a pair of opening internal wings, and a pair of fixed external wings. Both pairs of wings are decorated with reliefs on both sides. The altar is made of three types of wood: hard oak for the structure, lighter but equally strong larch for the background, and soft and flexible linden for the figures. The entire iconography is dedicated to the Virgin Mary and her role in God's plan of salvation.

The base of the pentaptych is a relief presenting the Tree of Jesse, depicting the ancestors of Christ. The main level of sculptures exhibits the Dormition of Our Lady surrounded by the apostles. Mary's Assumption into Heaven is presented above it. The high finial depicts her coronation as the Queen of Heaven and Earth. The reliefs on the wings present scenes from the lives of Jesus Christ and his Holy Mother. The wings of the open altar depict scenes of Mary's joys: the Annunciation, the Nativity of Jesus, the Adoration of the Magi, the Resurrection of Jesus, the Ascension of Jesus, and the Decent of the Holy Spirit.

The Assumption altarpiece is opened and closed each day with a trumpet call. In the closed position, the altar presents 12 scenes. On the left fixed wing are depicted the meeting of Joachim and Anne, the birth of Mary, and the presentation of Mary at the Temple. On the opening wings are shown the Presentation of Jesus at the Temple, the 12-year-old Jesus teaching at the Temple, the arrest of Jesus, the Crucifixion, the descent from the Cross, and the entombment of Jesus. On the right fixed wing are seen the appearance of the resurrected Christ to Mary Magdalene, the three Marys at the tomb, and the descent of Christ into the realm of the dead.

In her diary, St. Faustina described a visit to the church:

> When we had finished our business, we went to the Church of the Most Holy Virgin Mary. We attended Holy Mass, during which the Lord gave me to know what a great number of souls would attain salvation through this work [of art]. Then, I entered into an intimate conversation with the Lord, thanking Him for having condescended to grant me the grace of seeing how the veneration of His unfathomable mercy is spreading. I immersed myself in a profound prayer of thanksgiving. Oh, how great is God's generosity. Blessed be the Lord, who is faithful in His promises (*Diary*, 1300).

MEDITATION

• How does the image of Mary surrounded by the apostles at her death give me comfort as I contemplate my own death?

• What graces might God wish me to receive through the intercession of Mary today?

Reading: 1 Corinthians 15:50-58
This perishable body must put on imperishability, and this mortal body must put on immortality…

Response: "May your mother intercede for us, Lord."

As Mary welcomed the actions of the Holy Spirit into her life at the Annunciation, may we learn to listen to God's Word and let it be done in our lives. We pray. R.

As Mary cradled You as an infant and guided Your childhood, may we be guided by You throughout our lives and embraced in Your arms when our life is done. We pray. R.

As Mary trusted You to bring forth the new wine at Cana, may we always follow her motherly invitation to do whatever You tell us to do. We pray. R.

As Mary stood beneath Your Cross and was given by You to be the mother of your disciples, may we trust in her maternal care and call upon her in our needs. We pray. R.

As Mary prayed for the coming of the Holy Spirit in the Upper Room, may we open our lives to receive the gifts of the Spirit and be Your witnesses. We pray. R.

As Mary died and was brought to Heaven to share in Your glory, may we be surrounded at death by the prayers of the saints and await Your coming with joyful hope. We pray. R.

Prayer: Lord Jesus Christ, who dwelt in the ever-virginal womb of Mary, without You our humanity is trapped in sin and destined for eternal death. Through the intercession of Mary, shelter of orphans and guide for travelers, whom the grave could not contain, give us unshakable hope in the life of the world to come.

VII. Cardinal Stefan Wyszyński and the Church in Warsaw

After his ordination as a priest of the Diocese of Włocławek in 1924, Fr. Stefan Wyszyński traveled to Częstochowa to offer his first solemn Mass before the icon of Our Lady of Jasna Góra. After losing his mother to death when he was 9, he knew that Mary would be a mother who would never abandon him, and from his love for her, he drew the courage to risk everything throughout his heroic life. Wyszyński then spent the next four years in Lublin, where he earned a doctorate in canon law with an emphasis on socioeconomic science from the Catholic University of Lublin. As a young priest, he served as a seminary professor, editor of the diocesan weekly, and social activist, writing over a hundred publication between 1931 and 1939 dealing with economic issues, the rights of workers, and social justice. His early convictions led to his later belief, based on Catholic social teachings, that Poland should offer a third road, a political system that opposed not only the inherent problems of collectivism but also the self-interested faults of capitalism.

Hunted by the Nazis during the war, Fr. Wyszyński served as chaplain for the Polish underground resistance and for the insurgents' hospital during the Warsaw Uprising. After the war, he was made bishop of Lublin at the exceedingly young age of 44. Then, following the death of Primate August

Hlond in 1948, he became the Primate of Poland and the Archbishop of Gniezno-Warsaw. As the man chosen to lead the Church in Poland through one of the most difficult periods in its history, Archbishop Wyszyński combined the solidity of deep faith and steadfastness of principle with the flexibility of action that results from foresight, imagination, moderation, and the ability to grasp a complex situation.[52] He was the helmsman the Church needed to lead it through the torrents of the coming decades.

Although Wyszyński negotiated a first-ever agreement between a communist government and the Church in 1950, a new wave of persecution swept the Polish Church in 1953, leading to mass trials and internment of priests, including a

Statue of Cardinal Stefan Wyszyński in Warsaw.

three-year imprisonment of now-Cardinal Wyszyński. Yet, while in prison, he envisioned what would become his most distinguishing achievement: the dedication of the nation of Poland in submission to the Blessed Virgin Mary for the sake of the freedom of the Church in Poland and throughout the world. This act of national dedication would be preceded by an anticipatory novena of nine years, leading to the thousand-year anniversary of Polish Christianity in 1966.

The first act of this vast spiritual plan for Poland occurred while Cardinal Wyszyński was still confined. 1956 was the 300th anniversary of King Jan Kazimierz' vows at Jasna Góra, consecrating the nation to the protection of Our Lady and proclaiming her as Queen of Poland. For this occasion, the Primate wrote the king's vows in a form adapted to present times, then the Polish episcopate gathered about a million of the faithful at Jasna Góra to pronounce the Vows of the Polish Nation. Each verse was pronounced by Cardinal Wyszyński, standing before an image of Our Lady of Częstochowa from the cell of his confinement, while it was read to the crowd at Jasna Góra. Following each verse, the people responded loudly and full of emotion: "Queen of Poland, we promise!" The communist authorities stood by helpless, and within two months the Primate was freed to return to Warsaw and resume his pastoral leadership.

Following this event and during each year of the Great Novena of the Millennium, the bishops focused the nation on a theme of the Jasna Góra Vows. In this way, through catechesis, prayer, liturgy, pilgrimages, processions, works of charity, and social actions, Poland would experience a transformation of its national spirit in anticipation of the Millennium in 1966.

During the cardinal's final years, he was able to witness what he described as two "miracles": the election of his compatriot Cardinal Wojtyła as Pope in 1978 and the pastoral pilgrimage of Pope John Paul II to Poland in 1979, the first visit of a Pope to a communist country. Every Pole old enough to remember treasures the scene after the conclave when Cardinal Wyszyński and the other cardinals approached the newly elected Pope to pay their first homage. Before the eyes of the world, Cardinal Wyszyński fell to his knees and instantly the new Pope did the same, and the two men held each other in a long embrace. One week later, in his Letter to the People of Poland, Pope John Paul addressed these words to his mentor:

> This Polish pope, who today, full of fear of God, but also of trust, is beginning a new pontificate, would not be on Peter's chair were it not for your faith which did not retreat before prison and suffering. Were it not for your heroic hope, your unlimited trust in the Mother of the Church! Were it not for Jasna Gora, and the whole period of the history of the Church in our country, together with your ministry as Bishop and Primate![53]

On May 13, 1981, the day of the attack on the life of Pope John Paul in Rome, a communiqué about the deteriorating health of Cardinal Wyszyński was released. The Pope and the Primate spoke by phone and prayed for each other. How many sentiments must have penetrated their minds and hearts during that final conversation!

For more than three decades, until his death on the Feast of the Ascension in 1981, Stefan Wyszyński was the main spokesman for freedom and human rights in Poland. Because he addressed every national and social struggle in his public appearances and dialogue with the government, he gained an authority unknown to the spiritual leaders of other communist countries. When he died two months before his 80th birthday, he had been a priest for 57 years, a bishop for 35, archbishop of Gniezno and Warsaw and Primate of Poland for 32, and a cardinal for 28.

Saint John Paul gave Cardinal Wyszyński the title "Primate of the Millennium," which means not only that he created the program of national renewal to celebrate Poland's thousand-year anniversary, but also that he was one of the greatest Polish ecclesial leaders in 10 centuries. The cause for his canonization commenced in 1989, and in a great national celebration in Warsaw, he was raised to the altar with his beatification in 2021.

1. Warsaw, Cathedral Basilica of St. John the Baptist

One of Warsaw's most famous historical landmarks, the Zygmunt Column, stands in Castle Square to commemorate King Zygmunt III Wasa, who in 1596 moved Poland's capital from Kraków to Warsaw. The column is topped with a bronze statue of the king wielding a saber and leaning forward on a cross. The cathedral of the Archdiocese of Warsaw stands in the heart of the city's Old Town, between the Royal Castle and Old Town Square. The church was formerly connected to the castle by a long corridor, built after an assassination attempt on the king in front of the cathedral.

Originally built in the 14th century in Masovian Gothic style, the Church of St. John the Baptist took on increasingly more importance for the nation. In the 17th century, the church was one of the richest in Poland, the main altar funded by King Zygmunt III and the interior filled with works of art in the spirit of the Baroque, thanks to the patronage of nobility and city patricians. By the 18th century, the kings of Poland held their coronations there. After the resolution of the Constitution of May 3, 1791, at the end of the session at the Royal Castle, King Stanisław August Poniatowski went to the church to repeat the Oath of the Constitution in front of the altar. In 1798 the Church of St. John was elevated to the dignity of a cathedral when Warsaw was established as a diocese.

During the Warsaw Uprising of 1944, the cathedral was a place of struggle between insurgents and the advancing German army. The Nazis managed to bring a tank loaded with explosives into the cathedral, and the huge explosion destroyed a large part of the building. After the collapse of the uprising, the Germans drilled holes into the walls for explosives and blew up what remained of the cathedral. They did the same with most of the city's Old Town, a spiteful and strategically senseless operation by the Nazi regime, which was on the edge of collapse.

After the war, Cardinal August Hlond, Poland's Primate, stated in a 1947 pastoral letter, "Since the days of St. Peter, the church has not been subjected to a persecution such as that to which she is subjected today." Yet, he urged Warsaw to rebuild, establishing the Primate's Council for the

Reconstruction of the Churches of Warsaw. After Hlond's sudden death in 1948, his successor Stefan Wyszyński continued this work. After 15 years of painstaking rebuilding, Cardinal Wyszyński celebrated the achievement by consecrating the cathedral in 1960 and highlighting the historical unity of St. John's and the nation. The Nazis razed the church to the ground, he said, because "they knew that the strength of the nation was rooted in the cross, Christ's Passion, the spirit of the gospels, and the invincible church. To weaken and destroy the nation, they knew that they must first deprive it of its Christian spirit." Whatever our enemies attack, we should love and respect, he continued. "If they pack the churches with dynamite charges, we should fill them with the love of hearts faithful to God, the cross, the church, and her pastors."[54]

The cathedral was rebuilt based on its 14th-century appearance, not on its prewar appearance. Since very little of the church's furnishings survived, the interior reconstruction takes the church back to is raw Gothic look. It was enriched with new works of art, colorful stained glass evoking the history of Poland and its Polish saints, and the sound of the magnificent organ built in 1987. In the center stands a modern altar with a copy of the Black Madonna of Częstochowa.

Cathedral Basilica of St. John the Baptist in Warsaw's Old Town.

High altar of the Cathedral Basilica.

To the right of the central altar, the Baroque-styled Chapel of the Immaculate Conception, the so-called Literary Chapel, contains an image of the Virgin Mary from the destroyed St. Andrew Church, dating back to the 17th century. Beneath are the relics of St. Zygmunt Szczęsny Feliński, the 19th-century archbishop of Warsaw canonized in 2009. To the left of the central altar, the Baryczka Chapel features a surviving masterpiece of Gothic sculpture: a life-sized figure of Christ Crucified. The miraculous crucifix, with its expressive face full of sorrow and black human hair, has accompanied Warsaw through its turbulent history. It survived the two fires of 1598 and 1607, the collapse of the vault in 1602, the plunder by the Swedes, and the bombs of the Germans in 1939. Finally, the figure emerged intact though badly burned when the cathedral was raised to the ground in 1944. The crucifix has been venerated by Poland's rulers and faithful alike over the centuries.

Among the chapels on the left aisle stands the Chapel of St. John the Baptist, with its tomb of Cardinal August Hlond. Toward the entrance is the mausoleum and altar of Bl. Cardinal Stefan Wyszyński. Above his sarcophagus, there is a plate illustrating the life of the Primate of the Millennium: from the seminary, through his work as a priest, to his working with insurgent units, to his welcoming Pope John Paul to Warsaw.

The funeral Mass of Cardinal Stefan Wyszyński was held in Victory Square, after which the procession led to the Cathedral Basilica of St. John the Baptist, where the last part of the funeral took place. The vicar general of Warsaw read fragments of the spiritual testament that Wyszyński had composed in 1969. The Primate gave posterity an account of his struggles with the atheistic and mistaken policies of the communist government, forgiving all, including those who had attacked and imprisoned him. "I served the church in Poland according to my best understanding of its situation and needs," he declared. "I consider it a grace that, with the help of the Polish Episcopate, I was able to prepare the nation through the Great Novena and the Vows of Jasna Góra for the new millennium. I sincerely wish that the Polish people will remain faithful to these commitments."

The church crypt contains the tombs of kings, dukes, presidents, generals, writers, painters, musicians, and other archbishops of Warsaw. In recent years, the church has become an important center for the promotion of sacred music. It hosts the International Festival of Sacred Music with performances of oratorio-cantata, organ, and choral music, as well as frequent concerts of religious music throughout the year.

MEDITATION

• How can I prepare the way of the Lord like John the Baptist?

• How does Bl. Cardinal Wyszyński inspire me to live the call of my baptism?

Reading: John 1:29-34
The next day he saw Jesus coming toward him and declared, "Here is the Lamb of God…"

Response: "May we prepare the way of the Lord."

Saint John the Baptist, prophet of God, crying out in the wilderness, you prepared the way of the Lord. R.

Saint John the Baptist, calling God's people to repentance, you pointed to Jesus as the Lamb of God Who takes away the sins of the world. R.

Saint John the Baptist, unjustly imprisoned for speaking the truth, you were martyred in your witness to Christ. R.

Blessed Stefan Wyszyński, brave follower of Christ, you defended the Church and nation against the oppressions of Nazism and communism. R.

Blessed Stefan Wyszyński, model of courage and perseverance, you were unjustly persecuted and imprisoned for your witness to Christ. R.

Blessed Stefan Wyszyński, trusting always in Mary, you defended human dignity and forgave your persecutors. R.

Prayer: Lord God, through John the Baptist the forerunner of Christ and Stefan Wyszyński the Primate of the Millennium, you manifested Your Son to the world in the first and 20th centuries. Prepare our hearts for the coming of Christ so that we may trust in Him as the Lamb of God. Through our repentance, may we recognize and work toward the coming of your kingdom, where You reign with Christ our Lord.

2. Warsaw, Church of Divine Providence and Museum of John Paul II and Primate Stefan Wyszyński

The Temple of Divine Providence, located in southern Warsaw's Wilanów district, is a monumental building in the form of a Greek cross, comprising four equal-length arms, four gates, and a copper dome kissing the sky. Built and consecrated in 2016, the temple stands as a symbol of God's protection over the Polish people. The principal part of the structure is the church, formed by 26 columns supporting the dome. The Museum of John Paul II and Primate Wyszyński is found above ground in the ring surrounding the dome, and the Pantheon of Great Poles is the underground burial chamber for distinguished Poles.

The dome allows sunlight to fall through the glass circle in the center. The columns spire out over the altar, with lights that shine in the color of the liturgical season. A glass circle in the center of the floor, parallel to the circle in the dome, allows light to flood into the underground crypt. The architecture expresses how God never stops watching over the Polish people, dead or alive, and symbolizes God's dominion over the nation.

The idea of building the Temple of Divine Providence goes back to the reign of Stanisław August Poniatowski. Two days after the Sejm adopted the May 3 Constitution in 1791, the deputies and the king resolved to erect a church to express thanksgiving to "the Highest Ruler of the fate of nations" for the constitution's adoption. On the first anniversary of the constitution's adoption, the cornerstone was laid by the king and his brother, the Catholic Primate of the Polish-Lithuanian Commonwealth, Archbishop Michał Jerzy Poniatowski. However, the Russian Imperial Army invaded Poland in 1795, and three years later Poland disappeared from the map of Europe.

After Poland regained its sovereignty in 1918, a new design was drafted to celebrate Poland's independence. The Sejm budgeted the cost of construction as well as a perpetual endowment for Masses offered there for the intention of the homeland and for the souls of all Poles who died for the country. However, financial difficulties and inflation did not allow the young state to bear such costs. Another plan envisioned a tower, created to memorialize Marshal Józef Piłsudski after his death in 1935. But after Germany and the Soviet Union invaded Poland in 1939, the plans were stalled again. Another plan was presented after the war, but the communist government prevented its construction.

The recently constructed temple commemorates the providential events in Poland over the last 200 years: the Constitution of May 3, 1791; the rebirth of independent Poland in 1918; the 1920 Miracle on the Vistula;

Temple of Divine Providence at night.

Display of the intersecting lives of Pope John Paul II and Cardinal Stefan Wyszyński.

Upper level of the Church of Divine Providence.

Sacrament of Penance offered before Mass.

Cardinal Wyszyński pays homage to the newly-elected Pope John Paul II.

Requiem Mass on the battlefield, an exhibit in the Museum.

the founding of the Solidarity movement in 1980; the resumption of Polish independence in 1989; the pastoral ministry of Stefan Wyszyński; and the pontificate of Pope John Paul II. During his pilgrimage to Poland in 1999, the Pope blessed the cornerstone in Piłsudski Square and prayed that "this shrine become a place of special thanksgiving for freedom of the homeland."

Along the interior walls, reliquaries honor Polish saints such as St. John Paul, St. Faustina Kowalska, St. Maximilian Kolbe, and more. Each reliquary is designed to correspond to the story of the saint and to show how each person was an instrument used by God in Polish history. Some of the places remain empty, leaving room for collecting more relics of saints from the past and for future Polish saints.

The Museum of John Paul II and Primate Wyszyński tells the story of the two patrons of the Museum against the background of the century in which they lived. Its chronological framework covers the period from 1901, Stefan Wyszyński's birth year, to 2005, the year of John Paul II's death. The exhibition illuminates the activities of John Paul II and Cardinal Stefan Wyszyński, the close relationship between these two Poles, and the substantial contribution of the Church to the history of the Polish nation. The use of multimedia, sound, and light is intended to take the visitor through the course of these events, and invites them to be co-participants in Polish history.

Several exhibits highlight events of the 20th century expressing the special unity between the Polish nation and the Catholic Church, such as the Millennium of the Baptism of Poland in 1966; the first papal Mass conducted at Victory Square in Warsaw in June 1979; the Solidarity movement, which began in 1980; and the Great Jubilee of the year 2000. Other key exhibits include the following: the struggle of Wyszyński and Wojtyła to free Poland from two totalitarian systems during the Second World War; the imprisonment of Primate Wyszyński and persecution of the Church by the communist regime; the Great Novena of the Millennium; the role of Wojtyła and Wyszyński at the Second Vatican Council; the election of Karol Wojtyła as Pope; the John Paul II assassination attempt and the death of Primate Wyszyński; the gift of new freedom in 1989; and the Pope and youth leading the Church into the third millennium.

MEDITATION

- In what ways do I experience God watching over my life and my family?
- How does the kingship of Christ and the reign of his royal mother assure my freedom?

Reading: Luke 1:39-45
In those days Mary set out and went with haste...

Response: "Queen of Poland, we so pledge!"

O Queen of the world and Queen of Poland! Together with the nation of Poland, we place at your feet ourselves and everything we have: our families, houses of worship, homes, fields and workplaces, plows, hammers and pens, all of our efforts, our beating hearts, and our bursts of will. We promise to do everything in our power so that our nation may be truly your kingdom and your Son's kingdom, given over entirely to your rule in our personal, family, national, and social lives.[55] R.

O Mother of Divine Grace! We pledge to you to protect the gift of grace, which is the source of divine life in every heart. We hope that every one of us will live in sanctifying grace and be a temple of God, that we will live without mortal sin and become a house of God and a gate of heaven for the generations to come, passing under the leadership of the Catholic Church to our eternal homeland. R.

O Mother of Good Counsel! We pledge to you, with eyes focused on the manger of Bethlehem, that we will defend unborn life, every child, and every cradle as courageously as our ancestors fought for the existence and freedom of our nation, paying with their own blood. R.

O Mother of Christ and House of Gold! We pledge to you to strengthen the reign of your Son Jesus Christ in the family, to protect the honor of the name of God, to implant in the hearts and minds of children the spirit of the Gospels and love towards you, to guard the laws of God and Christian and national traditions. We pledge to you to raise the young generations in faithfulness to Christ, to defend them against godlessness and depravity and surround them with watchful parental protection. R.

O Mirror of Justice! We promise to work hard so that in our homeland all children will live in love and justice, in harmony and peace, so that among us there will be no hatred, violence, or exploitation. We promise to share among ourselves willingly the harvests of the earth and the fruits of labor, so under the common roof of our house there will be no hunger, no homelessness, no weeping. R.

O Victorious Lady of Jasna Góra! We promise to fight under your banner a most holy and most difficult struggle with our faults and vices. We promise to declare war on laziness and recklessness, wastefulness, drunkenness, and promiscuity. We promise to attain the virtues of faithfulness and conscientiousness, hard work and frugality, self-denial and mutual respect, love and social justice. R.

Prayer: O Mary our mother, we remember that you are the mother of our Way, Truth, and Life, that in your maternal face we will most surely recognize your Son, to whom you unfailingly point the way. In your hands we place our past and future, all our national and social life, the Church of your Son, and everything that is precious to us in God. Lead us through the land of Poland, which is devoted to you, to the gates of our heavenly homeland. And at the threshold of the new life show us Jesus, the blessed fruit of your womb. Amen.

VIII. Gdańsk, Solidarność, and Fr. Jerzy Popiełuszko

The city of Gdańsk lies on the coast of the Baltic Sea and is Poland's principal seaport. The Vistula River, the country's most important waterway, flowing first through Kraków and Warsaw, empties into the Baltic at Gdańsk Bay, near the city. Although much of the city was destroyed during World War II, the historic center has been completely rebuilt and is today one of Poland's most picturesque cities. The vast shipyards and port have been the city's most characteristic features since the Middle Ages, providing much of the city's income and prestige, and in the late 20th century gave rise to Solidarność, the Solidarity movement that transformed Poland.

Saint Wojciech evangelized the population in 997, but Gdańsk has had many other influences in its long history, with periods of Polish, Prussian, and German rule, and periods of autonomy or self-rule as a free city state. The Polish triumph over the Teutonic Knights in 1454 brought Gdańsk under Polish rule. Most exported grain left Poland through its port city, so Gdańsk became the wealthiest, most developed, and most autonomous of the Polish cities. The Crane (*Żuraw*), one of the city's defining symbols, is a spectacular example of a medieval port crane and represents what little is left of the city's great trading age. Located on the Motława River in the city, it was used to transfer cargoes and to put up masts on ships. At one time this

River view of Gdańsk with its medieval port crane.

was the biggest working crane in the world, but it also served a defensive function and as one of the gates to the city. Today it is part of the National Maritime Museum.

In the 16th and 17th centuries, Gdańsk became the largest and most distinguished city of the Polish Commonwealth, holding a near monopoly on the lucrative Baltic trade in grain, timber, and fish. During Poland's long partition, Gdańsk was swallowed up by the Prussian state, then became an autonomous city after the First World War, and finally was returned to Poland after the Second World War. After the war, the Main Town was rebuilt to look like the Gdańsk of 1450-1650.

Walking along Ulica Długa (Long Street), the visitor follows the Royal Route of the historic city center. At the western end, the Highland Gate and Prison Tower form part of the old city fortifications. The Golden Gate is a Renaissance city gate having both sides topped with figures symbolizing the qualities of the ideal citizen. The figures on the west side represent peace, freedom, wealth, and fame; and those on the east side signify prudence, piety, justice, and concord. The Latin inscription on the gate translates: "In agreement (*concordia*) small republics grow, because of disagreement great republics fall." The route leads to the Main Town Hall, which is today's Historical Museum of the City of Gdańsk. The street becomes the Długi Targ (Long Market), the centerpiece of which is the statue of Neptune, god of the sea. He's a fitting symbol for the city that dominates Poland's maritime life. The Royal Route continues past several magnificent residences and terminates at the Green Gate, which opens to the river.

In the heart of Main Town stands the Gothic Church of St. Mary, the world's largest brick church, begun in 1343 and requiring 159 years to complete. The exterior resembles a massive castle, and the vast interior space can easily accommodate 25,000 people. While the church was originally frescoed throughout, the Lutheran reformers whitewashed the entire space. The main altar displays a 16th-century triptych featuring the coronation of Mary, surrounded by the Trinity. The moving Priests' Chapel, with its statue of Christ weeping, commemorates the 2,779 Polish priests executed by the Nazis. The astronomical clock is a 42-foot-tall wooden clock from the 15th century. It not only tells time, but also gives the phases of the moon and calculates on which day each saint's feast falls in different years. On the top, Adam and Eve stand ready to ring the bell at the top of the hour. Toward the back of the church, 409 stairs lead to the church's tower, offering a magnificent view of the city.

Located between the church and the waterfront, the cobblestoned Ulica Mariacka is one of Poland's most atmospheric streets. Recreated after the war on the basis of old photographs and illustrations, this charming way features several ornamental details and enchanting gargoyles. The street includes several artisan shops selling amber jewelry, the city's most popular souvenir, and some great cafes.

In addition to the Basilica of St. Mary, the city holds many other churches, all of which gave refuge to the Polish people after the communist government declared martial law in 1981. When the riot police began cracking down on protesters, people flooded into the churches, knowing that the government forces wouldn't follow them. The Church became the only institution that could offer protection for those requiring it, and was also a forum for political meetings, lectures, discussions, and the dissemination of illegal literature. For all this, its leaders often paid a heavy price.

1. Gdańsk Shipyard and Solidarity Square

In the 1980s, Gdańsk was the birthplace of Solidarność, the movement that played a major role in bringing an end to communist rule in Poland and helped precipitate the collapse of the Eastern Bloc, the fall of the Berlin Wall, and the dissolution of the Warsaw Pact. This "cradle of freedom" — the shipyard gate, the worker's monument, and the European Solidarity Center — holds the memories of those brave workers who took on the communist empire and ultimately defeated it nonviolently.

Polish protests and uprisings against the government had occurred in 1968, 1970, and 1976, but they were brutally repressed. In December

The Gate of Freedom, Gate number 2 of the Gdańsk Shipyard, where the people of Poland gathered in support of the striking workers.

The 21 strikers' demands on the shipyard gate.

1970, a workers' protest at the Lenin Shipyard in Gdańsk was met with a hail of gunfire from the militia and the deaths of dozens of workers. But the election of Pope John Paul II in 1978 and his pilgrimage to Poland in 1979 removed the psychological barrier of fear from people's hearts. By 1980, the country was plagued with price increases and food rationing, resulting in a wave of public strikes. The epicenter was again at the shipyard of Gdańsk. The strike committee issued a list of 21 demands, including the right to strike, the right to form independent trade unions, and permission to erect a monument to their colleagues who had been killed in the 1970 uprising.

The Monument to the Fallen Shipyard Workers soars high above Solidarity Square, outside the entrance to Gate 2 of the shipyard. The memorial consists of three huge crosses, to which anchors are attached, representing faith and hope. Ten scenes with metal figures of dockyard workers are featured in the lower parts of the crosses. The monument was created by the shipyard workers within just four months of the August 1980 agreements with the government, the first monument to the victims of communist oppression to be erected in a communist country. Because it was dedicated on the 10-year anniversary of the massacre of December 1970, the government did not dare touch it because of its powerful significance.

The shipyard wall contains a list of the 44 workers murdered on that day. The bronze plaque, pockmarked with symbolic bullet holes, gives their names and their ages at death. The quote at the top is taken from the words of St. John Paul's homily at Victory Square in 1979: "Let thy Spirit descend and renew the face of the earth — of *this* earth." And the dedication below reads, "They gave their lives so you can live decently." To the left are plaques representing labor unions from around Poland and around the world. To the right is a verse from the Psalms: "May the Lord give strength to his people. May the Lord bless his people with the gift of peace" (Ps 29:11).

Monument to the Fallen Shipyard Workers soars high above Solidarity Square.

The leader of the 1980 strike and the emerging Solidarity trade union was a shipyard electrician, Lech Wałęsa. When the shipyard massacre took place in 1970, he had been at the forefront of the protests. Marked as a dissident, he was fired from his job in 1976. When he heard the news of the beginning of the strike in 1980, he raced to the shipyard and scaled the wall to get inside. His energetic determination won him the role of the workers' leader and spokesman. He represented 16,000 workers — manual laborers, forklift operators, welders, electricians, machinists — who stayed within the shipyard gates for the 18 days of the strike, sleeping on styrofoam, inspired by the new Polish Pope, elated about finally

Aging former president of Poland, Lech Wałęsa, continues to walk the streets of Gdańsk.

standing up to the regime, and terrified at the thought of being gunned down like their friends a decade before.

The renowned Gate number 2 of the Gdańsk Shipyard is the place where the people of Poland gathered in support of the striking workers. Spouses and families gathered here to communicate with their loved ones. Inside this gate, called the Gate of Freedom, Lech Wałęsa periodically pulled

222 *The Way of Mercy*

up in a truck, and standing atop its cab with a megaphone, addressed the thousands of people gathered outside. He updated the crowds on the progress of the talks and pleaded for food and supplies for the workers inside. His negotiations with the regime to hash out the August Agreements began a period of hope.

The current gate is a reconstruction, the original gate being run over by a tank during the first day of martial law in December 1981. It retains its original shape and is located in its historical place next to the authentic gatehouse and pass office. The gate today is decorated with authentic reproductions of its decorations during the strike: a copy of a painting of Our Lady of Częstochowa, a photo of Pope John Paul II, the Polish and papal flag, and a Solidarity banner. On the gate there are also containers with flowers in memory of bouquets hung on the gate in 1980, with which people expressed their support for the strikers. Above the gate, on two metal pillars, is an inscription made of steel letters painted in white: GDAŃSK SHIPYARD. On the right side of the gate, in red and black lettering, there is a copy of the sign listing the 21 strikers' demands.

Solidarity proved to be a nonviolent reform movement which, with its 10 million members, represented a broad section of the whole nation. Yet, in 1981, General Jaruzelski, the head of the Communist Party in Poland, was ordered by Moscow to crush Solidarity. He imposed martial law and ordered the army to occupy the country. Solidarity was officially abolished and all its leaders, including Lech Wałęsa, were imprisoned. The suppression was short-lived, however, as Solidarity went underground. It emerged again after martial law was lifted in 1983, triggered by the second visit of Pope John Paul to his homeland. That same year, Lech Wałęsa was awarded the Nobel Peace Prize for his work on human rights. After waves of strikes and protests in 1988, the Communist Party agreed to share political power. In the elections of 1989, communism was soundly thrashed and Solidarity won almost every seat it contested. In the presidential election of 1990, Wałęsa became the first president of Poland ever elected in a popular vote.

The events in Poland led to the collapse of communism throughout Europe. Other Eastern Bloc countries followed the example set by Solidarity, and the process became unstoppable. Like the images of the fall of the Berlin Wall in November 1989, Lech Wałęsa's personality and the Solidarity movement has come to symbolize popular demands for the end of communism in central Europe. In 1999, Poland became a member of NATO, returning to its thousand-year-old role of providing a shield for Europe.

The European Solidarity Center, opened in 2014 on the site of the Gdańsk Shipyard, is a museum devoted to the history of Solidarity and other opposition movements of communist Europe. The outside walls evoke the hulls of ships built at the site, while the interior houses a permanent exhibition and library.

MEDITATION

• What inspires me about the heroic struggles in Solidarity Square?

• How have my struggles led me to a sense of solidarity with the workers of the world?

Reading: Philippians 1:27-30
Live your life in a manner worthy of the gospel of Christ...

Response: "Jesus, worker and carpenter from Nazareth, hear our prayer."

O Jesus, worker and carpenter from Nazareth, we pray for all workers — men and women, young and old, of all races, ethnicities, and languages — that they experience a deeper understanding of Your presence in their labor and work to build human community where they are employed. R.

O Jesus, Lord of the Vineyard, Who has invited us who labor by the sweat of our brow to be workers in the vineyard and assist Your creative work to shape the world around us, help us respond to Your call by seeking Your reign upon the earth. R.

Make us attentive to those who seek work but cannot find it, and help us listen to the struggles of those who work hard to provide for their families but still have trouble making ends meet. R.

Open our eyes to the struggles of those who are exploited, and enable us to advocate for just wages and safe conditions, the freedom to organize, and time to enjoy Your gift of rest. R.

May our work always be a radiant expression of our human dignity and never a vehicle for exploitation. Fill us with Your Holy Spirit that You might work through us to let Your justice reign in all arenas of human labor. R.

Prayer: Lord Jesus, we join our hearts today with laborers throughout the world, praying for those who own companies and lead businesses, for union leaders responsible for speaking for workers, and for those employed to work in factories, fields, offices, hospitals, schools, and all arenas of human labor. May we realize the divinely given dignity of human work and build a spirit of solidarity among all who labor for a better world.

Amber Altar in St. Bridget's Basilica.

2. Gdańsk, St. Bridget's Basilica

Because of its proximity to the Gdańsk Shipyard, St. Bridget's Church became closely associated with Solidarność. Beginning with the strike of 1980 and throughout the struggle for Poland's freedom, resistance groups met here to worship, which during martial law was considered an act of political opposition. Lech Wałęsa, shipyard workers, port workers, and even leaders of free countries came here to pray in prayerful support of the homeland. St. Bridget's Basilica is still considered a sanctuary of Solidarity today, and a monument to Poland's 20th-century road to freedom.

The 14th-century penitential chapel of St. Mary Magdalene originally stood on the site. In 1374, the funeral procession carrying the remains of Bridget of Sweden, which was traveling from Rome to Vadstena in Sweden, made a two-week stop at the chapel, waiting for better weather conditions to make the voyage across the Baltic Sea. The residents of Gdańsk paid great homage to the sarcophagus and relics of St. Bridget, giving birth to a deep devotion to the saint. The Order of the Most Holy Savior, better known as the Bridgettines, settled here in 1386, and built a single-aisle church under the patronage of their founder. Fire and rebuilding resulted in the final form of the church and convent during the 18th century. Like most of the city, the church was destroyed during the Second World War in 1945 and was left in ruins for several decades.

When the church was rebuilt, beginning in 1970, it was not restored to the style of a past architectural period, but was reconstructed in a modern minimalism, creating a setting for contemporary works of art. Today the church is both an impressive and at the same time simple place of worship, containing sculptures and monuments recalling the difficult history of post-war Poland.

The remarkable Amber Altar, dedicated in 2017 by Archbishop Sławoj Głódź and President Andrzej Duda, is intended as a tribute to Divine Providence in thanks for St. John Paul and the regaining of Polish independence. It arches over the tabernacle and reaches upward as a vine with many branches, decorated with grapes and other figures of amber, gold, and silver. Amber is Poland's national stone, fondly referred to as "Baltic Gold." Whether in the form of rings, necklaces, or bracelets, as well as decorative items and jewelry boxes, amber is a visible element in Polish society and the most typical souvenir of the country. The stone consists of fossilized tree resin that has solidified and formed over thousands of years. Amber varies enormously in its size and shape, while its typical amber color can range to yellow, white, red, and green. Since the Baltic Sea continues to wash up amber from beneath the surface of the sand, Gdańsk is the heart of the amber trade, with guilds of amber craftsmen dating from the 15th century.

At the center of the Amber Altar is the figure of the Black Madonna, the Protector of Workers. Her long train is made from unique white amber, as is the white eagle soaring into the vaulted roof and the symbol of Solidarity below. On either side of the Blessed Virgin are the figures of the 14th-century St. Bridget of Sweden and the 20th-century St. Elizabeth Hesselblad.

Bridget raised eight children and was known for her care for the poor. After her husband's death, she sold her possessions and founded a double monastery for men and women, who lived apart but worshipped together. In the Jubilee Year of 1350, Bridget braved a plague-stricken Europe to make a pilgrimage to Rome. There she cared for the sick and dying, spoke out

*Chapel of Solidarity with memorial to Blessed Jerzy Popiełuszko,
the patron of Solidarność.*

against the injustices she saw, and sought papal authorization for her new community in Sweden. Toward the end of her life, she went on pilgrimage to the Holy Land, where she experienced Christ's presence in mystical visions. She died shortly after her return to Rome, and her coffin was solemnly transferred back to Sweden, where it is entombed at the monastery she founded.

Maria Elizabeth Hesselblad was born in 1870 and raised in a Swedish home, but she emigrated to New York at age 18 and studied nursing to help support her large family in Sweden. She worked as a home care nurse for the sick and aged, drawing increasingly close to the Catholic Church, which she joined in 1902. After a pilgrimage to Rome, she decided to begin a consecrated life there, welcomed by the Carmelites living at the House of St. Bridget of Sweden. In 1906 she received permission from Pope Pius X to profess vows as a spiritual daughter of St. Bridget and take the habit of the Bridgettines, including its most distinctive element, the silver crown with five red stones symbolizing the five wounds of Christ. For the rest of her life, she worked to revive the order in Sweden, where it had been suppressed by the Protestant Reformation, and in Rome. The branch of the Bridgettines she founded seeks to care for the poor and sick as well as to pray and work for the unity of Scandinavian Christians with the Catholic Church. During the war, she worked to save Jews and others persecuted by the Nazis by giving them refuge in Rome. Hesselblad became known as "the second Bridget" and her life ended in Rome in 1957. In 2004 she was recognized in Jerusalem as one of the "Righteous Among the Nations" for saving the lives of Jews who would have otherwise perished in the Holocaust, and in 2016, she was canonized by Pope Francis in Rome.

The church is a visual confirmation that Catholic devotion and national patriotism are intertwined. Seated on either side of the Amber Altar are figures of St. John Paul and Bl. Stefan Wyszyński, the two most influential religious figures of Poland in the 20th century. To the right of the main altar stands an image of Our Lady of Fatima. The metal grille around it depicts the Polish eagle from various periods of the nation's history. The treasury contains a unique collection, including an amber monstrance. The memorial to the Polish officers and intelligentsia murdered by the Soviets at Katyn contains soil from the places of Polish martyrdom.

One of the few remaining paintings from the old church is "The Coronation of St. Bridget," which was formerly situated at the main altar but now hangs on the side wall. Below the painting there is a reliquary containing St. Bridget's lower jaw. Further along the wall are crosses used in the shipyard during the Solidarity strikes. Particularly poignant, the Chapel of Solidarity contains a memorial to Bl. Jerzy Popiełuszko, the patron of Solidarność, who was murdered by the Polish secret police in 1984. The bronze doors at the end of the aisle depict scenes from the development of Solidarity.

MEDITATION

- In what ways do the white eagle and the black Madonna express the unity of the nation and its Catholic faith?

- How is the vine and its branches an appropriate image for the ideas expressed in the Amber Altar?

Reading: John 15:1-5
"I am the true vine, and my Father is the vinegrower…

Response: "Saints of God, hear our prayer."

Queen of Poland, Our Lady of Solidarity Workers, your face is marked with scars but radiates with your compassion. Throughout the long and difficult journey of the 20th century, you have remained steadfastly with your people. We thank you for your protection of this nation and the gift of freedom you have gained for the Polish people. R.

Saint Bridget, whose body rested in this place during its procession from Rome to Sweden, you learned the wisdom of the cross by experiencing the Passion of Christ in mystical contemplation and in caring for the sick and dying. Come to our aid as we strive to live our vocation worthily and to seek Christ in all things. R.

Saint Mary Elizabeth Hesselblad, in Rome and Sweden you revived the mission of your teacher St. Bridget, and you wore the crown of Christ's five wounds in imitation of her. Teach us to understand, by devoted daily practice, how love and humble service can be a primary tool to build a unified Church and a peaceful humanity. R.

Blessed Stefan Wyszyński, you served as Primate of the nation through the age of communist persecution and led the Church through a time of spiritual renewal in preparation for the Millennium of Christianity in Poland. Watch over the people of this land and guard them from the new dangers of relativism and consumerism. R.

Saint John Paul, your election as Bishop of Rome gave new courage to the people of Poland as they struggled to free themselves from religious persecution and political captivity. Teach us to be missionary disciples, fearlessly sharing the Gospel with the world around us. R.

Prayer: Lord God, in every age You give saints to Your people to inspire them with courage and determination for life's pilgrimage. Hear our prayer as we evoke Your saints and plead for their help to follow Your Son, Jesus Christ, in captivity and freedom, in sadness and joy, from death into life.

3. Warsaw, Sanctuary of Bl. Jerzy Popiełuszko

The grounds of St. Stanisław Kostka Church in Warsaw have been designated the Sanctuary of Bl. Jerzy Popiełuszko. During his life he was known as Solidarity's chaplain, and since his martyrdom he has been designated the Patron of Solidarity. Those who attended his funeral, estimated to be 1 million people, promised to continue the struggle for freedom through nonviolence. Lech Wałęsa said, "Rest in peace, Father Jerzy. Solidarity is alive because you have given your life for it." On that day, November 3, 1984, the end of communism in Poland and throughout Europe became only a question of time. His grave is situated beside the church and has become a place of pilgrimage, visited by Pope John Paul in 1987 and by millions from around the world. In 2010, he was beatified by Pope Benedict XVI as a martyr of the faith.

Father Jerzy Popiełuszko was ordained a priest in 1972 by Cardinal Wyszyński at St. John the Baptist Cathedral. He served several parishes in the Archdiocese of Warsaw and as chaplain of medical students and health personnel. In preparation for Pope John Paul's visit to Warsaw in 1979, Fr. Jerzy was put in charge of organizing first-aid stations with medical volunteers along the route of the Pope's travels. The next year he was assigned to assist Fr. Teofil Bogucki in St. Stanisław Kostka parish, where artists, writers, and journalists mingled with laborers from Huta

Jerzy Popiełuszko, priest and martyr, patron of Solidarność.

Warszawa, the imposing steelworks nearby. In August, the steel workers went on strike in support of the shipyard workers in Gdańsk. Shutting themselves in the steel mill, the workers requested a priest to offer the Mass, and when the call for a priest went out, Fr. Jerzy volunteered. Approaching the gate, he was met with the smiles, joyful tears, and applause of the workers. The altar had been prepared in the factory square and a cross set up. It was the turning point of his life, the apostolate where the Lord wanted him to serve. He would be the priest for those workers, the shepherd to give them courage and inspire them with the Gospel.

When Lech Wałęsa signed the accord with the government in Gdańsk to legalize the Solidarity union, new hope spread throughout the nation. But with the imposition of martial law, an iron hand took control of the country, searches and arrests became routine, and thousands were imprisoned. In response, Fr. Jerzy Popiełuszko was transformed from a timid and somewhat awkward young man into a confident, courageous leader, throwing himself body and soul into the resistance movement.

In February 1982, Fr. Jerzy began offering his famous "Masses for the Fatherland" at St. Stanisław Kostka Church. Celebrated every last Sunday of the month, the Masses were at first offered in the church, but soon they began drawing thousands and then tens of thousands and were staged on

*Father Jerzy offers "Masses for the Fatherland" from the balcony of
St. Stanisław Kostka Church.*

a balcony in front of the church in the presence of an immense crowd of
participants gathered in a park below. In December, Fr. Jerzy proclaimed to
the congregation:

> A regime that needs weapons to stay in existence dies by itself.
> Its violence is the proof of its moral inferiority. If Solidarność
> won hearts, it was not by struggling with power but by offering
> resistance on its knees, with a rosary in hand. In front of outdoor
> altars, it demanded the dignity of human work, freedom of con-
> science, and respect for man. Solidarność is a mighty tree; its top
> has been removed, and its branches have been cut, but its roots
> are deeply rooted among us, and new branches will grow back.[56]

He preached not political ideology but the universal message of the Church,
the message of human dignity and of the Truth Who makes us free.

Father Jerzy included in these Masses the Romantic poetry of the 19th
century, and after Communion the classics of Polish literature were read,
often by famous actors, intellectuals, and people of letters. Texts that evoked
the thousand-year history of Poland were chosen for their patriotic and
religious inspiration, and all the social strata of the nation were included to
express their unity of purpose in the struggle for human rights and freedom.
His sermons were broadcast on Radio Free Europe and published in news-

Saint Stanisław Kostka Church in Warsaw.

papers that circulated clandestinely. He never voiced any call for revenge, but advocated only forgiveness, reconciliation, and an optimistic hope.

He attended many of the sham trials brought against the opponents of the regime to offer his supportive presence, and from the parish he organized the distribution of medications and food, helped the imprisoned activists, and offered aid to their families. His homilies were an intolerable provocation for the regime, and during all his activities the intelligence agents never took their eyes off him. They published false accusations to sully his reputation, tried to intimidate him by throwing explosive charges through his window, and often arrested him on made-up charges. One day they planted grenades, bullets, and explosives in his apartment, then they searched the rectory accompanied by propagandists and accused him of sedition. Ceaseless provocations, surveillance, threats, and interrogations tried to limit his activities and his voice.

The communist authorities finally realized that the only thing that could stop Fr. Jerzy Popiełuszko was death. On October 9, 1984, employees of the Ministry of Internal Affairs detained the priest when he was returning to Warsaw from a speaking engagement. He was beaten, thrown into the trunk of a car, and cruelly murdered. After hearing that Fr. Jerzy had been abducted, all of Poland was on its knees. After a three-day search, his brutalized body was found submerged in a water reservoir formed from the Vistula by the Włocławek Dam, several hundred miles from Warsaw. The announcement of his ruthless assassination caused a national uproar of grief, but without violence his followers were determined to overcome evil with good. Pope John Paul, in a message to the Polish people, urged them not to be drawn into a spiral of hatred: "Let us pay our final respects to Fr. Popiełuszko in Christian dignity and peace. May the great significance of this death not be troubled or darkened in any way." The example of Poland's new martyr kept the people's hopes alive for a free Poland, which was realized a few years after his death.

At the morgue, Fr. Jerzy was clothed in his cassock, to which three insignia were pinned: one depicted Our Lady of Częstochowa against the white and red background of the Polish flag; the next bore the inscription "Solidarność, 1980-1984, Huta Warszawa" beneath an eagle's head; and the last presented a view of St. Stanisław Kostka Church, captioned, "Masses for the Fatherland, Warsaw." Over his cassock the priest was covered with a red stole and chasuble, representing the Passion of Christ and the fire of the Spirit. A cross was placed in his hand, along with a Rosary that he had received from John Paul II during his visit the previous year.

During his funeral, celebrated by the Primate of Poland, the immense but dignified crowd waved candles, flowers, crosses, and held Solidarity banners. As his body was being lowered into the ground, Fr. Teofil Bogucki stepped forward and declared, "The Polish ground has just received a new martyr. Only a great man, a saint, deserves a burial like this." The Jaruzelski government wanted the martyr to be buried back in the small town of his birth, knowing that he would be more dangerous to them dead than alive. But with the support of his family and friends, the Cardinal stood firm, insisting that he be interred in the church courtyard, in this plot of ground that has become a place of pilgrimage where Poles come to renew their courage and their hope.

A museum attached to the church chronicles the heroic life and death of Bl. Jerzy Popiełuszko, featuring items associated with his youth, priesthood, ministry to Solidarity, his Masses for the Fatherland, and his final martyrdom. The museum was established shortly after his death by the pastor, Fr. Teofil Bogucki. In 2004, another pastor, Fr. Zygmunt Malacki, gave the museum a modern, multimedia form featuring photos, film, and audio presentations.

The cornerstone of the Church of St. Stanisław Kostka was laid in 1930, but its consecration was only celebrated in 1963. Under Cardinal Wyszyński, the church became known as a bastion of the truth about contemporary Polish history, including a wall of remembrance under the slogan

"God and Homeland," commemorating Poles who fought and died during World War II and the victims of concentration camps. Above the tabernacle hangs a 17th-century crucifix with an ivory corpus, and the canopy is crowned with two Polish eagles.

Meditation

- In what ways does the blood of the martyrs become the seed of the Church?
- In what ways does the life of Fr. Jerzy Popiełuszko inspire me to work for the Gospel?

Reading: Romans 12:9-21
Let love be genuine; hate what is evil, hold fast to what is good…

Response: "Mother of faithful Poland, pray for us."

Mother of those deceived, betrayed, and arrested in the night.[57] R.

Mother of those who have been frightened, imprisoned, and subject to interrogations. R.

Mother of those who resist, who speak the truth, who cannot be corrupted. R.

Mother of those who are molested because they wear your image. R.

Mother of those who are forced to sign declarations contrary to their conscience. R.

Mother of orphans, of mothers who weep, and of fathers who grieve. R.

Mother of suffering Poland, of always faithful Poland. R.

Prayer: We beg you, O mother in whom resides the hope of millions of people, grant us to live in liberty and in truth, in fidelity to you and to your Son. Through the inspiration of the heroic life of Bl. Jerzy Popiełuszko and the witness of his martyrdom, may we seek to overcome evil with good and live in true freedom.

IX. Wrocław, St. Edith Stein

Dating back over a thousand years, the city of Wrocław was conquered by Duke Mieszko I of Poland in 985, and the Diocese of Wrocław was established in 1000 and placed under the Archbishopric of Gniezno. A city of mixed heritage as verified by its architecture, at various times it has been part of the Kingdom of Poland, Bohemia, Hungary, Austria, Prussia, and Germany. During the life of Edith Stein (1891-1942), the city of Wrocław (called Breslau) was a German city with a populous and active Jewish community. The Nazi regime brought discrimination and persecution to its Polish and Jewish inhabitants, including imprisonment in German labor camps and deportations to concentration camps. The city became part of Poland again in 1945 as a result of the border changes after the Second World War, which included the flight and expulsion of the majority of the prewar population of the city.

Born in Breslau (Wrocław) in 1891, Edith Stein was the youngest child in an observant Jewish family. Her birth on the Jewish feast of Yom Kippur, the Day of Atonement, would mark her destiny with its themes of prayerful repentance and return to God. Her father's untimely death, when Edith was 2 years old, cast a shadow over her happy childhood. From that time, her mother managed their family lumber business alone, strove to keep the children involved with the congregation of the White Stork Syn-

Medieval Town Hall of Wrocław.

Edith Stein, Wrocławian, philosopher, saint.

agogue, and provided an education for her children. Edith was a gifted and diligent student and stood out from the rest of the class with her zest for learning. After graduating at the top of her class from *Viktoria Schule*, Edith passed her examination in 1911 and began her studies at the University of Breslau (today's Wrocław University). There she chose courses in German language and literature, history, psychology, and philosophy. In addition to her studies, she worked in student organizations that focused on women's suffrage and equality.

Initially planning to study psychology, Edith changed her mind when she began to explore the philosophy of Edmund Husserl, the founder of phenomenology. This new philosophical school sought to explain the connection between the visible world and the world of ideas and values. At that time Edmund Husserl was a professor at the University of Göttingen, so Edith transferred there to study under his mentorship. In Göttingen, many of her teachers and peers had been born Jewish and became Christian. This philosophical school of thought provided fertile soil within which the seeds of ultimate truth might germinate within her. She first encountered the Catholic faith through the philosopher Max Scheler, one of Edith's teachers and the subject of Karol Wojtyła's doctoral thesis several decades later in 1954. This community of intellectuals brought Edith into a community where she could not blindly bypass an exploration of religious faith and spirituality.

When her studies were interrupted by the First World War, Stein trained as an assistant nurse and served in an Austrian field hospital. In 1916, she returned to Breslau where she taught in a secondary school while she prepared her doctoral thesis. Her research focused on "The Problem of Empathy," using the analytical tools and methods of phenomenology. Because Husserl had transferred to Freiburg, Edith followed him there to take her doctoral exams, and there she earned a doctorate in philosophy, summa cum laude, in 1917. She then worked as a teaching assistant to Husserl at the University of Freiburg. The next year, Stein sought against all odds to obtain a professorship. Yet, despite the highest endorsement of Husserl, she was rejected at Freiburg because she was a woman, and at Göttingen on account of her Jewishness. The prejudices of the times stood like an immovable wall blocking her academic advancement. Returning to Breslau, she offered instructions to university students and wrote articles and essays.

The entire life of Edith Stein was a quest for truth and meaning. At her canonization Mass, Pope John Paul said:

> Her mind never tired of searching and her heart always yearned for hope. She traveled the arduous path of philosophy with passionate enthusiasm. Eventually she was rewarded: she seized the truth. Or better: she was seized by it. Then she discovered that truth had a name: Jesus Christ. From that moment on, the incarnate Word was her One and All.[58]

Although Edith's road to Catholicism covered several years, her life changed forever during her summer vacation in 1921, when she read the autobiography of St. Teresa of Avila, the 16th-century mystic and founder of the Discalced Carmelites. Convinced of its truth, she bought a missal and a copy of the Catholic catechism the next day and began the process of conversion to Catholicism. Edith's experience with Teresa of Avila was much the same as what happened to Teresa herself four centuries earlier when reading the autobiography of St. Augustine. The conversions of these three saints came as they each learned to surrender what was keeping them from God. Edith was baptized on New Year's Day 1922, stating that from this point forward she belonged to Christ both spiritually and by blood.

From the day of her baptism, it had always been Edith's intention to enter the order of her beloved St. Teresa — when the time was right. Yet, her 11-year wait before joining a Carmelite monastery was due to her obedience to the advice of her spiritual directors, who recognized that her talents were needed in the world. Edith then spent the following years teaching at a girls' school of the Dominican Sisters in Speyer. There she lived in a room adjacent to the convent quarters, enabling her to attend daily Mass and the Divine Office with the sisters. She continued to penetrate the mystery of faith through her liturgical and contemplative prayer. During those years, she focused much of her lecturing and writing on inspiring women to the highest intellectual, professional, and spiritual development. Her students remembered her as an open-minded, understanding woman, ahead of her times in recognizing the true value of women. By the next decade, lecturing widely at congresses throughout Germany and abroad, she was recognized as the intellectual leader of Catholic feminism in Europe.

In 1931 she accepted a teaching position at the Institute for Scientific Pedagogy in Münster. But after Hitler seized power in 1933, the strict new racial laws forced her to leave her post. Deprived of the opportunity to work, nothing stood in her way to realize her long-prepared plans to enter Carmel. After visiting Breslau for the final time and saying goodbye to her mother, Edith entered the Discalced Carmelite monastery in Cologne, becoming Sr. Teresa Benedicta of the Cross. In the convent, she continued her writing, finishing her master work, *Finite and Eternal Being*, the culmination of her lifelong search for truth in all its philosophical, psychological, and spiritual dimensions. Her sister, Rosa Stein, who also converted to the Catholic faith, joined Edith at the Carmelite Monastery in Cologne, serving as an extern who handled the community's needs outside the monastery.

Following *Kristallnacht* in 1938 (the "Night of Broken Glass," when the Nazis destroyed Jewish synagogues, vandalized Jewish businesses and homes, and attacked Jewish citizens), the people of Jewish descent in Germany could no longer feel safe. It was decided to move Edith and Rosa to the Carmelite monastery in Echt, Holland. But soon the Netherlands was no longer a safe haven. When the Dutch Catholic bishops ordered the reading in all the churches of a statement condemning Nazi racism, the Nazis ordered the immediate arrest of converts of Jewish descent. Edith and her sister Rosa were arrested while in the convent chapel. Her last words in Echt were to her sister: "Come, we are going for our people." The two sisters arrived in Auschwitz where they were quickly sent to the gas chambers on August 9, 1942. Edith was 50 years old.

Teresa Benedicta of the Cross was beatified as a martyr in 1987 by Pope John Paul II, who described her as "a daughter of Israel, who, as a Catholic during Nazi persecution, remained faithful to the crucified Lord Jesus Christ and, as a Jew, to her people in loving faithfulness." John Paul went on to canonize St. Teresa Benedicta in 1998, and the following year, he proclaimed her as one of six co-patron saints of Europe.

Edith Stein's family home, 1910-1933.

1. Edith Stein House

Edith Stein's family in Wrocław moved during her life from a small rented apartment into larger apartments until her mother was able to acquire this beautiful villa in which the entire family, comprising several generations, found a place to live. Built in 1890, this Neoclassicist villa and the surrounding gardens were bought for the Stein family in 1910. It remained the Stein family home until 1939 when it was repossessed under the Nazi "Aryanization" laws and given to master bricklayer Oscar Jankel.

Edith Stein House, at 38 Nowowiejska Street, has been completely renovated. Since 1990, it has housed the Edith Stein Society, a research center dedicated to her ideas and testimony, devoted to Jewish-Christian understanding and Polish-German reconciliation. The society's program includes exhibitions, conferences, lectures, concerts, film screenings, lan-

Entrance to the University of Wrocław.

guage courses, and youth exchanges. Its permanent exhibition is entitled "Edith Stein: Wrocławian woman, philosopher, saint, patroness of Europe."

Edith Stein House invites anyone who wants to see the place where today's patron of Europe lived. Many come to learn about her and the turbulent road she took to discover life's purpose and meaning. She was an exceptional person, a saint who was ahead of her time, who today can be a guide for all people who are searching for meaning and fulfillment in their lives.

Edith settled here with her Jewish family at the age of 19. In the large living room on the first floor, birthday parties were held for children and grandchildren and Seder suppers were celebrated. From this house Edith used to commute to Breslau University, today's University of Wrocław. From here she departed to Göttingen to continue her studies there. After receiving her doctorate in philosophy and working as a teaching assistant to Professor Husserl, she returned here. In the living room, she conducted her private philosophical seminar. A couple of years later, she returned to this house in 1921 to tell her mother and other family members that she wanted to be baptized in the Catholic Church. Finally, in 1933, from this house she embarked on a journey to Carmel in Cologne, never to return.

Numerous sites connected to Edith Stein are found throughout Wrocław. Since the beginning of the 20th century, the University of Wrocław, attended by Edith Stein in from 1911 to 1913, has produced nine Nobel

Prize laureates and is renowned for its academic quality. With a large student population today, Wrocław is arguably one of the most youth-oriented cities in the country.

The medieval Market Square is one of Europe's largest, with 11 streets leading to the market from all directions of the city. The Old Town Hall is a striking Gothic building at the center of the square. Concerts as well as civic and cultural events are held in its Great Hall. Its Burghers' Hall Museum holds a bust of Edith Stein. The Gothic-style Cathedral of St. John the Baptist is marked by its elegant double-spires and its elaborate portal. A panoramic view of the city is available from the top of one of its towers.

The White Stork Synagogue, the only synagogue in Wrocław to escape the torches of *Kristallnacht*, was built in 1829, taking its name from the inn that once stood in its place. Attended by the Stein family, the synagogue was restored and rededicated in 2010. Here members of the Jewish community were rounded up for deployment to the death camps. The synagogue was then used by the Nazis as an auto repair shop and to store stolen Jewish property. It now serves as a worship space and cultural center housing an exhibition on the history of Jews in Wrocław.

The Old Jewish Cemetery, established in 1856, is a testament to the former strength of Wrocław's prewar Jewish community. Closed in 1942, the cemetery quickly fell into disrepair and in 1945 it became a Nazi fortress. It saw fierce fighting as evidenced by the eerie bullet holes in many of the gravestones. Following renovation, it was opened in 1991 as the Museum of Jewish Cemetery Art in tribute to the craftsmanship, beauty, and diversity of its sepulchral art. Many noteworthy figures are buried here, including Edith's parents, Siegfried and Augusta Stein.

MEDITATION

• How did the Scriptures, prayers, and feasts of Judaism prepare Edith Stein for her future life in Christ?

• In what ways can I live my life with the open heart of St. Edith Stein?

Reading: Psalm 131
O LORD, my heart is not lifted up, my eyes are not raised too high…

Response: "St. Edith Stein, pray for us"

"O my God, fill my soul with holy joy, courage and strength to serve you. Enkindle your love in me and then walk with me along the next stretch of road before me. I do not see very far ahead, but when I have arrived where the horizon now closes down, a new prospect will open before me, and I shall meet it with peace."[59] R.

"To suffer and to be happy although suffering, to have one's feet on the earth, to walk on the dirty and rough paths of this earth and yet to be enthroned with Christ at the Father's right hand, to laugh and cry with the children of this world and ceaselessly sing the praises of God with the choirs of angels — this is the life of the Christian until the morning of eternity breaks forth." R.

"The limitless loving devotion to God, and the gift God makes of himself to you, are the highest elevation of which the heart is capable; it is the highest degree of prayer. The souls that have reached this point are truly the heart of the Church." R.

"Do not accept anything as the truth if it lacks love. And do not accept anything as love which lacks truth! One without the other becomes a destructive lie." R.

Prayer: God of our ancestors in Israel, Who bound Your people to Yourself in covenant, grant our prayers as we cry out to You through the intercession of Your daughter, St. Edith Stein. May we continue to search for life's meaning and fulfillment that can only be found in You, through our Messiah and Lord, Jesus Christ.

2. Church of St. Michael the Archangel

Although the first chapel of St. Michael on this site was built around 1100 as part of Ołbin abbey, the present neo-Gothic church was erected in the years 1862-1871. It was Edith Stein's preferred house of worship during her visits to Breslau (Wrocław), from the time of her baptism in 1922 until her last visit to her home city in 1933 before entering the Carmelite monastery.

A chapel dedicated to St. Edith Stein (Teresa Benedicta of the Cross) is in the northern tower of the church, on the left from the main entrance. The chapel was consecrated on the hundredth anniversary of the saint's birthday in 1992. The main element of the chapel is a marble altar stylized as an open Bible and a marble candlestick in the shape of a stack of paper sheets. The inscription on the altar contains an excerpt from the ancient hymn *"Ave Crux, spes unica"* (Hail the Cross, the only hope) and the date of Edith Stein's death. The chapel holds an urn containing earth and ashes from

Auschwitz, as well as other relics, including a fragment of the saint's habit. To the right is an oil painting of Stein by Jolanta Kornecka, and on the left, two images of Stein and John Paul II. The church's main altar also includes a large sculpture of the saint.

Edith Stein described two decisive moments on her path to conversion. The first occurred after the death of her beloved teacher, Adolf Reinach, who was killed at the war front in 1917. Edith went to see his widow, Anna Reinach, fearful that she would find a broken and distraught woman. Instead, Edith found a committed Christian, suffering, but at peace. Edith said later:

Church of St. Michael the Archangel.

> It was my first encounter with the Cross and the divine power that it bestows on those who carry it. For the first time, I was seeing with my very eyes the Church, born from her Redeemer's sufferings, triumphant over the sting of death. That was the moment my unbelief collapsed and Christ shone forth — in the mystery of the Cross.[60]

Edith's second episode occurred when she was strolling through Frankfurt with her friend Pauline Reinach. While visiting the cathedral, Edith noticed a woman who had obviously been shopping come into the empty church and kneel silently in a pew. Edith had never seen this before, having only seen people praying during services in Protestant churches and Jewish synagogues. She later wrote, "Here was someone interrupting her everyday shopping errands to come into this church, although no other person was in it, as though she were here for an intimate conversation. I could never forget that."[61]

Main altar of St. Michael the Archangel.

Chapel dedicated to St. Edith Stein, "Ave Crux, spes unica" (Hail the Cross, the only hope).

Although these two moments did not occur in Wrocław, we can be sure that these and many more events and insights continued to lead her to the One who would fulfill the searching of her mind and the yearning of her heart. Through liturgical and contemplative prayer, in this church and others, she was led to the Incarnate Word, the fullness of truth and of love.

Exiting the front entrance of St. Michael's Church, the pilgrim may take a right down St. Edith Stein Street to follow the same five-minute walk she would take between her mother's house and the church. In the opposite direction, at the intersection of Prusa and Cardinal Wyszyński Streets, stands the European Peace Cross, erected in 2008. It consists of two parts: wooden and metal. 365 nails are hammered in the wooden part, symbolizing the suffering that affects people every day. The metal part contains an inscription in Hebrew from Psalm 31: "Father, into your hands I put my spirit." The cross commemorates the victims of World War II, in particular St. Edith Stein and her death at Auschwitz.

MEDITATION

• What feelings might Edith and her mother have felt when one went to church and the other to synagogue?

• What has been a decisive moment in my life that has led to my ongoing conversion?

Reading: Galatians 6:14-18
May I never boast of anything except the cross of our Lord Jesus Christ...

Response: "St. Teresa Benedicta of the Cross, pray for us"

"I have an ever deeper and firmer belief that nothing is merely an accident when seen in the light of God, that my whole life down to the smallest details has been marked out for me in the plan of Divine Providence and has a completely coherent meaning in God's all-seeing eyes. And so I am beginning to rejoice in the light of glory wherein this meaning will be unveiled to me."[62] R.

"When night comes, and you look back over the day and see how fragmentary everything has been, and how much you planned that has gone undone, and all the reasons you have to be embarrassed and ashamed: just take everything exactly as it is, put it in God's hands and leave it with Him. Then you will be able to rest in Him — really rest — and start the next day as a new life." R.

"Learn from Saint Thérèse to depend on God alone and serve Him with a wholly pure and detached heart. Then, like her, you will be able to say 'I do not regret that I have given myself up to Love.'" R.

"The walls of our monasteries enclose a narrow space. To erect the structure of holiness in it, one must dig deep and build high, must descend into the depths of the dark night of one's own nothingness in order to be raised up high into the sunlight of divine love and compassion." R.

Prayer: O God, you brought St. Teresa Benedicta of the Cross to know Your crucified Son and to imitate Him even until death. Through the intercession of Your holy martyr, grant that all people may come to acknowledge You as the world's Redeemer and to behold You for eternity.

X. Frédéric Franciszek Chopin

Often called the poet of the piano, Chopin is Poland's most important musical composer and one of history's greatest Romantic composers. Born in 1810 at Żelazowa Wola near Warsaw, he spent the first half of his life in Poland, then in 1930, he left his homeland to travel, eventually making his career in Paris before his untimely death at the age of 39. The people of Poland love Chopin, and his music is filled with the rhythms, harmonies, emotions, and moods of his homeland.

After moving to Warsaw, the parents of the young Frédéric Chopin purchased a grand piano and provided music teachers for their son. He played his first public concert in the Radziwiłł Palace (now the Presidential Palace) at the age of 8. The boy progressed so rapidly that he was soon taught by Joseph Elsner, the director of the Warsaw Conservatory, who nurtured his student's extraordinary talent. News of the child prodigy spread quickly; his first compositions were published in a Warsaw newspaper, and he was famous outside Poland by the time he was 15.

At the age of 20, Chopin embarked on an artistic tour of Europe, visiting Vienna, Munich, Stuttgart, and Paris, expecting to continue to London. Before leaving Warsaw, a local choir sung for him a cantata, written by Elsner his teacher as a farewell: "Born among Polish fields, May your talent bring you fame wherever you go. Although you leave your native

*Chopin absorbed the folk music of his
native Mazovia.*

land, Still will your heart remain with us!" Elsner presented Chopin with a silver urn containing Polish soil with the advice for Frédéric to never forget his Polish homeland.

Three weeks later, while in Vienna, Chopin learned of the November Uprising in Poland, an armed rebellion in the heartland of partitioned Poland against the Russian occupying forces. Although he wanted to return and fight, like nearly all his relatives and friends, he was convinced to remain in Vienna. Regretting leaving his homeland and seeing no rational way out of the situation, he began pouring out his extreme emotions on the piano and wrote the first sketches of some of his most dramatic works. The next year, while in Stuttgart, he received news that the uprising had been brutally crushed and Warsaw captured. As a result, Chopin, the internationally known patriot who refused to take a Russian passport, was never able to return to his homeland. Throughout the rest of his life, he longed for Poland, for his family and friends left behind. His nostalgia for Poland and grief over his homeland's cruel defeat became Chopin's inspiration for his "Revolutionary Étude."

Chopin was enchanted with Paris and decided to settle there. The young composer quickly captivated a circle of Parisian elite, making a living in part by teaching piano to their children. He despised the forceful virtuosi of his time and chose to perform in the city's smaller salons rather than the grand concert halls. The subtle delicacy of much of his music, his gradations of sound and myriad colors, earned him the title "the Raphael of the piano." Because his passport had been drawn up for England, inserted within it were the words, "passing through Paris." Many years afterwards, when he seemed naturalized in France, he would smilingly say he was in Paris "only in passing."

In 1837, at the age of 27, Chopin fell in love with Aurore Dupin, the French novelist who wrote under the pseudonym George Sand. Dupin was a fiery intellectual who had fled an unhappy marriage, and her writings made her a celebrity in the name of women's freedom. The two artists had a stormy relationship during their nine years together, and Chopin's fame kept the newspapers filled with gossip about their life. Their illustrious friends — Hugo, Balzac, Liszt, Berlioz, Schumann, Dumas, and Delacroix, among others — shared their artistic and intellectual intensity. In 1838, Chopin became ill with tuberculosis. Dupin cared for him in Paris and at her estate in central France. Despite his health, Chopin was musically creative, perhaps in poignant appreciation of his fleeting life. He continued to work through his fevers and poured the pain of illness and war into his music. By 1847, Chopin's relationship with Dupin had frayed irreparably.

Chopin died on October 17, 1849, surrounded by friends and in the company of his older sister Ludwiga. Franz Liszt wrote:

> When the holy Viaticum was administered to him, he received it, surrounded by those who loved him, with great devotion. He called his friends a short time afterwards, one by one, to his bed-side, to give each of them his last earnest blessing; calling down the grace of God fervently upon themselves, their affections, and their hopes — every knee bent — every head bowed — all eyes were heavy with tears — every heart was sad and oppressed — every soul elevated.[63]

As the mourners took their places in the Church of St. Magdalene in Paris for his funeral, the organist played the funeral march from Chopin's own Sonata in B-flat Minor. Then, the choir of the Paris Conservatory sang the opening verse of Mozart's "Requiem": "*Requiem æternam dona eis, Domine*" (Eternal rest, grant unto them, O Lord), and the priest chanted the High Mass for the Dead. Chopin was laid to rest at the famous cemetery of Père Lachaise, between Bellini and Cherubini, fellow musicians. And although his body remained in Paris, in testament to Chopin's unwavering loyalty to his homeland, his heart was dispatched with his sister to Poland and sealed in a pillar of the Church of the Holy Cross in Warsaw. His heart lives on in spirit, palpably present in the hundreds of compositions Chopin left to the world.

1. Żelazowa Wola, Birthplace of Frédéric Chopin

The biographical museum of Frédéric Chopin in Żelazowa Wola includes a charming manor house surrounded by an extensive park, containing exotic species of trees and shrubs maintained in the style typical of 19th-century noble residences. The manor house with the park is a branch of the Frédéric Chopin Museum in Warsaw, managed by the Frédéric Chopin Institute.

Birthplace of Frédéric Chopin at Żelazowa Wola.

Żelazowa Wola lies in the historic region of Mazovia, which developed its own folk songs, architecture, dress, and traditions. The village was purchased at the turn of the 19th century by the family of Count Skarbek, who lived in a manor with two outbuildings. (The present birthplace is the former eastern outbuilding.) In 1802 Mikołaj Chopin, originally from southwestern France, came to this manor house to serve as a tutor for the four children of Kacper and Ludwika Skarbek. He had settled in Poland in 1787 at the age of 16 and became greatly attached to the country. A few years after Mikołaj's arrival at the manor, Justyna Krzyżanowska was employed as a housekeeper and nanny for the Skarbek household. Within a year of their meeting, Justyna and Mikołaj Chopin married at the St. Roch parish church in Brochów in June of 1806, and the wedding procession returned through the landscape of Żelazowa Wola for a sumptuous wedding party at the manor. After the celebration, the couple must have looked toward their future life in the quiet night surrounded by the whispering linden trees.

The Chopins lived in the eastern outbuilding of the manor (the present birthplace), and they often entertained guests of the Skarbeks with musical concerts. Justyna played the piano and sang; Mikołaj played the violin and flute. Because they often moved between Żelazowa Wola and Warsaw with the Skarbek family, their first child, Ludwika, was born in Warsaw in 1807. Then in 1810, their only son, Frédéric, was born at the white manor house, which serves today as the birthplace and museum. He was baptized in the same parish church in Brochów where his parents were married.

The next year, Mikołaj Chopin was offered a post as a teacher of French at the Warsaw Lyceum. As the family permanently settled in Warsaw, they lived in an apartment provided to faculty for the lyceum in the Saxon Palace. To supplement the family income, they took in students as boarders and Justyna managed the household. Here their two other daughters, Izabela and Emilia, were born. Justyna taught piano to Ludwika and Frédéric, however her son's talent was apparent and surpassed what his mother could teach him, so a tutor was hired. In 1817, the family moved to faculty housing in the Kazimierz Palace, where they remained for the next decade.

Concert room in Chopin's family home.

Young Frédéric often visited his birthplace and the Skarbek family during the summer and family holidays. He listened to the Mazovian folk tunes at the manor and at village events, harvest festivals, and parish fairs. The Polish themes, which manifested themselves in his compositions, have their roots in his experiences at Żelazowa Wola. During the composer's visits to the Skarbek estate, the piano was taken to the garden, where Frédéric gave concerts in the familiar landscape to the gathered family and guests. Chopin's final visit to Żelazowa Wola was in the summer of 1830, when the entire Chopin family was on summer vacation.

Although the Skarbek manor burned down during the Napoleonic Wars in 1812, the outbuildings survived, including Chopin's birthplace. In 1894, on the initiative of the Russian composer Milij Bałakiriew, a monument to Chopin was unveiled in the park. In 1928, the Warsaw Society of the Friends of the Chopin House purchased the birthplace. During World War II, German soldiers were stationed there, and many valuable items were lost, including a Pleyel concert piano and two armchairs belonging to Chopin.

The birthplace is entered through a front porch with two columns and a triangular pediment. The rectangular building contains seven rooms with a hallway along the axis of the building. The beamed ceilings are decorated with polychrome floral motifs. Although the furniture, instruments, and paintings from the Chopin house have not survived to our times, the house is filled with early 19th-century keepsakes that evoke the haunting spirit of Chopin that lingers throughout. On the whitewashed walls are hung images of members of the Chopin family as well as views of Warsaw. Visitors will also find facsimiles of the marriage certificate of the composer's parents and his birth and baptism records, as well as musical manuscripts, drawings, and letters. The mother's room contains a 19th-century Leszczyński piano, and the music lounge contains a contemporary grand piano on which concerts are frequently played.

The nicely landscaped gardens outside feature several Chopin monuments, including the obelisk dating from 1894, a bronze monument made by Józef Gosławski, and a bust by Stanisław Sikora. The trees of great variety offer cool shade in the summer and echo with the songs of birds as the Ultrata River flows through the park. In autumn the trees assume a more austere appearance, rustled by the wind, and seem to invite visitors to the warmth inside the house.

MEDITATION

• What memories arise within me when I return to the place of my birth?

• What feelings are associated with homesickness?

> Reading: Psalm 71:17-24
> *O God, from my youth you have taught me, and I still proclaim your wondrous deeds...*
>
> Response: "My lips will shout for joy when I sing praises to You, O Lord."
>
> As the devout in prayer, so he poured out his soul in his compositions, expressing in them those passions of the heart, those unexpressed sorrows, to which the pious give vent in their communion with their Maker.[64] R.
>
> What they never say except on their knees, he said in his palpitating compositions; uttering in the language of the tones those mysteries of passion and of grief which man has been permitted to understand without words, because there are no words adequate for their expression. R.
>
> Chopin had that reverential worship for art which characterized the first masters of the middle ages ... As for them, so art was for him, a high and holy vocation. Like them he was proud of his election for it, and honored it with devout piety. R.
>
> When having scrupulously fulfilled the last duties of a Christian, he left all of earth which he could not bear with him to the skies. He had linked his love for art and his faith in it with immortality long before the approach of death. R.

Prayer: Faithful God, who raised up Frédéric Chopin among the sons of Poland, we offer You joyful praise for the magnificence of his art. Those passions of the heart that we seek to express to You in prayer, he poured out in his compositions. May his music inspire us with the nobility of our humanity and lift up our souls to participate in Your divinity.

Frédéric Chopin Museum in Warsaw.

2. Warsaw, Frédéric Chopin Museum and Holy Cross Church

Refurbished for the 200th anniversary of Frédéric Chopin's birth in 2010, the multimedia Chopin Museum covers 12 themes located on the four levels of Warsaw's historical Ostrogski Palace. The exhibition includes original musical manuscripts of Chopin; a gold watch given to him by Angelika Catalani in 1820 that he kept throughout his life; a Pleyel piano belonging to the composer in the last years of his life; personal calendars from 1834, 1848 and 1849, the content of which can be viewed in a virtual form; a tablecloth with the initials FC embroidered by George Sand; a lock of Sand's hair belonging to Chopin; a pendant belonging to Chopin with the initials FC; a cast of his left hand; portraits of the composer; a lock of Chopin's hair; and a death mask. The original objects are presented with scenery and Chopin's music, creating a sense of immersion in history and close contact with the

Chopin's last piano (Playel Company) 1848-1849.

Holy Cross Church, "Let us lift up our hearts".

artist. In the Composer's Hall, Chopin's music is presented through recordings of the most outstanding pianists made on pianos from the composer's time, evoking the original sound of Chopin's works. In the Concert Hall, recordings are presented from the Fryderyk Chopin International Piano Competitions, which are held here every five years.

Nearby stands Holy Cross Church, the Baroque parish church of the Chopin family. After Chopin's death in Paris, the doctor removed Chopin's heart, in accordance with Chopin's own wishes, and preserved it in a crystal jar filled with alcohol. In his dying wish, he told his sister Ludwika, "I know that Paskiewicz (the tsarist governor of occupied Warsaw) will not allow you to bring my body to Warsaw, so at least bring my heart there." His sister Ludwika brought the jar back home to Warsaw, and eventually it found its permanent resting place within a pillar of Holy Cross Church.

The whole world has come to know and love Chopin's music for the piano, telling in glorious melody of the beauty of his beloved Poland. Both Frédéric's father and his teachers encouraged him to pay attention to the music of his homeland and listen for the hearts of the people in their folk songs. The people of Poland were passionate about their country's history and their desire for independence, and their songs demonstrated their deep emotions and expressed the powerful feelings in their hearts.

Chopin's Polish childhood and youth provided him with ample exposure to a vast repertoire of religious songs, both in church and at home. On Sundays and religious holidays the whole family participated in church services, often singing Polish songs during the Mass

Detail of Holy Cross Church, "Here rests the heart of Frederick Chopin".

and other services. During his youth, Chopin was the organist at Warsaw's Church of the Visitation, intoning and accompanying the songs. From his earliest years as an émigré, Chopin sought to remember and enter into the soul of this Polish music.

During numerous trips across Poland and vacations spent with his friends in the country, Chopin discovered and studied Polish folk music in a much deeper way than anyone before him, music that would become a source of profound inspiration for him, adding a unique quality to his works. His "Polonaise in A Major" is almost entirely played forte. During the 1939 invasion of Poland by Germany, Polskie Radio broadcast this piece daily as a nationalistic protest and to rally the Polish people.

He held dear everything that reminded him of Poland: his family, his happy childhood and adolescence, and therefore also Polish music, both religious and folk, with which he was involved on a daily basis in his native land. These songs provided a creative inspiration, as he drew from the beginning or ending of a song, sometimes from the refrain, as the source material for motifs, phrases, and larger formal units.

In his brief 39 years, Chopin composed over 180 works for piano, and except for three piano sonatas and two concertos, most of them last no more than three to five minutes. The traditional dances of the stately polonaise and the haunting mazurka were major elements in his writings. His 24 études, which are some of the most technically challenging exercises for piano students, are also works of artistic genius. His nocturnes are slow pieces with a clear tune played in the right hand, expressing the calm of night. Chopin's 24 preludes, which he wrote as a tribute to Bach, were written in all 24 major and minor keys in a harmonious order. Chopin's four scherzos converted the playful scherzo form into rather serious and dramatic pieces. His four ballades, inspired by Polish epic poems, were a new musical form invented by Chopin, full of dramatic intensity.

Chopin was one of the initiators of the Romantic period in music, however the music he really loved was written by Bach (from the Baroque period) and Mozart (from the Classical period). His own work blended Classical restraint with Romantic feeling, as he detested any exaggeration that would turn sentiment into sentimentality. To recognize this distinction is to play Chopin's music the way he himself played it, the way he wanted it played. Yet to play his music as he felt it means to free it of all earthly bonds. This is the pianist's greatest challenge.

MEDITATION

• Why did Chopin desire that his heart be brought back home to Warsaw?

• Where is my treasure, the desire of my heart?

Reading: Matthew 6:19-21
Do not store up for yourselves treasures on earth, where moth and rust consume...

Response: "Where your treasure is, there your heart will also be."

"Listening to him, one yields with one's whole soul, as to a singer who, oblivious of accompaniment, lets himself be carried away by his emotion. In short, he is unique among pianists." (Ignace Moscheles) **R.**

"It was an unforgettable picture to see Chopin sitting at the piano like a clairvoyant, lost in his dreams; to see how his vision communicated itself through his playing, and how, at the end of each piece, he had the sad habit of running one finger over the length of the plaintive keyboard, as though to tear himself forcibly away from his dream." (Robert Schumann) R.

"There is something fundamentally personal and at the same time so very masterly in his playing that he may be called a really perfect virtuoso." (Felix Mendelssohn) R.

"Music was his language, the divine tongue through which he expressed a whole realm of sentiments that only the select few can appreciate ... The muse of his homeland dictates his songs, and the anguished cries of Poland lend to his art a mysterious, indefinable poetry which, for all those who have truly experienced it, cannot be compared to anything else." (Franz Liszt) R.

"Chopin is a pianist of conviction. He composes for himself, plays for himself and everyone listens with interest, with delight, with infinite pleasure. Listen how he dreams, how he weeps, with what sweetness, tenderness and melancholy he sings, how perfectly he expresses the gentlest and loftiest feelings." (*La France Musicale*) R.

Prayer: O God, source of our deepest desires, from the heart of Chopin flow the sentiments that moved the nation of Poland. As Your word counsels us, "Keep your heart with all vigilance, for from it flow the springs of life" (Prov 4:23), guard our hearts so that from them may surge streams of truth, goodness, and beauty.

3. Chopin Monument in Łazienki Park

The large bronze statue of Frédéric Chopin, which stands today in the upper part of Warsaw's Łazienki Park, was designed by Wacław Szymanowski to commemorate the centenary of Chopin's birth in 1910. Its execution was delayed, however, because tsarist Russia banned putting up monuments in Poland. The statue was finally cast and erected in 1926 after Poland received its independence following the First World War. In 1940 German occupying forces blew up the monument on the order of Governor-General Hans Frank in an attempt to destroy Polish culture. It was the first of many monuments destroyed by the Nazis in Warsaw.

Chopin Monument in Łazienki Park.

Since the original mold for the statue had survived the war, a replica of the monument was cast and erected at the original site in 1958. The impressive Art Nouveau monument presents a seated figure of Chopin with a stylized willow tree evoking the pianist's hand and fingers and the head of the Polish eagle on the right end. It is inscribed with a quote from Adam Mickiewicz's narrative poem "Konrad Wallenrod": "Flames will consume our painted history, sword-wielding thieves will plunder our treasures, the song will be saved." Since 1959, piano concerts of Chopin's compositions have been performed at the statue's base on summer Sunday afternoons from May through September.

The music of Chopin still expresses for Poland its long struggle for freedom and independence. Public performances of Chopin's music were censured as subversive by tsarist Russia and banned by Nazi Germany. In 1863, Russian troops even destroyed the piano Chopin had played as a child prodigy in Warsaw, throwing it out the second story of a building in symbolic revenge for a failed assassination attempt against the Russian governor of Poland. After hearing Chopin's quintessentially Polish "Mazurkas," Robert Schumann described the music of his contemporary as "cannons hidden among blossoms." The Germans sought to destroy Poland's national heritage, and this certainly included the music of Chopin, which stirred patriotic sentiments like nothing else.

What is it about Chopin that draws the listener into his world and gives his music such emotional power? Franz Liszt tells us that one evening in Paris, Chopin was asked by one of the aristocratic ladies present, overcome by the music he had just played, to identify the source of its melancholy. After some reflection Chopin could find no appropriate expression except in his own language: the Polish word *żal.* The term can mean "longing," "regret," "nostalgia," "melancholy," "grief," and even a combination of these things. Chopin's music is shot through with this inexpressible quality, familiar to all who hear it, elusive to all who attempt to analyze it.[65]

Whatever might have been his transitory pleasures, he had never been free from this feeling which might almost be said to form the soil of his heart. "Zal! In very truth, it colors the whole of Chopin's compositions," wrote Franz Liszt. Chopin's fellow exiles gathered in Paris heard laments for their homeland in the languorous rubato of the mazurkas, with their heart-catching drop from major to minor keys, a mood often shattered by discordant expressions of unleashed rage. It is a feeling of losing everything, of deep loneliness, of passing away.

Drenched in nationalistic sentiment, the compositions and performances of Chopin were set against a backdrop of a swelling desire for Poland's independence from its Russian masters. Producing music in many different styles, Chopin repeatedly reminds his listeners of the various instruments and musical styles of his homeland. His use of Polish folk songs in his compositions influenced a whole generation of nationalistic composers — such as the Norwegian Edvard Grieg and the Czech Antonín Dvořák. As the greatest Polish composer of all time, he developed folk melodies as the basis of his complex piano works and thereby brought Polish music to international salons and to the attention of the world.

MEDITATION

• What emotions does the Chopin monument evoke in me?

• Why did the enemies of Poland want to suppress the music of Chopin?

Reading: Psalm 37:1-9
Do not fret because of the wicked; do not be envious of wrongdoers...

Response: "Let us listen with the ear of the heart." (St. Benedict)

"It was impossible to know whether the master [Chopin] had imparted his soul to the piano or himself embodied the piano's soul." (Arthur Rubinstein) R.

"To play Chopin, you have to try to be a poet like him. You can be as clever or passionate as you like, but if you don't make the piano sing, you're not playing Chopin. That doesn't mean being sentimental. ... You only need to hear his music to be in touch with his immense inner strength and sense of discipline and craftsmanship." (Angela Hewitt) R.

"I was wary of the Romantics as a young pianist, but listening to older recordings taught me how classical Chopin is in his clarity of form. The key to playing his work is a restraint that only comes after years of playing it. I'd held back performing the E minor Concerto until the other day, when I did it for the first time in Lincoln. I suddenly felt young and vulnerable again. After all, his music is partly why we become pianists." (Peter Donohoe) R.

"I'm from a Polish family, so playing Chopin was unavoidable. Although he's a national hero, his real value is universal. His connection with the piano is so complete, it feels almost as if the instrument was created to allow his music to come into the world. I have to work hard to get it right, but the notes fall under the hands so beautifully that playing him is overwhelmingly pleasurable." (Emanuel Ax) R.

"Chopin was not a greater composer than Bach or Mozart, Beethoven or Schubert, an absurdity in itself. But for me, Chopin is unique. He understood as no other composer did what the piano can do. Chopin gave us the full emotional range of what a piano can express." (Walter Witt) R.

Prayer: God of all nations, whose creative power lifts up the Polish people through the music of Frédéric Chopin, help us perceive the joy, sadness, and longing of our hearts expressed in music. May the music of this Polish genius, who made such a great contribution to the culture of Europe and the world, bring us close to You and help us discover the depth of the human spirit.

XI. JEWISH HERITAGE AND HOLOCAUST MARTYRS

Poland represents both the most distinguished and the most tragic account of European Jewish history. From the time of the Middle Ages until World War II, Poland was home to Europe's largest and most significant Jewish community. Compared to the situation of Jews in most other European countries, the Jewish people of Poland were secure and prosperous, developing an incredibly rich culture of their own. Ultimately, however, Poland wound up being the largest cemetery in Europe, the place where the Nazi dream of exterminating the Jewish race was almost perfectly realized.

When Nazi Germany invaded in 1939, there were about three and a half million Jews in Poland, which was over 10 percent of the population. Warsaw's Jewish population was 375,000, one-third of the city's population. In Kraków, there were 60,000 Jews, about one-quarter of the inhabitants. In some smaller towns and villages, the residents were over half Jewish. Everywhere, the Jewish culture, its music and rituals, its feasts and customs, enriched the tradition of the nation.

In the first year of the German occupation, several hundred synagogues were blown up or burned by the Nazis, who sometimes forced the Jews to do it themselves. In many cases, synagogues were transformed into factories, places of entertainment, or prisons. Rabbis were shorn of their beards, humiliated in public, forced to dance in their prayer shawls, and many were set on fire or hanged. All Jews were required to register, and the word "Jude" was stamped in their identity cards. Many restrictions and prohibitions targeting Jews were announced and brutally enforced. For example, Jews were forbidden to walk on the sidewalks, use public transport, or enter theaters, museums, places of leisure, and libraries. By the end of 1941 all Jews in German-occupied Poland had to wear an identifying badge shaped like the Star of David. German tabloids printed in Polish routinely ran anti-Semitic articles urging local people to adopt an attitude of indifference towards the Jews.

Between 1939 and 1942, a system of ghettos was imposed by the occupiers for the confinement of Jews in most cities and villages throughout the country. The Warsaw Ghetto was the largest, confining the entire Jewish population to a little over one square mile. Overcrowding, uncollected filth, lice, hunger, and lethal epidemics such as typhoid all resulted in countless deaths. All Poles were forbidden from buying from Jewish shops under penalty of execution. When Jews tried to escape the ghettos and were caught, the escapees were murdered and their bodies left in plain view as a warning to others.

While the Nazi policy towards Jews was ruthless, their policy towards Christian Poles who helped Jews was equally brutal. Execution was automatic for even the most basic help rendered to Jews. To discourage Poles from giving shelter to Jews, the Germans often searched houses and introduced ruthless punishments. The penalty applied not only to those who did the helping, but it was also extended to their family, neighbors, and sometimes to entire villages. This principle of collective responsibility was designed to encourage neighbors to inform on each other in order to avoid punishment. These policies were widely publicized by the Nazis as they sought to terrorize the Polish population. Thousands of non-Jewish Poles were executed for harboring Jews, helping them escape the ghettos, or offering simple assistance.

Some individuals blackmailed Jews in hiding, taking advantage of their desperation by extorting them for money and valuables in exchange for not informing on them. Sometimes, after robbing their victims of everything of value, they would turn them over to the Germans for the bounty. These extortionists, called *szmalcowniks* (literally, greasy-palmers), did substantial damage to the Jewish community: stripping Jews of assets they needed to survive, threatening rescuers, forcing those in hiding to move, and increasing their risk of capture and death. These extortionists and informers were condemned by the Polish Underground State, which fought against them and punished them with the death penalty.

Hiding in a Christian society to which the Jews were unassimilated was a formidable undertaking. They needed to quickly acquire not only a new identity, but a new body of knowledge. They had to minimize their Yiddish accent, learn different gestures and facial expressions, and learn the minimum of Christian prayers and doctrine. Those with specific physical characteristics associated with Jews were particularly vulnerable. Food rations for Poles were minimal and black-market prices for necessary goods were high, factors which made it difficult to hide people and almost impossible to hide entire families, especially in the cities. Yet, in spite of these severe measures imposed by the Nazis, Poland has the highest number of people honored as "Righteous Among the Nations" for rescuing Jews.

Beginning in 1940 the Nazis established a number of concentration and forced-labor camps in Poland, six of which were later refashioned to function as extermination camps. An estimated 3 million Jews were killed in these camps on Polish soil as part of the "Final Solution." These camps were all located near the rail network so that the victims could be easily transported. Before departure, Jews were usually told that they should bring small valuables with them because they were moving to a new location. These treasures were then confiscated upon arrival at the camp. Shortly after arrival, most were killed, although often able-bodied Jews were forced to work and then beaten to death.

After the war, many of the estimated 200,000 Jewish survivors left the Polish People's Republic for the nascent State of Israel, North America, or South America. Their departure was hastened by the lack of any remaining Jewish institutions and the hostility of the Communist Party to both religion and private enterprise. Then, following the fall of the communist regime in 1989, the situation of Polish Jews became normalized and those who were Polish citizens before the war were allowed to renew their Polish citizenship. In recent years there has been a renewed interest in Jewish culture, including new study programs at Polish secondary schools and universities, Kraków's Jewish Culture Festival, and Warsaw's Museum of the History of Polish Jews. Although most physical traces of Jewish heritage were destroyed by the Nazis or under the communist regime in the decades afterward, there are still many Jewish heritage sites, synagogues, cemeteries, schools, and other structures that have been rebuilt or restored throughout Poland.

Memorial of the Umschlagplatz, the "collection point," shaped like an open freight car.

1. *The Warsaw Ghetto and Its Uprising*

Boundary markers and memorial plaques were erected in 2008 "to the memory of those who suffered, fought and perished" in the former Warsaw Ghetto. Each marker consists of a bronze plaque with a map representing the ghetto's borders on a map of Warsaw and a pin indicating the featured site. Information and historic photos accompany the markers on acrylic glass, describing the gates, footbridges, and buildings important to the ghetto inmates. A 10-inch-wide strip along the ground, made with cast iron lettering, reads: "MUR GETTA/GHETTO WALL: 1940-1943" and indicates the exact location of the ghetto walls.

The ghetto was established in 1940 by the German governor-general Hans Frank. It was surrounded by a 10-foot wall and cut off from the rest of the city. After 110,000 non-Jewish Poles had been forcibly evicted from the area, approximately 360,000 Warsaw Jews and 90,000 from other towns were herded into the ghetto. The German occupying authorities selected Adam Czerniakow to take charge of the Jewish Council, called *Judenrat*, made up of 24 Jewish men commanded to establish Jewish labor battalions as well as Jewish Ghetto Police responsible for maintaining order within the ghetto walls. Over time, the demands made on the *Judenrat* became increasingly cruel, and the slightest sign of noncompliance was punished with execution. Average food rations in 1941 for Jews in Warsaw were limited to 253 calories. Poles were allowed only 669, while Germans received 2,613 calories. An estimated 100,000 Jews died in the ghetto of starvation and diseases, especially typhoid.

The summer of 1942 witnessed the beginning of the mass deportation of the Warsaw Ghetto inhabitants. The Jewish Ghetto Police were ordered to escort the ghetto inhabitants to the *Umschlagplatz* (collection point) at the train station, where they were transported by freight train to the Treblinka extermination camp. Adam Czerniakow committed suicide when he was forced to collect daily lists of Jews to be deported to the camp. Today a stone monument marks the *Umschlagplatz*, where the Jews were assembled for deportation. The memorial resembles an open freight car, marked with four plaques in Polish, Yiddish, English, and Hebrew: "Along this path of suffering and death over 300,000 Jews were driven in 1942-1943 from the Warsaw Ghetto to the gas chambers of the Nazi extermination camps." Also engraved on the wall are the 400 most popular Jewish-Polish first names, in alphabetical order from Aba to Żanna. Each one commemorates 1,000 victims of the Warsaw Ghetto. The middle opening of the monument is surmounted by a gravestone showing a shattered forest, a symbol of the eradication of the Jewish people.

The Warsaw Ghetto Uprising of 1943 was the largest single revolt by Jews during the war. The heroic effort opposed the attempt of the Nazis to transport the remnant ghetto population to the death camps. The remaining Jews began to build bunkers and smuggle weapons and explosives into the ghetto. The left-wing Jewish Combat Organization (ŻOB) and right-wing Jewish Military Union (ŻZW) began to train and prepare. Most of the Jewish fighters did not believe their revolt would be successful, yet they fought for the honor of the Jewish people and to protest the world's silence. The first resistance effort in January was partially effective and spurred the Polish Underground to support the Jews in earnest. The final uprising started on April 19, when the ghetto refused to surrender to the police commander, *SS-Brigadeführer* Jürgen Stroop. The overwhelming German forces were incapable of crushing the Jewish resistance in open street combat, so after several days they decided to switch strategy and set fire to all the buildings in which the Jewish fighters hid. Of the 56,000 Jews who fought in the ghetto uprising, about 13,000 were killed in the fighting, about half of them burned alive or suffocated from smoke inhalation. The commander of the ŻOB, Mordechai Anielewicz, died while fighting at the organization's command center on 18 Mila Street, committing suicide by ingesting cyanide rather than surrendering. Today the site is memorialized by Anielewicz Mound, a grass knoll and monument where Anielewicz and dozens of fighters are buried.

The block-by-block destruction of the ghetto finally ended on May 16, with most of the remaining fighters captured and shipped to the death camps. After the end of the fighting, Heinrich Himmler ordered that the Great Synagogue on Tłomackie Square be destroyed as a celebration of German victory and the end of the Warsaw Ghetto. *SS-Gruppenführer* Jürgen Stroop, who pushed the detonation device, recalls:

> After prolonging the suspense for a moment, I shouted: "Heil Hitler" and pressed the button. With a thunderous, deafening bang and a rainbow burst of colors, the fiery explosion soared toward the clouds, an unforgettable tribute to our triumph over the Jews. The Warsaw Ghetto was no more. The will of Adolf Hitler and Heinrich Himmler had been done.[66]

The Monument to the Ghetto Heroes, sculpted by Nathan Rapoport, was unveiled in 1948. The 36-foot-high wall of the memorial was designed to evoke both the ghetto walls and the Western Wall in Jerusalem, Judaism's holiest site. The western side of the monument displays a bronze sculpture of insurgents — men, women, and children, armed with guns and Molotov cocktails. The central standing figure is Mordechai Anielewicz, leader of the ŻOB, during the uprising. The eastern side depicts the persecution of Jews at the hands of the Nazi oppressors. The sign in three languages reads: "Jewish nation to its fighters and martyrs."

Facing the Monument to the Ghetto Heroes stands the POLIN Museum of the History of Polish Jews, which opened in 2014, featuring its multimedia exhibition about the Jewish community that flourished in Poland for a thousand years up to the World War II Holocaust. Its minimalist exterior, clad in glass, encloses a dramatic interior of undulating walls, showing how Poland became home to the world's largest Jewish community. According to legend, Jews fleeing persecution came east. When they arrived in a forest, they heard the word *"Polin,"* which sounds like "here you will dwell" in Hebrew, indicating that this was the place to settle. *Polin* is the Hebrew word for Poland and the inspiration for the name of the museum. Visitors will enter a salon, tavern, home, church, synagogue, train station, and schoolroom, encountering artifacts, documents, photographs, and films.

The Warsaw Jewish Cemetery, located on Okopowa Street next to the Catholic Powązki Cemetery, is one of Europe's largest Jewish cemeteries.

Monument to the Ghetto Heroes with POLIN Museum behind.

Memorial plaques marking sites important for the ghetto inmates.

Bronze sculpture of insurgents on the Monument to the Ghetto Heroes.

The Jewish necropolis was established in 1806 and contains over 250,000 marked graves, as well as mass graves of victims of the Warsaw Ghetto. Many of the markers are simple, others are elaborately carved and richly decorated. Of special note is the monument dedicated to Janusz Korczak, a Polish Jewish educator and children's author. After spending many years working as the principal of an orphanage in Warsaw, the Germans offered him

Monument to Janusz Korczak at the Warsaw Jewish Cemetery.

sanctuary because of his fame, but he chose to stay with the children and their nurses when they were sent from the Ghetto to the Treblinka extermination camp in 1942. The bronze monument depicts Korczak leading the children through the Ghetto, holding one by the hand and carrying another, to the *Umschlagplatz* and then to their death in the camp. The cemetery also contains the poignant Memorial to the Child Victims of the Holocaust.

Following the Warsaw Ghetto Uprising, a group of surviving fighters escaped through the sewers and reached the forest in the outskirts of the city. Many became active in the Polish Underground, hiding other Jews, and forging identity documents. A year later, after the ghetto had been totally destroyed, the general Warsaw Uprising began on August 1, 1944, led by the Polish Home Army in an attempt to liberate the city from German occupation. In addition to ending the occupation, they sought to assert Polish sovereignty over the capital before the Soviet Red Army could assume control. Among the defenders, hundreds of surviving Polish Jews, men and women, took part in combat against the Nazis during the insurrection.

The Warsaw Uprising was intended to last a few days until Soviet-controlled forces arrived to end the Nazi occupation. But Stalin gave instructions to cut off the Warsaw resistance from any outside help. Although the Poles established control over most of central Warsaw, the Soviets ignored Polish

Warsaw Uprising Monument.

attempts to make radio contact with them and did not advance into the city. The Germans then bombarded the city through the use of heavy artillery and tactical bombers, against which the Poles were unable to effectively defend. The uprising was fought heroically for 63 days until the Polish resistance was defeated. Thousands of resisters were evacuated through the sewers, and those who remained were either shot or transported to concentration camps. In retaliation, the German occupiers burned and demolished the remaining buildings and houses of the city, focusing especially on historical monuments, Polish national archives, and places of interest to Polish culture.

The Warsaw Uprising Monument on Krasiński Square was unveiled on August 1, 1989, the 45th anniversary of the uprising. The bronze figures represent insurgents actively engaged in combat and running from a collapsing building. Another section shows insurgents descending into a manhole, a reference to their use of Warsaw's sewer system to move across German-held territory. The Warsaw Uprising Museum in Warsaw's Wola district was opened in 2004, marking the 60th anniversary of the uprising. It displays hundreds of artifacts on several floors, remembering the people and events of those 63 days from August 1 to October 2, 1944. The incredible heroism of the insurgents still resonates, charging us to live lives that pay tribute to their resistance and sacrifice. May their memory forever be a blessing and inspiration to us.

MEDITATION

- What emotions do I experience while imagining the former Jewish ghetto?
- How can I be blessed and inspired by the memory of Warsaw's wartime inhabitants?

> Reading: Genesis 4:8-10
> *Cain said to his brother Abel, "Let us go out to the field."*
>
> Response: "May their memory be a blessing."

"Be still, and know that I am God!" (Ps 46:10). We have seen the evidence. We have heard the witness. Millions were torn from their homes, uprooted from all that was familiar, and relocated with orchestrated cruelty. We share the silence of remembering together. R.

"He has sent me to bring good news to the oppressed, to bind up the brokenhearted, to proclaim liberty to the captives, and release to the prisoners" (Is 61:1). We struggle to understand how it came to be: that humanity could become so inhuman. But these captives will not be torn from our hearts, for today they have a home in the silence of our shared remembering. R.

"Then hear from heaven your dwelling place their prayer and their pleas, maintain their cause and forgive your people who have sinned against you" (2 Chr 6:39). Forgive us for forgetting Your presence in our world and its peoples. Enable us to pause and ponder Your image in all those we encounter. R.

"You shall love your neighbor as yourself: I am the LORD" (Lev 19:18). Forgive us for the limits we have placed on love and grant us the discernment to recognize the full consequences of our actions. May we grow in our desire to extend the boundaries of our love and to encompass all within our care. R.

"I have set before you life and death, blessings and curses. Choose life so that you and your descendants may live" (Dt 30:19). May what happened in those dark years never be forgotten, so that new generations may be warned against the rise of prejudice and intolerance of others. Forgive us for the decisions that have wrought agony and destruction, and grant us the courage to speak for all that gives abundant life. R.

Prayer: God of all peoples, Whose many gifts include memory and empathy, we hold in remembrance before You those countless Jewish people who were terrorized, displaced, and murdered in the horror of Nazi persecution and whose communities were destroyed. In Your mercy, cleanse our hearts of all bigotry and help us accept differences without fear, so that every human community may flourish and every home be secure, to the advancement of Your loving purposes and the glory of Your Holy Name.

The iconic entrance to Auschwitz I.

2. Auschwitz I and Auschwitz II-Birkenau

Auschwitz, which became Europe's largest concentration and extermination camp, is rightly known as the world's preeminent monument to evil. In cinder and stone, it stands as a reminder of the stunning depravity of which human beings are capable.

The Nazi occupation selected the site for two main reasons. First, the area had few inhabitants. The farmers and villagers living in the area around the Polish town of Oswiecim were ordered to leave, and an area of 15 square miles was zoned off with observation towers, armed patrols, and signs warning "Forbidden area — Trespassers will be shot without warning." Within this

The entrance into Auschwitz II–Birkenau, where prisoners were brought in by railway cars.

area, the original Auschwitz concentration camp, a huge sister camp called Birkenau, and several satellite camps were eventually built.

The second reason the Nazis chose this site for Auschwitz was its practicality. This area at the fork of Poland's Vistula and Sola rivers was at the center of Nazi-occupied Europe. This location, crossed by Europe's rail system, made transporting the victims to the camps most convenient.

The original camp was formed in 1940 from a group of abandoned Polish military barracks. The site was secured from escape with concrete posts supporting a double barbed-wire fence through which passed a 220-volt, three-phase current. On the inner side of the entire fence a wide graveled zone formed a death belt, within which any prisoner could be shot. While the Nazis directed the work of the camp, they brought in hard-core German criminals to exercise authority over the prisoners. Known as "kapos," many of these men were perverted sadists, vying for who could use the vilest methods to torture prisoners.

The first transport of prisoners, in June of 1940, consisted of 728 Poles who were immediately put to work enlarging the camp. Since Hitler had ordered that the Polish leadership and intelligentsia be destroyed, the camp was established as a quarantine camp for Polish political prisoners. By November the first mass execution occurred — 40 Polish men shot in the back of the head against the so-called "Death Wall" in front of which thousands would be executed over the next four years. The first experimental gassing took place in mid-1941, when a group of Soviet prisoners of war were killed when the authorities cast Zyklon B crystals into their basement cell in block 11. The camp morgue was later converted to a gas chamber able to hold 800 people. The prisoners died as Zyklon B was dropped into the room through slits in the ceiling.

In accord with the Nazi's "Final Solution to the Jewish Question," freight trains began delivering Jews from all over occupied Europe to Auschwitz and other extermination camps in the spring of 1942. At this time, Auschwitz II-Birkenau was constructed, where the gas chambers were located in what prisoners called the "little red house" and "little white house," brick farmhouses that had been turned into gassing facilities by bricking up the windows to create insulated rooms. Soon increasingly larger and more efficient gas chambers and crematoria were constructed. The dressing rooms held wooden benches along the walls and numbered pegs for clothing. Victims would be led along a corridor that led to the opening of the gas chambers where nozzles were fixed to the ceilings to resemble showerheads. The total capacity of the crematoria — one at Auschwitz I and four at Auschwitz II — allowed for the burning of several thousand bodies per day. Although all the gas chambers and crematoria were destroyed by the Germans before the liberation of the camps in 1945, the ones at Auschwitz I have been reconstructed and may be somberly visited today.

An inmate's first experience at Auschwitz, unless they were sent directly to the gas chamber, took place at the prisoner reception center near the gate with the iconic "*Arbeit Macht Frei*" (Work Makes You Free) sign. Here prisoners were tattooed with a number on their arms, shaved, disinfected, and given a striped prison uniform. "Selection," whereby new arrivals were chosen either for work or the gas chamber, was conducted regularly beginning in 1942. The slave labor of the prisoners was a source of enormous profit for the Nazis and their industrialist allies. It is estimated that 1.1 million people died at Auschwitz. The death toll includes over 960,000 Jews (865,000 of whom were gassed on arrival), 74,000 non-Jewish Poles, 21,000 Roma (gypsies), 15,000 Soviet prisoners of war, and up to 15,000 other Europeans. Those not gassed died of starvation, exhaustion, disease, medical experiments, individual executions, or beatings.

A tour of Auschwitz I includes exhibitions in the prisoner blocks 4-7: methods of extermination, evidence of crimes, life of the prisoner, and sanitary conditions. Block 10 was used for medical experiments and block 11 was the camp jail. The basement of the jail was used for the darkest tortures. Here St. Maximilian Kolbe died of starvation along with other prisoners in reprisal for an escape of a fellow prisoner. In the basement the Nazis also carried out the first mass murder with the use of Zyklon B. The yard outside the block holds the Wall of Death and posts for hangings and flogging. Outside the camp boundary stands the Nazi hospital, administrative building, commandant's office, the Gestapo building where prisoners were interrogated and tortured, and the reconstructed gas chamber and crematorium.

Auschwitz II-Birkenau, a short drive away, is recognized by its iconic entrance gate through which runs the railroad tracks that brought Jewish prisoners for extermination. Over the gate stands the tower that served as the main guard house for the camp. Within the gate, the tracks run alongside the concrete unloading platform. Here families were divided by sexes as they exited the railcars, and then Nazi doctors made the decisions about who was qualified for labor and who would be killed immediately. The railroad spur along this ramp runs up to the ruins of two gas chambers and crematoria. Between these ruins stands the International Monument to the Victims of the Camp, including over 20 plaques, each in the language of a nation or ethnic group that was persecuted at Auschwitz. The camp held over 300 buildings, mostly wooden and brick barracks, destroyed after the war to use for construction materials in the towns and cities. A few of these buildings served as warehouses for the loot confiscated from the Jewish victims when they arrived at the camp. Nicknamed "Kanada" by the prisoners, referring to the land of plenty to which some of their relatives had immigrated, the wealth of these storehouses was shipped to Nazi beneficiaries throughout Germany.

A dramatic final chapter of the story of Auschwitz involves the camp commandant, Rudolf Höss, who was sentenced to death by the Polish Supreme National Tribunal and hanged for war crimes in 1947. His gallows still stand next to the reconstructed gas chamber and crematorium of Auschwitz I. Visible in the distance is the spacious villa in which Höss lived with his wife and five children while he administered what he called in his memoirs "the largest killing center in all of history." [67]

While he awaited his execution, Höss was sent to the prison in Wadowice, the birthplace of Karol Wojtyła, for the last days of his life. Höss feared not death but torture, which he felt certain to receive as his Polish captors sought revenge. Yet, he was wholly confounded when he met kindness instead from the guards, several of whom showed him their tattoos from Auschwitz. If persons whom he had caused such suffering could forgive him, he thought, then perhaps God could forgive him as well.

On Good Friday, April 4, 1947, Höss asked to see a priest. Since the prisoner spoke no Polish, a priest was sought who spoke German, but none were found in the circumstances. Then Höss recalled a seemingly insignifi-

In this pond lie the ashes of men, women, and children who fell victim to the Nazi genocide.

cant event that took place in 1940. The Gestapo had arrested the Kraków Jesuits and sent them to Auschwitz, but the Jesuit superior, Fr. Władysław Lohn, SJ, was absent at the time. When he discovered the deportation of his community, he traveled to Auschwitz to find them. He was quickly captured and brought before the commandant to decide his fate. Fr. Lohn's courage

Author with the late Eva Mozes Kor, liberated from Auschwitz at age 10 after she and her twin survived Dr. Mengele's medical experimentations.

impressed Höss, who released the priest unharmed. Seven years later, Höss the prisoner remembered the brave priest who spoke fluent German and requested a visit from him.

The prison authorities finally located Fr. Lohn in Łagiewniki, where he was serving as chaplain of the convent of the Sisters of Our Lady of Mercy there. When asked to meet with Höss, Fr. Lohn dreaded his mission and asked the sisters to pray for him. He spent several hours with Höss on April 10, and at the end of their conversation, Höss made a formal profession of Catholic faith, thus returning to the Church he had left a quarter-century before, and made his Confession. The next day, the Friday of Easter Week, Fr. Lohn returned and gave Holy Communion to Höss, who knelt in the middle of his cell. The former Nazi commandant, trained to conceal every sign of weakness, openly wept.[68]

On the same day, Rudolf Höss wrote moving farewell letters to his wife and children, and the next day, four days before his execution, Höss acknowledged the enormity of his crimes in a message to the state prosecutor, asking for forgiveness from the Polish people:

> My conscience compels me to make the following declaration. In the solitude of my prison cell, I have come to the bitter recognition that I have sinned gravely against humanity. As Commandant of Auschwitz, I was responsible for carrying out part of the cruel plans of the "Third Reich" for human destruction. In so doing I have inflicted terrible wounds on humanity. I caused unspeakable suffering for the Polish people in particular. I am to pay for this with my life. May the Lord God forgive one day what I have done. I ask the Polish people for forgiveness. In Polish prisons I experienced for the first time what human kindness is. Despite all that has happened I have experienced humane treatment which I could never have expected, and which has deeply shamed me. May the facts which are now coming out about the horrible crimes against humanity make the repetition of such cruel acts impossible for all time.[69]

The repentant commandant was brought to Auschwitz and led to a cell in Block 11, the "Death Block" where St. Maximilian Kolbe and so many others had died. Here Höss was to wait. Two hours later the handcuffed prisoner was led through the camp to the waiting gallows. The sentence was read out as the hangman placed a noose around the neck of the condemned man, and there he died in silence.

Although only God knows the final state of his soul and the eternal destiny of Rudolf Höss, it seems that in the end even his horrific sins weren't bigger than the mercy of God. By God's grace, divine life penetrated his heart; apathy evolved into deep-seated repentance and trust in God.

MEDITATION

• What are some of the feelings within me as I linger over the images of Auschwitz?

• Why is it so critically important to teach children and every new generation about the Holocaust?

Reading: Joel 1:2-3
Has such a thing happened in your days, or in the days of your ancestors?...

Response: "Your steadfast love never ceases, your mercies never come to an end."

God, we fear Your action, but we protest Your inaction even more. Why did you let Your people be led like lambs to the slaughter? How could You look on as they were transported and humiliated, worked to death, and deprived of dignity and hope? R.

These are Your people whom You called by name. They were brought here, starved, and murdered. Did this cause You as much pain as it caused Your people? How can anyone ever trust again, believe again, hope again, restore and build and plan? How will this indescribable scar ever be healed? R.

You watched parents killed beside their children, Your people systematically exterminated and almost obliterated from the earth. How can such evil be possible in Your creation? What demon can have possessed those who did it? What remote good could ever come from it? What punishment could ever do justice to it? R.

You have shown us the evil we are capable of. We recognize ourselves in the many who knew but remained silent, who colluded and denied. Yet You are the God who works good out of evil. In the depths of Your mercy, show us that You are Lord even over this apocalypse of horror. Make our every step one of wisdom, truth, humility, and courage. R.

Prayer: God of the past, present, and future, great is Thy faithfulness. We remember the 6 million Jews murdered in the Holocaust and the countless other victims of Nazi persecution and other genocides. We bring to mind the survivors of this tragedy, who have shared their stories and spoken the truth. We honor those who courageously stood up against evil, offered aid, and saved lives. We pray that You will help us to remember, to stand together for the sacred dignity of every human life, and to glorify You in our words and actions.

The Old Synagogue in Kazimierz.

3. Kraków, the Districts of Kazimierz and Podgórze

The town of Kazimierz was established in 1335 and named after its founder, King Kazimierz the Great. It was originally an island, formed by two branches of the Vistula, just south of Wawel Cathedral. In the 19th century, the northern branch of the river was drained and filled in, and the area became a district of Kraków. The charming Christian-Jewish neighborhood of Kazimierz developed over many centuries with a character distinct from the royal pageantry of neighboring Kraków. The medieval town had its own market square and town hall, and soon monumental churches and many synagogues were built.

The Basilica of Corpus Christi was the parish church of Kazimierz. Its structure is a fine example of Polish Gothic, and its interior decor is impressive Baroque. The grandeur of the high altar is emphasized by the light flowing down from its stained-glass windows. Especially notable are the elaborately decorated stalls and the pulpit in the shape of a boat, complete with masts and rigging, all supported by mermaids and dolphins. To the left of the church entrance stands the altar and sarcophagus of St. Stanisław Kazimierczyk. This saint of the 15th century has for centuries been a special patron of the inhabitants of Kazimierz. As a priest and a professed member of the Canons Regular of the Lateran, he became noted for his ardent devotion to Christ's Passion and the Eucharist, which was reflected in his skillful preaching, spiritual guidance, and dedication to the ill and poor. Although the veneration of Stanisław of Kazimierz developed right after his death, he

The Remuh Synagogue in Kazimierz.

was only recently beatified by Pope John Paul II in 1993 and canonized by Pope Benedict in 2010.

At the end of the 15th century, after a fire destroyed a large part of Kraków, a Jewish quarter was created in the eastern part of Kazimierz. At the request of the Jewish community, a wall was erected to mark the boundaries of what became known as the *Oppidum Judaeorum*, the Jewish City, governed by internal Jewish authorities and subject only to the king. At about this time, the Old Synagogue was completed, which is the oldest synagogue building standing in Poland. Today it houses a museum dedicated to the history and culture of Jews in Kraków. The Remuh Synagogue, built in the 16th century, is an active synagogue honoring the famous commentator on the Torah, Rabbi Moses Isserles, known as Remuh. The Jewish cemetery behind the synagogue is one of the oldest in Europe, serving as the main Jewish burial place for Kraków, with many tombstones dating back to the 16th, 17th, and 18th centuries. Besides being the gravesite of Rabbi Remuh, it holds the graves of other celebrities of the Jewish world: Natan Spira, Wolf Popper, members of their families, and also representatives of other notable families of Kraków Jews: the Landaus, Jakubowiczes, and Meiselses.

The *Oppidum* became the main spiritual and cultural center of Polish Jewry, hosting many of Poland's finest Jewish scholars, artists, and craftsmen. In the early 20th century, as Jews moved to other parts of Kraków, most Jewish families stayed relatively close to the historic synagogues, especially because of the rabbinical teaching against travel on the Sabbath. Although by the 1930s, Kraków had 120 officially registered synagogues and Judaism was flourishing, during the Second World War most Jews of the city were killed in the ghetto or death camps. Devoid of Jews, Kazimierz was neglected by the communist authorities after the war, but in recent years, a new generation of Poles who grew up without Poland's historic Jewish community have been introduced to Jewish culture.

The magic of the old Jewish town can once again be felt. Historical sites have been restored and some Jews are even moving to Kazimierz from Israel and America. Every June, Kazimierz hosts the Jewish Cultural Festival, which draws visitors from throughout the world, and Jewish art galleries, restaurants, clubs, bookstores, and souvenir shops abound in the neighborhood, especially around Nowy Square and Szeroka Street.

During the early 1940s, the Nazis forced all the Jews of Kraków into a crowded ghetto in the district of Podgórze, across the river from Kazimierz on its south bank. In 1942, many inhabitants of the ghetto were systematically moved to a new forced-labor camp erected in nearby Płaszów. Thousands were killed there, mostly by shooting. The German industrialist Oskar Schindler established an enamelware factory adjacent to Płaszów, attempting to protect his Jewish workers, some 900 people, from abuse in Płaszów and from deportation to killing centers. Two years later, when the Kraków Ghetto was liquidated, the Jewish population was either murdered inside the ghetto, driven to the nearby Płaszów camp, or transported to the gas chambers of Auschwitz or Bełżec.

The Kraków Ghetto is memorialized at Plac Bohaterów Getta (Ghetto Heroes Square) in Podgórze. As the ghetto's largest open space, the plaza was the location for the residents' greatest relief and also the scene of their greatest horrors. It was a place for people to socialize and escape the oppressive overcrowding of the tenements, but it became the site of families being torn apart, mass deportations to the death camps, and beatings and executions. Today, the "empty chairs" memorial consists of 70 well-spaced metal chairs meant to symbolize the departure and absence of the Jews and their rich culture from Kraków. The Eagle Pharmacy, on the edge of the plaza, has been renovated to look as it did during the occupation and serves as a five-room museum with artifacts, photographs, and testimonials describing life in the Kraków Ghetto. Because the pharmacy's Polish owner, Tadeusz Pankiewicz, decided to stay, he and his staff were the only Poles allowed to work in the ghetto over the two years of its existence. The pharmacy became a center of social life and aid in acquiring food and medicine, falsified documents, and preventing

Empty Chairs memorial in Ghetto Heroes Square, Podgórze.

The Eagle Pharmacy in Podgórze.

Memorial of Torn-Out Hearts on the grounds of the Płaszów camp.

deportations. Pankiewicz and his staff risked their lives in many clandestine operations, bearing witness to tragedy through the pharmacy windows as the ghetto and its inhabitants were ultimately decimated.

The Oskar Schindler Factory Museum opened in 2010 and hosts the permanent exhibit entitled "Kraków under Nazi Occupation 1939-1945." Through multimedia installations, documents, photos, radio and film recordings, and period artifacts, the museum presents life under occupation, the fate of the Jews, and the underground resistance, as well as the heroic work of Oskar Schindler. Further south, the area of the Płaszów camp is dominated by the haunting Memorial of Torn-Out Hearts, depicting five figures representing the five countries of the victims, with heads bent under the weight of the massive stone block from which they are carved and a horizontal crack across their chests, symbolizing their abruptly ended lives. The barren field found there today indicates that nothing is left of the dreaded prison, surrounded by electrified barbed wire and 12 watchtowers equipped with machine guns and spotlights. A series of outdoor photographic exhibits throughout the grounds offers brief explanations of sites associated with the camp, including the main guard post, the quarters of the camp commandant Amon Goeth, and the infamous Grey House, used as a jail and torture chamber by the Nazis. A rough estimate of the number of prisoners executed here over its two-year history would be in the neighborhood of 150,000.

MEDITATION

- Which images from Kraków's historic Jewish community speak most powerfully to me?
- What signs of hope have I experienced in the renovated Jewish districts?

Reading: Jeremiah 33:10-11
There shall once more be heard the voice of mirth and the voice of gladness, the voice of the bridegroom and the voice of the bride.

Response: "We will stand together."

We pray for God's ancient people, the Jews, the first to hear His Word — for greater understanding between Christians and Jews, for the removal of our blindness and bitterness of heart, so that God will grant us grace to be faithful to His covenant and to grow in the love of His Holy Name. R.

In the face of the classification of people and racial supremacy, in the face of injustice and coldness of heart, in the face of demeaning behavior and the denial of human rights and dignity. R.

For too long we walked different ways, we let what separates us define us. For too long we turned a blind eye and did not stand together when it mattered most. R.

In the face of discrimination and extremism, in the face of the incitement to hatred, persecution, and oppression, in the face all hints of anti-Semitism and racism. R.

We did not see the sights they saw, hear the sounds they heard, or feel the pain they felt, through persecution and unparalleled levels of brutality. But now we have watched and listened, and we have come to walk together with them, to seek truth, to remember, and to commit to a new relationship. R.

May we be chastened and renewed, uneasy with the status quo, challenging resistance, and refusing to stand idly by. Let us repent of all untruth, show humility to the first-called children of Israel, and work for reconciliation between all who claim the faith of Abraham. R.

Prayer: Fiercely loving God, You reveal yourself in myriad ways, speaking through different voices to enlighten our world and enrich our lives. As pilgrims in Your world, we visit the past in order to confront the present and protect the future. Strengthen, console, and guide us as we seek to follow Your way. May we stand together as Your people, speaking the truth with clarity and compassion, committed to transforming the world with Your everlasting mercy.

4. Markowa, Ulma Family Museum of Poles Who Saved Jews

After invading Poland, the Nazis quickly began large-scale persecutions of both Poles and Jews. By 1941, as the focus turned to the massacre of Jews, the German authorities plastered posters across Poland warning that Jews who fled ghettos would be executed, as would anyone who assisted them. Nowhere else in Europe were punishments for helping Jews so harsh. Even seemingly small gestures of aid or sympathy were punished with death, and sometimes by the deaths of their neighbors as well.

Ulma Family Museum of Poles Saving Jews in World War II.

As some Jews managed to flee from the ghettos, the reactions of the Polish people varied widely. Most were simply trying to survive a horrific occupation, yet some took the extraordinarily heroic risk of hiding Jews. Historians believe that between 50,000 and 80,000 Jews survived the Holocaust thanks to Polish help. Of course this was only part of the story, as other Poles made a living out of blackmailing fugitive Jews or handed them over to the Germans, a crime punished with the death penalty by the Polish government-in-exile and resistance movement.

When a strange Jew knocked at the window of a peasant cottage — asking for a morsel of food, a few moments inside to get warm, or permission to stay for a few days — the family was faced with an extremely difficult moral dilemma with four different options: the first, to turn over the Jew in accordance with the law imposed by the German occupiers, which was tantamount to the death sentence for the victim; the second, to refuse not only to denounce but also to help; the third, to render immediate assistance; and the fourth, to provide care and refuge for a longer period of time. The third and fourth choice risked death for one's family and neighbors. The brutality of the Nazi regime elicited the best of the human spirit right alongside the very worst.

Among the Poles who acted heroically were Wiktoria and Józef Ulma and their six children: Stanisława, Barbara, Władysław, Franciszek, Antoni, and Maria. The Ulmas were a Catholic family of simple farmers. Józef was a pioneer in fruit growing as well as beekeeping and silkworm breeding. He built a small electric windmill for charging an accumulator, thus becoming the first person in the village to replace kerosene lamps with electricity. Also passionate about photography, he took hundreds of pictures of his family and his village, many of which are preserved today.

The Ulma family lived in Markowa, a village in the Subcarpathian province of southeastern Poland. The 4,500 people who lived there before the war included 120 Jews. In the fall of 1942, 55 Jews were being hidden by Markowa's residents. In rural areas, hiding Jews was much

Ulma family who gave their lives for saving Jews.

more difficult than in the large cities. Villages lack the anonymity of big city living, and people easily find out what is happening to their neighbors. When the Germans decided to raid the village searching for Jews, the town's mayor was able to warn the people in advance. During the search, the Germans succeeded in tracking down almost half of the hidden Jews, often tipped off by locals.

Despite the raid, at least eight families in Markowa continued to hide Jewish fugitives. The Ulmas took eight Jews under their roof, and Józef had built a dugout for eight other Jews, who were eventually found by the Germans and shot. Undeterred, the Ulmas continued to shelter their Jewish neighbors in their home, including the Szall and Goldman families. On March 24, 1944, a group of German gendarmes and Polish Blue Policemen came to the Ulmas' house and shot Wiktoria, Józef, their six children (all of whom were between the ages of 2 and 8), and the eight hidden Jews. During the execution, Wiktoria — in her ninth month of pregnancy with her seventh child — went into labor. One of the gendarmes, Josef Kokott, was heard to say while killing the children, "Look at how Polish swine die for concealing the Jews." After plundering the house and carrying off three carts of loot, the gendarmes ordered the locals of the village to dig graves for the 16 victims. Finally, the village elder was ordered to bring three liters of vodka, and the executioners ended the day with a drinking spree. [70]

Despite the shocking murders of the Ulmas and the Jewish fugitives they were sheltering, several families in Markowa continued to hide Jews. A total of 21 Jews survived the Holocaust by hiding in the village. Seven members of the Weltz family survived thanks to the help of Antoni and Dorota Szylar; Michał and Maria Bar along with their five small children saved Chaim and Rózia Lorbenfeld with their daughter; the five-member Riesenbach family was hidden by Józef and Julia Bar; Michał and Katarzyna Cwynar rescued a Jew named Władysław; Jakub Einhorn, along with two other Jews, was hidden by Michał Drewniak and the Przybylak family. Abraham Segel survived the war herding cattle at the farm of Jan and Helena Cwynar and their two daughters, Maria and Czesława.

After the war, Abraham Segel, whose parents and siblings were murdered by the Nazis, moved to Israel but often visited the town of Markowa. He worked tirelessly to bring Poles and Jews closer together, fighting against stereotypes and making the story of the Polish rescuers of Jews better known in his adopted homeland. Before his 2019 death at his home in Haifa, he was awarded the Knight's Cross of the Order of Merit of the Republic of Poland in 2016 for "nurturing the memory and disseminating the knowledge about Poles who saved Jews" and for his commitment to creating the Ulma Family Museum.

In recent years, the story of the Ulma family has become increasingly known in both Catholic and Jewish circles, in Poland and around the world. In 1995 the Yad Vashem Institute posthumously honored Józef and Wiktoria with a Righteous Among the Nations medal. The Catholic Church opened their cause for beatification in 2003. In 2013, Pope Francis blessed the cornerstone to the museum, and during his 2016 visit to Auschwitz met with relatives of the Ulma family.

The Ulma Family Museum of Poles Saving Jews in World War II was opened in 2016 and is operated by the Subcarpathian Province and Poland's Ministry of Culture and National Heritage. The building is austere and minimalistic, designed in the shape of a simple house. reminiscent of the history of prewar Markowa. In its center, a glass cubicle is a mock-up of the original house of the Ulma family.

In front of the museum building, the open square encompasses illuminated tablets containing the names of Poles killed for saving Jews. The middle of the square holds a slab with an inscription to the memory of the Jewish victims of the *Shoah* (Holocaust) and their anonymous Polish helpers in distress. The wall next to the building contains nameplates of Subcarpathian residents who helped the Jews.

In the vicinity of the museum, fruit trees mark the beginning of the Orchard of Remembrance, evocative of both Józef Ulma's passion for fruit horticulture and the Garden of the Righteous at Yad Vashem in Jerusalem. Throughout the orchard, illuminated plaques contain the names of 1,500 cities, towns, and villages throughout Poland where Jewish residents were rescued by the 6,700 persons recognized as the Polish Righteous Among the Nations. There were also many anonymous heroes, whom we also remember here. Within the orchard stands the Monument to the Ulma Family, funded by the local community on the 60th anniversary of the Markowa murder.

Ulma family grave at their parish church.

The museum's interactive permanent exhibit presents archive materials (prints, photographs, notations, and documentaries) and includes the following sections: Poles and Jews before 1939 in the Subcarpathian region; residents during the German occupation; Poles saving Jews; shelters and hiding places; Poles killed for helping Jews; the Ulma family; and the postwar period.

Markowa is now a pilgrimage destination where both Christians and Jews from around the world come to pay their respects to the Ulmas, who, despite enormous risks, became their Jewish brothers' keepers and paid the ultimate price. Markowa is near other important Jewish sites, including the famous synagogue in Łańcut and the tomb of Rabbi Elimelech in Leżajsk. The Ulma family tomb is at the nearby parish cemetery, which is usually fully lined with small stones, an ancient Jewish tradition for remembering the dead.

When pondering World War II and the Holocaust, humanity spends much time pondering the mystery of evil, but not enough time on the equally mysterious mystery of good. The awful juxtaposition of these two mysteries is never so evident than at places like Auschwitz and Markowa.

MEDITATION

- Would I have been a persecutor, bystander, resister, or rescuer in wartime Markowa?
- How have I been a bystander when I could have stood up for the oppressed?

Reading: Luke 10:29-37
But wanting to justify himself, he asked Jesus, "And who is my neighbor?"

Response: "Through your mercy, Lord, teach us not to be bystanders."

The Holocaust and subsequent genocides took place because communities allowed intolerance and persecution to take root. While some actively supported or facilitated policies of persecution, the vast majority stood by silently — at best, afraid to speak out; at worst, indifferent. R.

Like the Good Samaritan of Jesus' parable, the people of Markowa willingly cared for the suffering victims at great risk to themselves. May we learn from them not be bystanders, but to stand up for the oppressed. R.

"Wherever human beings endure suffering and humiliation, we must always take sides. Neutrality helps the oppressor, never the victim. Silence encourages the tormentor, never the tormented" (Elie Wiesel). R.

Those who refused to be bystanders while persecution took place around them not only acted as rescuers of victims, but also resisted the prevailing beliefs that some people's lives were worth less than others. R.

Those who refused to be bystanders offered shelter to save the lives of others, organized rescue efforts, arranged safe passages for families, and accompanied children to safety. R.

As we remember this war-torn land of Poland, let us not only reflect on the fate of victims, but also learn how to resist policies that discriminate, to rescue victims of oppression, and to work for justice and the common good of all. R.

Prayer: God of all nations, those of us who haven't experienced the atrocities of genocide cannot imagine its horrors. Show us how to imitate the Good Samaritan and to overcome the fears and apathy that would enable us to be bystanders in the face of evil done to our neighbor. Give us the courage to speak and act in the name of justice.

XII. Returning Home

After completing a pilgrimage through Catholic Poland, the traveler is filled with pleasant memories, scattered images, and fragmentary insights. Part of the task of returning home is savoring these memories, reminding ourselves of each sacred place along the way, and continually assimilating our many images and insights into everyday life.

The final words of every Mass are critically important for the pilgrim: "*Ite Missa est*": "Go, You are sent forth," "Go and announce the Gospel of the Lord," "Go in peace, glorifying the Lord by your life." After gathering to receive God's Word and to share intimately in the sacrifice of Christ's Body and Blood, we are sent forth to be His disciples in the world. Similarly, after our pilgrimage, having encountered the living Lord in sacred places and the living memory of God's saints, we are obliged to proclaim the Good News and glorify the Lord because of the transformation we have experienced along the road.

A pilgrimage is different from a vacation because it changes us interiorly, increasing and deepening our spiritual desires. After a journey through Catholic Poland, we are left wanting more — more encounters with the Merciful Lord, His Blessed Mother, and His saints, richer experiences of the holy sacrifice of the Mass in beautiful churches, continuing experiences of Scripture and prayer along the road. Because pilgrimage deepens these desires, it encourages us to continue on the road of discipleship, a journey that is never complete until we reign with the Lord in glory.

Because pilgrimage changes our hearts, it also transforms our lives. Having experienced the sights and sounds, the aromas and tastes, and the truths and emotions of sanctity in Poland, we can learn to experience all of life as holy. Every person, place, and event can be viewed as a sacred encounter, as part of our journey of discipleship with Christ, when we live with the heart of a pilgrim.

1. The Call to Holiness and Mission

Our experience of discipleship draws us in two directions as we continue the pilgrimage of the Christian life: inwardly to holiness and outwardly to mission. As the Gospels show us, the first appeal of Jesus to his disciples was "Come and see" (Jn 1:39); His final appeal was "Go into all the world and proclaim the good news" (Mk 16:15). Those disciples first grew close to Jesus by following in His way, then they were impelled to go out and share what they had experienced with the world. This double vocation — the call to holiness and the call to mission — is necessary to be authentic and effective followers of Jesus Christ. Travel that doesn't lead us to a deeper connection to holiness and mission is merely spiritual tourism, not Christian pilgrimage.

When we return home from a pilgrimage, we must continue the spirit of pilgrimage if we are to be transformed by our journey. Ongoing pilgrimage is the lifelong pursuit of holiness and mission, until we reach our goal. For as the French novelist Léon Bloy wrote, "The only great tragedy in life, is not to become a saint."[71]

In the four Gospels and the Acts of the Apostles, the sacred writers narrate this double call of discipleship. In the gospels, we are led toward Jerusalem, toward an increasingly deep and more personal encounter with Jesus. Through His teachings and healings, His Death and Resurrection, we come to know and love Him more intimately. Then, in Acts, we are led away from Jerusalem, in the way of missionary discipleship, the outward-reaching evangelization of the world.

The final words of Jesus before His Ascension were these: "You will be my witnesses in Jerusalem, in all Judea and Samaria, and to the ends of the earth" (Acts 1:8). The first sphere of Christian witness is Jerusalem, the place where the disciples lived. For us this call to witness corresponds to our home, the domestic space within our families. The second area of mission is Judea, the area surrounding Jerusalem, which corresponds to our neighbors,

The porter's gate where St. Faustina encountered Jesus in the beggar at the gate.

our parishes, and our local communities. The next sphere is Samaria, which the Jews of Jerusalem avoided. This relates to our mission toward those who are shunned and rejected. And ultimately, the mission of the whole Church together is to the ends of the earth, the missionary mandate of Christ to bring the Gospel to the whole world.

Because it is difficult in our culture today to be followers of Jesus, we need models to follow and to give us inspiration. Our materialistic culture has blurred our vision and muffled our hearing, diverting our attention from what really matters. Surrounded by consumerism, we can no longer discern what we most truly desire. But there is nothing that cuts through this superficial culture more effectively than the saints from the past and people who are living lives of sanctity today, who are filled with God's mercy, have a deep sense of joy despite life's struggles, and show a compassionate concern for others.

One of the great challenges for the Church today is the rapid rate of people leaving the church and giving up a belief in God. This is a tragedy for which we are all, in some way, responsible. Thomas Merton warned, "Do not be too quick to condemn the man who no longer believes in God, for it is perhaps your own coldness and avarice, your mediocrity and materialism, your sensuality and selfishness that have killed his faith."[72] Jesus and the great tradition He founded hold the answers to the questions the world is asking, the best answers to the questions that well up from every human heart.

Let us continue, then, to cultivate the spirit of pilgrimage within ourselves, investing time in Scripture reading, meditation, and prayer to come to know Jesus Christ more personally, so that we can become more effective witnesses for the sake of God's people.

Living the works of mercy in the world;
the works of mercy, caring for the poor and the lost.

2. The Spiritual and Corporal Works of Mercy

The experience of God's mercy, as it is encountered in a pilgrimage to Catholic Poland, is expressed through our double vocation to holiness and mission. We grow in holiness through the change of heart brought about by Divine Mercy, nurtured by continuing prayer, reflecting on Scripture, and living the Sacraments. And we grow in mission by showing God's mercy to others through actions that help them to meet their physical and spiritual needs.

Experiencing God's mercy while on pilgrimage encourages and obliges us to become witnesses of mercy when returning home. If God treats us mercifully and forgives us, then we too must forgive and show mercy to one another. In our acts of mercy, God's mercy for our neighbor becomes concretely realized. These acts of witnessing mercy to others have been traditionally categorized as the seven spiritual works and seven corporal works of mercy.

The spiritual works of mercy are acts of compassion by which we help others with their emotional and spiritual needs. These seven are the following: counsel the doubtful, instruct the ignorant, admonish the sinners, comfort the afflicted, forgive offenses, bear wrongs patiently, and pray for the living and dead. These works are a kind of preventive medicine for the spiritual afflictions of shame, doubt, and despair, which drain life of its energy, joy, and sense of purpose. Think about each of these seven spiritual works of mercy and consider how you could begin to practice one or more of them as you return home.

The corporal works of mercy are compassionate deeds by which we help others with their material and physical needs. These seven are the following: feed the hungry, give drink to the thirsty, clothe the naked, welcome the stranger, visit the sick, visit the imprisoned, and bury the dead. These corporal works of mercy come from a variety of places throughout Scripture, but especially the Last Judgment scene of Matthew 25. Those on Jesus' right receive eternal life because when they did these works of mercy to the least of their brothers and sisters, they did them for Jesus (see Mt 25:34-40). Saint John Chrysostom called these works of mercy "the sacrament of the brother and sister." As we encounter Christ in the seven Sacraments, we encounter Christ in doing these seven works of mercy for others. So think about this list of the corporal works of mercy and consider how you could begin to practice one or more of them as you return home.

Jesus teaches us to be merciful like God: "Be merciful, just as your Father is merciful" (Lk 6:36). Jesus ministered to people in need, and He calls all of his followers to care for the lost, the poor, and the despised. Saint John of the Cross said, "At the evening of life, we shall be judged on our love." All of these works of mercy — both spiritual and corporal — are ways of entering more deeply into the heart of God.

The image of the Merciful Jesus is a wondrous expression of God's care for suffering humanity. The heart of Jesus is forever wounded, forever pouring out salvation and redemption into our lives. In the sacrifice of the Mass, Jesus is continually offering Himself for our sins and the sins of the whole world. Christ's eternal wounds are now radiant and glorious, an eternal sign that he is forever our wounded healer. From His pierced Heart flows saving love for all the people of the world.

Jesus invites us to unite our heart with His own. In that union of hearts, our own struggles can participate in the redemptive sacrifice of Christ. God usually doesn't take away suffering, failure, and pain from our lives, but He invites us to unite our hearts with that of His Son. In that way, our failures can become the means to our growth and our ability to help others who struggle. Our pains can give us deeper compassion and impel us to become healers for others. Our suffering can become the means to unite us more deeply to Christ and transform us into a source of strength and hope for others.

The tendency in our culture today is to try to deny pain and make suffering go away. But covering up our wounds may deny us their deeper gifts. When we unite our hearts to the Heart of Christ, we will know that our suffering is never wasted. When we open our lives to this transformation, we are becoming imitators of God and draw close to the Sacred Heart of Jesus.

Jesus told St. Faustina that there are essentially three ways of mediating God's mercy:

> **I demand from you deeds of mercy ... You must not shrink from this or try to excuse or absolve yourself from it.**
>
> **I am giving you three ways of exercising mercy toward your neighbor: the first — by deed, the second — by word, the third — by prayer. In these three degrees is contained the fullness of mercy, and it is an unquestionable proof of love for Me. By this means a soul glorifies and pays reverence to My Mercy** (*Diary*, 742).

In Paul's letter to the Ephesians, we read: "Therefore be imitators of God, as beloved children, and live in love, as Christ loved us and gave himself up for us, a fragrant offering and sacrifice to God" (Eph 5: 1–2). This pattern of "*imitatio Dei*," the imitation of God because we are His beloved children, is the foundation of the Christian life. As we seek a civilization of love, the message of Divine Mercy has consequences for the life of every Christian, for the pastoral praxis of the Church, and for the contributions that Christians should render to the humane, just, and merciful structuring of society.

The family of God is worldwide, and God's children include all who are in need of life's basic necessities: food, hospitality, clothing, health care, education, counseling, prayer, pardon, and companionship. The radical love of neighbor that Jesus demands is possible for us only because we have first received the love of God in the form of Divine Mercy. Only by imitating God, in His gift of mercy to the world, can we make talk about God's mercy credible and persuasive; only in this way can we make it a message of hope for the world.[73]

NOTES

1 Stephen J. Binz, *Holy Land Pilgrimage* (Collegeville, MN: Liturgical Press, 2020).

2 Mikhail Tukhachevski's orders on July 2, 1920.

3 George Weigel, *Witness to Hope: The Biography of Pope John Paul II* (New York: Cliff Street Books, 1999), 77.

4 Stephen J. Binz, *Divine Mercy* (New London, CT: Twenty-Third Publications, 2015).

5 Michael E. Gaitley, *The Second Greatest Story Ever Told* (Stockbridge, MA: Marian Press, 2015), ebook edition.

6 Tertullian, *Apologeticus*, 50.

7 Louis de Montfort, *True Devotion to Mary: With Preparation for Total Consecration*, n. 55.

8 Pope Francis, Homily, Celebration of Divine Mercy Sunday, Vatican Basilica, April 11, 2015.

9 Pope John Paul II, Homily, Mass in St. Peter's Square for the Canonization of Sr. Mary Faustina Kowalska, April 30, 2000, n. 5.

10 Grzegorz Górny and Janusz Rosikoń, *Trust: In Saint Faustina's Footsteps* (San Francisco: Ignatius Press, 2014), 19.

11 Sister Sophia Michalenko, *The Life of Faustina Kowalska: The Authorized Biography* (Cincinnati: Franciscan Media, 1999), 72.

12 Sister Maria Elżbieta Siepak, ZMBM, *Sister Faustina's New "Congregation": The Apostolic Movement of the Divine Mercy* (Kraków: Misericordia, 2005).

13 Henryk Ciereszko, *Endless Mercy: God's Way to Holiness — The Life of Blessed Michael Sopoćko* (Dublin: Divine Mercy Publications, 2013), 62.

14 Father Michael Sopoćko, *Journal*, n. 4, 24.

15 Cardinal Stanisław Dziwisz, quoted in Fr. Kazimierz Chwalek, MIC, "Father Michael Sopoćko, Our New Blessed," September 29, 2013, www.thedivinemercy.org/articles/father-michael-sopocko-our-new-blessed.

16 Blessed Fr. Michael Sopoćko, "A Prayer of Trust."

17 Pope John Paul II, Homily, Dedication of the Shrine Of Divine Mercy, Kraków-Łagiewniki, Apostolic Voyage to Poland, August 17, 2002, n. 5.

18 Pope John Paul II, Message on the occasion of the dedication of the chapel of Blessed Sacrament, April 3, 2005.

19 Written by Maximilian Kolbe early in 1941, in the last edition of *Knight of the Immaculata* before his arrest. Maximilian Kolbe, *The Collected Writings of St. Maximilian Maria Kolbe, Vol. 2: Various Writings*, ed. by Antonella Di Piazza, (Nerbini International: 2016), 2152-53.

[20] Patricia Treece, *A Man for Others: Maximilian Kolbe the "Saint of Auschwitz"* (Libertyville, IL: Marytown Press, 1993), 42.

[21] Saint Maximilian Kolbe, *Gli Scritti di Massimiliano Kolbe, eroe di Oswiecjm e Beato della Chiesa*, vol. III (Florence: Citta di Vita, 1975), 690, quoted in Br. Francis M. Kalvelage, FI, *Kolbe: Saint of the Immaculata* (New Bedford, MA: Franciscans of the Immaculate, 2001), 224.

[22] The Kolbe Foundation, "Who is Maximilian Kolbe?" www.kolbefoundation.org/gbookswebsite/studentlibrary/greatestbooks/kolbe/whokolbe.html

[23] Kalvelage, *Kolbe: Saint of the Immaculata*, 8.

[24] Zdzisław Józef Kijas, OFM Conv, "The Process of Beatification and Canonization of Maximilian Maria Kolbe," Studia Elbląskie, XXI (2020), http://studiaelblaskie.pl/assets/Artykuly/CB-11-A17-Kijas-Rew-1.pdf.

[25] Polish bishops, source unknown, quoted in Mary Craig, *Blessed Maximilian Kolbe, OFM Conv.: Priest-Hero of a Death Camp*, (London: Catholic Truth Society, 1982), 15.

[26] Pope John Paul II, Homily for the Canonization of St. Maximilian Maria Kolbe, October 10, 1982.

[27] Pope John Paul II, Homily for the Inauguration of His Pontificate, St. Peter's Square, October 22, 1978, n. 5.

[28] Pope John Paul II, Homily, Victory Square, Warsaw, Apostolic Journey to Poland, June 2, 1979, n. 3a.

[29] Pope John Paul II, Homily, Holy Mass in Honor of St. Stanislaus, Kraków, Apostolic Journey to Poland, June 10, 1979, n. 5.

[30] Adam Bujak, *The Pope's Wadowice* (Kraków: Bialy Kruk, 2014), 128.

[31] Gian Franco Svidercoschi, *Letter to a Jewish Friend: The Simple and Extraordinary Story of Pope John Paul II and His Jewish School Friend* (New York: Crossroad, 1995).

[32] Darcy O'Brien, *The Hidden Pope: The Untold Story of a Lifelong Friendship That Changed the Relationship Between Catholics and Jews* (Emmaus, PA: Rodale Books, 1998).

[33] Pope John Paul II, Homily, Visit to the Marian Shrine of Kalwaria Zebrzydowska, Apostolic Pilgrimage to Poland, June 7, 1979, n. 2.

[34] Pope John Paul II, Homily, Kalwaria, Apostolic Voyage to Poland, August 19, 2002, n. 1.

[35] Adapted from "Prayer for the Gifts of the Holy Spirit," taught to young Karol Wojtyla by his father.

[36] Antonio Socci, *Tajemnice Jana Pawła II* (Kraków: Rafael Dom Wydawniczy, 2014), 30.

[37] George Weigel, *City of Saints* (New York: Image, 2015), ebook edition.

[38] Quotes from John Paul II, *Love and Responsibility*, trans. H. T. Willetts (San Francisco: Ignatius Press, 1993), ebook edition.

[39] Kalvelage, *Kolbe: Saint of the Immaculata*, 34.

[40] Francis of Assisi, "The Canticle of the Sun (Canticle of the Creatures)," trans. Bill Barrett, from the Umbrian text of the Assisi codex.

[41] Cardinal Stanisław Dziwisz, *A Life with Karol: My Forty-Year Friendship with the Man Who Became Pope* (New York: Image, 2008), 33.

[42] Pope John Paul II, remarks after Mass for the Beatification of Maria Bernadina Jablonska and Maria Karlowska, Zakopane, Poland, June 6, 1997.

[43] Pope Francis, Act of Entrustment to Mary, Virgin of Fatima, Saint Peter's Square, October 13, 2013.

[44] Adapted from the Jubilee Prayer to St. Vojtěch for the 1000-year anniversary of the death of St. Vojtěch, 1997.

[45] Andrzej A. Napiórkowski OSPPE, *Skałka: Between Heaven and Earth* (Kraków: Salwator, 2013), 130-131.

[46] Pope John Paul II, Homily at Mass and Canonization of Blessed Kinga, Stary Sącz, June 16, 1999, n. 4.

[47] Robert E. Alvis, *White Eagle, Black Madonna: One Thousand Years of the Polish Catholic Tradition* (New York: Fordham University Press, 2016), 45.

[48] John Paul II, Homily, Holy Mass and Act Of Consecration to the Mother of God, Apostolic Journey To Poland, Częstochowa, Jasna Góra, June 4, 1979, n. 3.

[49] John Paul II, Homily, Częstochowa, Jasna Góra, June 4, 1979, n. 3.

[50] Petitions adapted from John Paul II, Act of Consecration to the Mother of God, Częstochowa, Jasna Góra, June 4, 1979.

[51] *The History of the Shrine of Our Lady of Licheń* (Licheń: Zakład Godpodarczy "Dom Pielgrzyma," 2013), 34.

[52] Andrzej Micewski, *Cardinal Wyszynski: A Biography* (San Diego: Harcourt Brace Jovanovich, 1984), 41.

[53] Pope John Paul II, Letter to the People of Poland (October 23, 1978).

[54] Alvis, *White Eagle, Black Madonna*, ix.

[55] Petitions adapted from Stefan Wyszyński, "The Pledge of Jasna Góra," 1956.

[56] Bernard Brien, *Blessed Jerzy Popiełuszko: Truth Versus Totalitarianism* (San Francisco, Ignatius Press, 2017), 49.

[57] Adapted from Bl. Jerzy Popiełuszko, "Litany to Our Lady of Częstochowa," May 1982.

[58] Pope John Paul II, Homily for the Canonization of Edith Stein, October 11, 1998, n. 5.

59 Selected quotes from St. Edith Stein, see *The Collected Works of Edith Stein*, ed. L. Gelber, Michael Linssen, trans. Waltraut Stein (Washington, DC: ICS Publications, Institute of Carmelite Studies).

60 Saint Edith Stein, quoted in Waltraud Herbstrith, *Edith Stein: A Biography/ the Untold Story of the Philosopher and Mystic Who Lost Her Life in the Death Camps of Auschwitz*, 2nd English ed., trans. Bernard Bonowitz, OCSO (San Francisco: Ignatius Press, 1992), 56.

61 Maria Ruiz Scaperlanda, *Edith Stein: St. Teresa Benedicta of the Cross* (Huntington, IN: OSV Publishing, 2001), 75-76.

62 Selected quotes from St. Edith Stein, see *The Collected Works of Edith Stein*, ed. L. Gelber, Michael Linssen, trans. Waltraut Stein (Washington, DC: ICS Publications, Institute of Carmelite Studies).

63 Franz Liszt, *Life of Chopin*, trans. Martha Walker Cook (public domain), 87.

64 Franz Liszt, *Life of Chopin*, trans. Martha Walker Cook (public domain), 48-49, 55.

65 Walker, *Fryderyk Chopin: A Life and Times* (New York: Farrar, Straus and Giroux, 2018), 193-194.

66 Jürgen Stroop, quoted in Kazimierz Moczarski, *Conversations with an Executioner* (Hoboken, NJ: Prentice Hall, 1984), 164.

67 Rudolf Höss, *Death Dealer*, ed. Steven Pakuly (Amherst, NY: Prometheus Books, 1992), ebook edition.

68 Marc Massery, "Divine Mercy and the Commandant of Auschwitz," January 24, 2020, www.thedivinemercy.org/articles/divine-mercy-and-commandant-auschwitz.

69 Rudolf Höss, quoted in John Jay Hughes, "A Mass Murderer Repents: The Case of Rudolf Hoess, Commandant of Auschwitz," Archbishop Gerety Lecture, Seton Hall University, March 25, 1998.

70 Mateusz Szpytma, *The Risk of Survival: The Rescue of the Jews by the Poles and the Tragic Consequences for the Ulma Family from Markowa* (Warsaw and Kraków: Institute of National Remembrance, 2009), 75-79.

71 Léon Bloy, *The Woman Who Was Poor*, quoted in Pope Francis, *Gaudete et Exsultate*, Apostolic Exhortation on the Call to Holiness in Today's World, March 19, 2018, n. 34.

72 Thomas Merton, *New Seeds of Contemplation* (New York: New Directions, 1961), 177.

73 Stephen J. Binz, *Divine Mercy* (New London, CT: Twenty-Third Publications, 2015), 7-8.

Index of Proper Names and Places